D1334281

Introduction to the Gold First Exam Maximiser

The **Gold First Exam Maximiser** is specially designed to maximise your chances of success in the Cambridge English: First examination.

The **Exam Maximiser** will help you prepare for the Cambridge English: First exam by offering you:

- further **practice and revision** of all the important vocabulary, grammar and skills (reading, writing, listening and speaking) that you study in the Gold First Coursebook.
- more **information about the kinds of questions** you will have to answer in the Cambridge English: First exam.
- guidance with the **strategies and techniques** you should use to tackle exam tasks.
- **exam-style exercises** so that you can practise using the techniques.
- regular **extra Use of English sections** to help you practise the language and strategies you have learned.
- details of **Common errors** in the Cambridge English: First exam and how to avoid them.
- a complete **Practice exam** which you can use for preparation just before you sit the exam. This means that you will know exactly what to expect in each paper and that there are no unpleasant surprises.

How can I use the Gold First Exam Maximiser?

The **Exam Maximiser** is very flexible and can be used by students in a variety of situations and in a variety of ways. Here are some typical situations:

> **1**
> You are doing a Cambridge English: First course with other students, probably over an academic year. You are all planning to take the exam at the same time.

You are using the **Gold First Coursebook** in class. Sometimes you will also do the related exercises or even a whole unit from the **Exam Maximiser** in class, though your teacher will ask you to do exercises from it at home as well. You will use the entire **Exam Maximiser** or you will use it selectively, depending on your needs and the time available.

> **2**
> You have already done a Cambridge English: First course and you are now doing an intensive course to prepare for the exam.

Since you have already worked though the **Gold First Coursebook** or perhaps another Cambridge English: First coursebook, you will use the **Exam Maximiser** in class. This, together with the **Practice Tests Plus Cambridge First 2 New Edition (2014)**, will give you a concentrated and highly focused short exam course.

> **3**
> You have a very short time in which to prepare for the Cambridge English: First exam.

Your level of English is already nearing Cambridge English: First exam standard, though you have not been following a coursebook. You now need exam skills. You will use the **Exam Maximiser** independently, without a coursebook, because you need practice in the exam tasks and how to approach them.

> **4**
> You are retaking the Cambridge English: First exam as unfortunately you were not successful in your first attempt.

You may be retaking the exam because you were not sufficiently familiar with the exam requirements. You will not need to follow a coursebook, but you will use the **Exam Maximiser** to develop your exam techniques and build up your confidence.

> **5**
> You are preparing for the exam on your own.

Maybe you are not attending a Cambridge English: First class, but wish to take the exam and prepare for it independently. You will get the practice and preparation by using the **Exam Maximiser** by itself. You can give yourself additional practice by using the **Practice Tests Plus Cambridge First 2 New Edition (2014)** just before taking the exam.

What is in each unit?

The Exam Maximiser follows the structure of the Gold First Coursebook and each unit provides further work on the language, skills and exam strategies you looked at in the Coursebook unit.

Each unit contains **Vocabulary** sections. These practise the words and expressions which you studied in the Gold First Coursebook and introduce you to some new words and expressions as well. There are plenty of exercises to do, including exam-style tasks from the Reading and Use of English paper and crosswords and wordsearch grids for some fun.

You will find two **Grammar** sections in each unit. By doing the exercises in these sections, you can practise and revise the grammar points you have studied in the Gold First Coursebook. Once again, there are exam-style tasks from the Reading and Use of English paper.

There is a **Speaking** section in every unit to work on language and strategies to help you do well in the Speaking exam. In these sections, you listen to or read examples of candidates performing the speaking tasks and complete the activities to develop your own speaking skills.

Every unit has a **Listening** section. These sections help you train for each of the four parts in the Listening paper. First, you read some information about the paper and are given some advice on the strategy you should use in that particular part. You do an exercise to help you practise the strategy and then an exam-style listening task. The tasks get more difficult as you move through the units in the Exam Maximiser, so that by the end of the book they are at the same level as the exam.

There is also a **Reading** section in each unit. Like the Listening sections, these provide you with information about the exam and strategies to use in each of the four parts of the Reading paper. You do some exercises to help you with the strategy and then you do an exam-style task. There is a vocabulary activity at the end of most Reading sections as well, so that you can practise dealing with unfamiliar words and phrases. Like the Listening sections, the Reading sections are easier at the beginning of the book, but are at the level of the exam at the end.

At the end of each unit you will find a **Writing** section. Again, you are given information about the exam and the kinds of writing tasks you have to do in Parts 1 and 2 of the Writing paper. You are also given a strategy to follow and then have an opportunity to put it into practice by doing some exercises, often using sample answers. You write your answers to these exercises in the Exam Maximiser. Finally, you look at an exam task and write your own answer to this task.

There are **Use of English** sections in exam format after every two units. These provide practice in the tasks and are based on the topic areas of the two units, giving you the opportunity to review the vocabulary you have learned.

At the back of the book, there is a section giving examples of **Common errors in the Cambridge English: First exam** for each paper. There is also a short section on common language errors.

Once you have worked through all the units, you will be ready to try the **Practice exam** at the back of the book. Then you'll be really well prepared for the Cambridge English: First exam.

Good luck!

Bands and fans

1

Vocabulary
music and free time activities

1 Find eight words in the wordsearch connected with music, bands and fans.

o	t	k	j	i	n	s	t	r	u	m	e	n	t
p	e	r	f	o	r	m	a	n	c	e	o	k	d
q	u	e	h	i	n	s	t	r	r	m	g	n	r
a	u	d	i	e	n	c	e	u	m	f	u	l	u
p	j	l	z	p	e	r	t	t	l	u	i	x	m
i	u	g	b	v	j	l	u	i	t	a	t	o	m
q	k	n	k	y	u	w	i	p	u	m	a	u	e
q	x	p	k	c	o	n	c	e	r	t	r	n	r

2 Find and correct the mistakes with collocations in sentences 1–8 below.

1 I really think listening music is relaxing.

2 Can you play at a musical instrument?

3 I try to go as many live concerts as possible – they're great!

4 I watch at television in the evenings after work.

5 It's much easier if I can make the shopping at the weekends.

6 I tend stay at home on Sundays.

7 Making yoga helps me switch off from problems at work.

8 I'm really in rock music – I love the strong beat.

Speaking

Listening to and answering questions (Part 1)
▶ CB page 7

▶ CB page 7

1 ▶ 01 Listen to the questions an examiner asks. Match questions 1–7 to answers A–I. There are two answers you do not need to use.

A My older brother actually. I can talk to him about almost anything.

B It's hard to say but I hope I'll be working as a doctor. I've just started studying medicine.

C All kinds really. Hip hop, rock, jazz. I really like classical music too.

D I play the violin.

E Yes, a brother and a sister. My brother is three years older than me and my sister is a year younger.

F We usually go to the seaside, but this year we're going to visit my brother in Madrid. He's studying there.

G The people. The town itself is very beautiful with a cathedral and a wonderful square, but it's the people that make it special.

H I was studying at school.

I English! I liked the science subjects too but English is my favourite.

About the exam:
In the Speaking exam, Part 1, you are asked a few questions in which you give personal information and opinions. Listen to the questions an examiner asked.

Strategy:
- Give interesting answers but don't say so much that you dominate the conversation.
- Make sure your answers are quite short.

Reading

Gapped text (Part 6) ▶ CB page 8

About the exam:

In the Reading exam, Part 6, you read a text with missing sentences. After the text you find the sentences in jumbled order. You decide where they go in the text. There is always one extra sentence that does not fit anywhere.

Strategy:

- Read the whole text first and make sure you understand it.
- Look at the words like pronouns (e.g. *it*, *she*), demonstratives (e.g. *this*, *that*) and possessive adjectives (*her*, *their*) in the sentences that have been removed from the text and decide what they refer to.
- When you have chosen the missing sentences, read the whole text through again with the sentences in place to make sure that it all makes sense.

1 **You are going to read a newspaper article about musicians raising money for charity. Read the article and decide which of titles 1–3 summarises the article best.**

1 Where did all the money go?

2 The concert that changed what it means to be a musician

3 The first charity concert

2 **Six sentences have been removed from the article. Choose from sentences A–G the one which fits each gap (1–6). There is one extra sentence which you do not need to use.**

A What is far clearer is the benefits they have for the musicians themselves.

B They ended up making over a thousand times that much.

C It was recorded in just under twenty-four hours in a studio in London.

D It was this that gave Geldof the idea of recording a song for the African famine.

E In fact it was difficulties with transporting the aid once in Africa that led to the next phase of the effort and the famous Live Aid concert itself.

F The result was one of the biggest-selling singles of all time.

G Live Aid was not the first concert aimed at raising money for charity.

Musician Bob Geldof wanted to make a difference and not just in the world of pop music. Stuart Maconie tells us how he did it.

The day after seeing a TV report about a famine in Ethiopia, pop singer Bob Geldof noticed that his wife had <u>stuck</u> a note on the fridge door. It read, 'Ethiopia: everyone who visits this house from today onwards will be asked to contribute £5 for famine relief.' **[1]** The problem was that he didn't think his own band would be able to raise enough money if they recorded a song on their own.

He asked another musician friend, Midge Ure, to help him write the music and lyrics and they then recruited forty-five of the most popular Irish and British musicians of the early eighties. Each musician in the group, which came to be known as Band Aid, sang a <u>line</u> of the song *Do they know it's Christmas?* **[2]**

The success of the song probably had more to do with the status of the performers than the quality of the music, but its <u>release</u> had an immediate effect on the British public. The BBC played it once an hour. The singer who was number one at the time told people to buy the Band Aid single instead of his own record. Geldof and Ure had hoped to make £70,000. **[3]**

Even then not everyone was convinced that it had been such a good idea. There were criticisms of Geldof and Ure's choice of musicians and the lyrics of the song and doubts about whether the money raised would reach its <u>target</u>. The journalist who had filed the report which had inspired Geldof's wife was very suspicious of the performers' motives. But when he returned to Ethiopia and saw eight huge planes with the Band Aid logo at the airport, he was impressed.

[4] The food and supplies were <u>held up</u> because the local trucking companies would not move the goods or allow anyone else to move them. Geldof realised he had to do something to protest about this so he set about organising the Live Aid concert.

Geldof not only managed to get the truck drivers to cooperate, he also started a new trend that continued over the next three decades. **[5]** There had been 'benefit concerts' before. The difference was that pop stars were now expressing opinions about world events.

Doubts are often raised about the contribution these concerts make. Some even argue that they have a negative impact. **[6]** These include fame and celebrity, but surely, it can never be a bad thing to try and raise money for those in need.

3 Look at words 1–3 from the article in Activity 2 and cross out the word that <u>cannot</u> be used with it.

1 raise *money/your hand/doubts/your mind*

2 record *a song/your answers/a dish/a message*

3 file *a jacket/a report/a complaint/a document*

4 Choose the definition, A or B, that matches the meaning of words 1–5 in the context of the article in Activity 2.

1 stuck

  A put   **B** glued

2 line

  A a group of words   **B** a long thin mark

3 release

  A freedom   **B** availability

4 held up

  A stolen   **B** delayed

5 target

  A a board with circles that you try to hit when you are shooting

  B an amount you are trying to achieve

5 Find words in the article to match definitions 1–4.

1 when a large number of people become ill or die because they do not have enough food

2 the words of a song

3 found new people to work

4 a new situation with changes or development

6 Look at sentences 1–3 from the article. Choose the sentence, A or B, that is closest in meaning to the original. Look at the article again and use the whole context to help you.

1 The success of the song probably had more to do with the status of the performers than the quality of the music.

  A The success of the song was due to the status of the performers rather than the quality of the music.

  B The success of the song was based on a combination of the status of the performers and the quality of the music.

2 They ended up making over a thousand times that much.

  A Eventually they made more than they had expected.

  B By the time it was over they had made more than they expected.

3 It can never be a bad thing to try and raise money for those in need.

  A It's always good to try to raise money.

  B It can sometimes be wrong to try to raise money.

7 Read the complete article again. Which of the opinions below do you agree with? Think of three reasons you would give for your opinions.

> Concerts like Live Aid are a good thing.

> Raising money to help others should be done by politicians not musicians.

> Celebrities have a duty to help others.

Grammar

simple and continuous forms in the present ▶ CB page 10

1 Underline the correct alternative in sentences 1–10.

1 I *have/am having* a ticket for the concert on Friday and I *get/am getting* really excited!

2 The group *come/are coming* from the same school as I went to, which makes it even more exciting.

3 They *perform/are performing* all over Europe now, or at least that's what my friend *tells/is telling* me.

4 They *become/are becoming* more popular now as more people *know/are knowing* about them and *download/are downloading* their music.

5 I *understand/am understanding* that the concert is sold out, so I just can't wait to *hear/be hearing* them play!

6 I *know/am knowing* one of the roadies and he *works/is working* backstage on some of their gigs here in the UK.

7 He *says/is saying* that the band *are really looking forward/really look forward* to coming back to their home town to play on Friday.

8 Their fans *love/are loving* them wherever they *play/are playing*, but we're special for them.

9 They've changed their style of playing a bit over the years. On their latest record they *sound/are sounding* more like Coldplay but I *like/am liking* it a lot.

10 Some people *criticise/are criticising* them for that, but I *disagree/am disagreeing*. I'm still their biggest fan.

Use of English

Multiple-choice cloze (Part 1)
▶ CB page 11

1 **For questions 1–8, read the text below and decide which word (A, B, C or D) best fits each gap. There is an example at the beginning (0).**

Music on your mind

You know the feeling – you're listening to music and suddenly your whole **(0)** _A mood_ changes from sad to happy. This mind-altering power of music is amazing, and internet music sites are using sophisticated ways of **(1)** .... us in touch with new artists. They search our downloaded files or online listening habits **(2)** .... patterns, and the results are often surprising – would you believe that AC/DC fans may well enjoy Beethoven?

Musicians have been **(3)** .... unforgettable music for centuries, using accepted ideas about the emotional appeal of certain combinations of musical sounds. It's **(4)** .... knowledge that major chords sound upbeat **(5)** .... minor chords sound mournful – in tests, even children as young as three connect music in major keys to happy faces. Scientists investigating the subject have been **(6)** .... various experiments such as scanning the brains of people while they listen to music. One thing they **(7)** .... across is that music triggers activity in the motor regions of the brain, which could explain why we often need to **(8)** .... our feet to music. The possibilities for medicine and business are exciting!

0	**A** mood	**B** atmosphere	**C** temper	**D** idea
1	**A** placing	**B** putting	**C** making	**D** doing
2	**A** looking out	**B** looking for	**C** looking up	**D** looking after
3	**A** constructing	**B** forming	**C** inventing	**D** composing
4	**A** great	**B** usual	**C** common	**D** wide
5	**A** while	**B** during	**C** since	**D** so
6	**A** taking	**B** making	**C** doing	**D** having
7	**A** came	**B** went	**C** brought	**D** took
8	**A** tap	**B** bang	**C** hit	**D** strike

2 **Read the complete text again. Underline:**

1 two phrasal verbs.
2 three collocations.
3 one fixed phrase.

Listening

Multiple matching (Part 3)
▶ CB page 12

1 ▶ 02 **You will hear five different people talking about a live pop concert they have been to. Choose from the list (A–H) what each speaker disliked most about the concert. Use each letter only once. There are three extra letters which you do not need to use.**

A The type of music played
B The arena and the stage
C The location of the venue
D The audience participation
E The quality of the music
F The price of the tickets
G The facilities at the venue
H The queue to get in

Speaker 1 ☐
Speaker 2 ☐
Speaker 3 ☐
Speaker 4 ☐
Speaker 5 ☐

Grammar

would and *used to* for past habit
▶ CB page 13

1 Read the extracts about music and cross out the incorrect verb form in each sentence.

1   Throughout history, parents *would/did/used to* make sure their children had classical music lessons from a young age. Some parents *did/had used to do/used to do* this because they thought it was good for mental discipline. Others *believed/used to believe/would believe* that knowledge of important works of classical music was part of a good general education.

2   Classical music has regularly featured in pop culture, and has often been used as background music for movies, television programmes and advertisements. As a result many people *are used to/would/have got used to* regularly and often unknowingly listening to classical music. This means that people who *didn't use to/wouldn't/hadn't used to* buy classical music have actually been enjoying it without realising.

2 Sentences 1–6 below each have a word missing. Complete the sentences with the words in the box.

would	to (×2)	used
got	get	

1   When I was a child I used hate classical music, but I loved rock.

2   Every time I went to a concert I buy a T-shirt to remind me of it.

3   My brothers to go to football matches instead of coming to rock concerts with me.

4   After a while I used to going to music events on my own.

5   My mother could not used to me doing different things from my brothers.

6   Now I think she's got used it.

Use of English

Key word transformations (Part 4)

About the exam:
In the Use of English paper, Part 4, there are six unconnected sentences. For each one you complete a new sentence so that it has a similar meaning, using a word given in bold. You must not change this word.
This part tests a range of grammatical structures and vocabulary.

Strategy:
- Don't change the key word.
- Only write between two and five words, including the given word. Contractions (e.g. *won't*) count as two words.

1 Complete the second sentence so that it has a similar meaning to the first sentence, using the word given. Do not change the word given. You must use between two and five words, including the word given. Here is an example (0).

0   I decided not to learn to play the piano as it seemed very difficult.
    UP
    I decided not *to take up learning* to play the piano because it seemed very difficult.

1   I lived in London when I was a child, but now I live in Paris.
    USED
    I live in Paris now, but .... London when I was a child.

2   When I lived in London, I went to the music shop on the corner every Saturday.
    WOULD
    Every Saturday .... the music shop on the corner when I lived in London.

3   It's become easy for me to sing live as I do it so much.
    GOT
    I've .... as I do it so much.

4   I find watching TV quite relaxing in the evenings.
    FEEL
    Watching TV .... in the evenings.

5   I don't go to live concerts very often.
    HARDLY
    I .... live concerts.

6   I only found your message by chance when I was looking for something else.
    ACROSS
    I .... accident when I was looking for something else.

Writing

Informal email (Part 2)   ▶ CB page 14

About the exam:
In Part 2 of the Writing paper you may have the opportunity to write a letter or email. You will be given part of a letter or email to reply to, and you should write 140–190 words. The letter or email may be semi-formal or informal.

Strategy:
Read the instructions and the whole task very carefully. Identify:
- who you are writing to
- why you are writing
- what you have to write about
- whether you need to use a semi-formal or informal style

You will probably need to use functions such as explaining, giving information, suggesting. Make sure you cover all the points mentioned in the email or letter in the task.

1 Look at the task and decide if statements 1–5 below are true (T) or false (F).

> You have received an email from your English-speaking friend, Julia.
>
> From: Julia
> Subject: Music Club
>
> I'm going to start a music club here! I want to play music from all over the world, and I'd like to visit your country to get ideas. When's the best time to come? What's the best way to find out what kind of music young people like?
> Can you recommend some local music clubs I could visit?
> Reply soon,
> Julia

1 You should write in a formal style.
2 Your reply should provide various kinds of information.
3 You have to ask some questions as well.
4 You can use abbreviations and smileys in your answer.
5 You should write 140–190 words.

2 Write your email for the task. You must use grammatically correct sentences with accurate spelling and punctuation in an appropriate style.

3 Match the sentences below to the functions in the box. You can use two of the functions more than once.

explaining   inviting   refusing an invitation
stating preferences   making offers
making suggestions

1 What I'd rather do is go to the evening performance.
2 I'm afraid I won't be able to make it in November.
3 Maybe we could meet outside the box office at seven.
4 The thing is, the venue's a difficult place to find so it's better to go together.
5 I'm going to the gig in the park tonight – do you fancy coming along?
6 July is the best month for festivals so that would be a really good time to come.
7 Would you like me to buy the tickets?
8 Unfortunately, that's when I have some of my exams.

4 Look at the task below. Then read the email the student has written.

Identify any missing information.

Underline any sentences that are too formal.

Correct any language mistakes.

> You have received this email from your English-speaking friend, Jo.
>
> From: Jo
> Subject: Next week
>
> Hi Inga – I'm really looking forward to coming to stay with you next week. If you can't meet me at the station at 3, I'll get a taxi.
>
> Tell me about the music festival we're going to! Do I need to bring anything special?
>
> See you soon!
>
> Jo

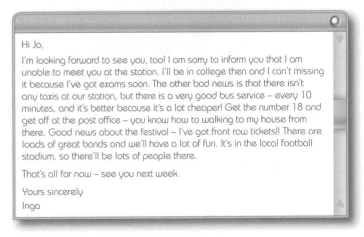

Hi Jo,

I'm looking forward to see you, too! I am sorry to inform you that I am unable to meet you at the station. I'll be in college then and I can't missing it because I've got exams soon. The other bad news is that there isn't any taxis at our station, but there is a very good bus service – every 10 minutes, and it's better because it's a lot cheaper! Get the number 18 and get off at the post office – you know how to walking to my house from there. Good news about the festival – I've got front row tickets!! There are loads of great bands and we'll have a lot of fun. It's in the local football stadium, so there'll be lots of people there.

That's all for now – see you next week.

Yours sincerely
Inga

Relative values

Vocabulary

formation of adjectives ▶ CB page 17

1 Look at the adjectives of feeling in the box. Which five are negative?

imaginative	practical	relaxed	harmful
independent	encouraging	depressing	confusing
frustrating	irritated		

2 Complete sentences 1–6 with a suitable adjective from Activity 1.

1 She found the lecture very .... and couldn't understand her own notes afterwards.

2 She's a very .... person who likes to do things on her own.

3 I feel most .... when I'm sitting outside in the sun.

4 When newspapers write stories about celebrities that are not true it can be .... to their careers.

5 Too much rain can be rather .... when you want to have a picnic!

6 I get very .... by people who talk loudly on mobile phones in public.

3 Complete the paragraph about Jamie with the adjective form of the words in the box.

pessimist	create	emotion	social	sympathy
reliability	real	thought		

Jamie is a very **(1)** .... person. He always seems to see the negative side of everything. He can be quite **(2)** .... and gets upset if he is criticised, but this does not affect his work. In his work he is **(3)** .... and puts forward lots of unusual and interesting ideas. He gets on well with colleagues and is very **(4)** ...., often inviting them to evenings out. Colleagues describe him as **(5)** .... to people in difficulties, always prepared to spend time with them and offer advice. He is able to set **(6)** .... targets which are possible to achieve. He is always **(7)** .... when meeting deadlines and he never lets others down. He brings a **(8)** .... approach to his work, never jumping in too quickly and making mistakes.

Use of English
Word formation (Part 3)
▶ CB page 17

1 **For questions 1–8, read the text below. Use the word given in capitals at the end of some of the lines to form a word that fits in the gap in the same line. There is an example at the beginning (0).**

Gossip is good for you!

Gossip has a bad name. Many people say it is
(0) *unkind* and others claim that it is often   **KIND**
(1) .... and therefore a waste of time.   **ACCURATE**
Talking about someone behind their back can cause
(2) .... to break down and create   **RELATE**
great **(3)** .... But can it have a   **HAPPY**
positive function as well? The most popular television
programmes are soap operas which often have
rather **(4)** .... storylines in which   **DEPRESS**
strange characters indulge in creating and circulating
(5) .... and vicious rumours that in   **PLEASE**
the real world would be **(6)** .... – and   **ACCEPT**
yet we all take great delight in discussing the ups and
downs of their lives. Why is this? Could it be that they
give us an alternative family which we can gossip
about without **(7)** .... creating   **ACTUAL**
trouble? Taking an interest in other people is
considered to be a **(8)** .... activity in   **HEALTH**
some circles – it gives the feeling of being informed
about what's happening in the wider world. So
gossiping may be good for us after all!

Listening
Multiple choice (Part 4)
▶ CB page 18

1 ▶ **03 You will hear an interview with a young actor called Danny Fisher, talking about his relationships during his career. For questions 1–7, choose the best answer (A, B or C).**

1 How does Danny feel about his family?
   A glad that he came from a big family
   B grateful for the support of his parents
   C happy that his parents wanted him to be an actor

2 What does Danny say about his relationships at school?
   A They were difficult to maintain.
   B They helped him deal with life outside school.
   C They were upsetting because of the attitude of others.

3 Danny thinks that being rich and famous is
   A better than he'd been told.
   B fun because he has money to spend.
   C different from what other people think.

4 What does Danny say about his relationships with the people he works with?
   A They were sometimes rude to him.
   B They are very critical of his acting.
   C They change his mental attitude.

5 Danny says his best friend is important to him because of her
   A approach to her work.
   B attitude to others.
   C acting ability.

6 How does Danny feel about his life?
   A He is angry that others criticise him.
   B He is sorry he didn't have a normal childhood.
   C He is pleased that he has earned a lot of money.

7 What is Danny's attitude towards winning awards?
   A He finds it embarrassing.
   B He thinks he does not deserve them.
   C He dislikes the whole awards system.

Grammar

adverbs and extreme adjectives
▶ CB page 19

1 **Find and correct the mistakes with adverbs in sentences 1–8 below. There are four mistakes.**

1 We followed her directions as close as we could, but we still got lost on the way to the farm.

2 In the afternoons we were free to do whatever we liked.

3 She handed in her essay too lately and the teacher refused to mark it.

4 As hardly as I try, I can never manage to remember all my relatives' birthdays.

5 I'm not as close to my sister as I am to my brother.

6 She spent her money so free that at the end of the month she had nothing left.

7 I've been seeing a lot of Alicia lately. We've become really good friends.

8 It's strange that we get on so well because we have hardly anything in common.

2 **Complete sentences 1–8 below with an appropriate adjective from the box.**

difficult	intelligent	angry	frightened
tired	enormous	big	terrified	exhausted
impossible	brilliant	furious	

1 The test was really .... and most of the students got low marks.

2 Max is certainly very clever but his brother Albert is absolutely ....

3 I'm a bit .... with Tim. He completely forgot my birthday.

4 We really wanted to meet up but it was completely .... in the end.

5 I'm going to have an early night. I'm absolutely ....

6 She was very .... of dogs when she was a child, but now she loves them.

7 Fauzia's new house is absolutely ....! It's got so much more space than her last place.

8 If you're really ...., a coffee might help.

Reading

Multiple matching (Part 7)
▶ CB page 20

About the exam:

In the Reading paper, Part 7, you match questions or statements to several short texts.

Strategy:
- Read the text through quickly to get a general idea of what it is about.
- Underline key words and phrases in the questions.
- Find expressions in the text that have a similar meaning to the key words.

1 **You are going to read a magazine article about people who discovered they had a relative they didn't know about. Read the texts quickly and decide if the statements are true (T) or false (F).**

1 All the people are unhappy about what happened to them.

2 All the people only met recently.

2 **For questions 1–10, choose from the sections of the article (A–D). The key words and expressions have been underlined for you. The sections may be chosen more than once.**

Which two people

live near one another?	1
do the same work?	2
met thanks to someone else?	3
blame someone else for what happened to them?	4
plan to meet for the first time soon?	5
had a good relationship before they found out the truth?	6
were not equally knowledgeable about their family history?	7
plan to publish something about their experience?	8
were at the same event when they were very young?	9
were the victims of a cruel experiment?	10

Finding family

Ever wondered if you had a relative you knew nothing about?
It's not as rare as you might think.

A Harry and Samuel Quintana

Harry Quintana and his cousin Samuel have a lot in common, even if they didn't know that until they met again recently after fifty years. Samuel grew up in South Africa and only visited the USA, where his cousin Harry lived, once as a very small child. Both children attended a family wedding. After that neither boy's parents talked about their relatives overseas. As a result, the cousins grew up on different sides of the Atlantic Ocean, unaware of each other and the parallel lives they were leading. Harry Quintana graduated in dentistry and decided to specialise in the treatment of children. Until he saw Samuel's name in a conference programme, he had no idea that over in South Africa his cousin had already become well established in exactly the same profession. When the cousins met recently they found out they like the same foods and have both recently taken up golf.

B Andrea Ives and Sandy Dixon

They look alike and sound alike, wear similar clothes and have often been taken for sisters. But it still came as a huge shock to Andrea Ives and Sandy Dixon when, more than fifteen years into their friendship, they discovered that they really are related. Ives was adopted as a child but earlier this year learnt the identity of her biological parents. She realised at once that her father had the same name as her best friend's dad. A DNA test later confirmed that he was in fact the same man. The women, who live a mile apart, met through a mutual friend. They soon became so close that Andrea was a bridesmaid at Sandy's wedding. When confirmation of the test result came through, Ives sent Dixon a text saying 'Hi, Sis!' 'It was a shock,' Dixon said, 'but I had always longed for a sister, and what better sister could I have than my best friend?'

C Petra Holmes and Elisa Manning

Petra Holmes and Elisa Manning have lived very similar lives. Both born in New York, they edited their high school newspapers and studied the same thing at university. It was only at the age of thirty-five that they discovered each other and just how similar they were: identical twins who had been separated as babies and gone to live with new families as part of a scientific study of child

development. The truth came out when Elisa decided to try to trace her birth mother. She was able to look at the records and saw that she had an identical twin, Petra. When she finally found her sister, they put the pieces of the story together. 'Nature intended for us to grow up together, so we think it is a crime we were separated,' said Elisa. They have taken this up with the psychologist responsible, but according to the twins he didn't even apologise. The sisters are working on a book about their experience.

D Brenda McLaughlin and Allison Burroughs

Brenda McLaughlin had spent years compiling an extensive family tree in which she had recorded all her father's relatives' names along with the dates they were born, when they married and when they died. Brenda, who lives in Sydney, Australia, knew about their various offspring, including the children of her father's youngest cousin, Irene. Meanwhile, Allison Burroughs, Irene's daughter, was living on the other side of the country in Perth. Although Brenda knew about her and her younger brother, there had been no contact. Then, out of the blue, she received an email from Allison, who had also been looking into the McLaughlin family and had found Brenda's name on a website devoted to genealogy. Allison knew virtually nothing about the family and was amazed and delighted with Brenda's research. 'We've arranged to have a family reunion next Christmas,' says Brenda. 'Better late than never is what I say.'

---

3 **Find phrasal verbs in the texts A–D in Activity 2 with the same meanings as the underlined words and phrases in sentences 1–8 below. There are two phrasal verbs in each of the texts.**

1 I've been <u>investigating</u> ways of getting from Barcelona to Montpellier and the train seems the best option.

2 As children <u>get older</u>, their interests often change.

3 Finally, the real reason Tom had run away from home <u>emerged</u>. He had always hated his stepfather.

4 The student representative has <u>raised</u> the issue of access to the computer room with the school director.

5 Tamara had always <u>wanted</u> a dog and now she had one – a gorgeous Golden Retriever puppy.

6 When her exam results <u>arrived</u> she was overjoyed to see that she had passed everything.

7 I've just <u>started doing</u> yoga. I love it.

8 William <u>discovered</u> that the person he had thought was his uncle was actually not related to him at all.

Grammar

verb patterns with *-ing* and infinitive
▶ CB page 22

1 Underline the best ending for sentences 1–4.

1 I stopped running because *it was raining too hard/I needed the exercise.*

2 I tried to write an email but *he wouldn't accept my apology/I couldn't think what to say.*

3 I remembered buying the milk *but I couldn't remember where I put it/so I put it in the fridge.*

4 I regret to tell you that *I was breaking up with you/you have not got the job.*

2 Complete sentences 1–6 with the correct form of the verbs in brackets.

1 I started .... when I was only three. (*dance*)

2 Do you ever regret .... her about the problem? (*tell*)

3 Sadly, although I wanted .... his friend, he didn't like me. (*be*)

4 I want .... a new mobile phone, but what should I get? (*buy*)

5 I actually enjoy .... to the cinema on my own. (*go*)

6 I can't stand .... football – it's so boring! (*watch*)

3 Find and correct the mistakes with *-ing* and infinitives in sentences 1–6. Tick the sentences that are correct.

1 She made him help her do the cooking, but he wasn't very good at it!

2 I stopped to smoke over five years ago and now I feel great!

3 He tried to phone her number, but she didn't answer.

4 I'll never forget to see the Royal Wedding on television – it was beautiful.

5 I regret informing you that your application for the job has been unsuccessful.

6 I'm keen on doing as much sport as possible to keep fit.

Speaking

agreeing and disagreeing (Part 3)
▶ CB page 23

1 ▶ 04 Complete dialogues 1–3 with the phrases in the boxes. Then listen to the recording and check your answers.

1
| I hadn't thought of that. | I'm not sure about that. |
| So do I. | What about you? | Exactly! |

A: I think it's so important to get on well with your parents.

B: **(1)** .... I have a great relationship with my folks. I think it's more important than getting on with your brothers and sisters.

A: Hmm. **(2)** .... I mean, I think it's important to have a good relationship with them too.

B: It's much more difficult if you come from a very large family.

A: **(3)** .... I guess it's almost inevitable that there will be someone you don't get along so well with if there are a lot of you.

B: **(4)** .... There are five of us and though I get on fine with my older brother and with my two sisters, my younger brother and I just don't have anything in common. **(5)** ....

A: Well, I've only got one sister and I really enjoy doing things with her.

2
| Good point. | I'm not convinced. | Well, actually … |
| I see what you mean but … | What's your view on that? |

A: I saw a programme about relationships last night that said that friends were more important than family.

B: I saw it too – but **(6)** .... Certainly friends are pretty crucial – it'd be a poor social life without them! But family must always come first.

A: **(7)** .... some things the programme said are certainly true for me. They said your friends have a lot more influence on you when you're young than your parents do. **(8)** ....

B: **(9)** .... in my case it was the other way round. I learnt my values from my parents. I think it's their responsibility to teach you how to behave.

A: **(10)** .... Parents do need to teach their children how to behave, but I think you can also learn from your friends.

3
| Neither do I. | I'm not sure about that. | I suppose so. |
| That's very true. | What do you think? |

A: They say that people are having fewer and fewer children.

B: **(11)** .... I don't plan to have a large family myself.

A: **(12)** .... But in some ways, it's a pity. It must be fun to grow up with lots of brothers and sisters. I mean you always have someone to play with.

B: **(13)** .... I'm an only child so I don't really know what it would be like. My friends who come from large families seem much more sociable than me. Being part of a big family might help you to get on better with other people. **(14)** ....

A: **(15)** .... It depends a lot on the family.

Writing

Essay (Part 1)   ▶ CB page 24

About the exam:

In Part 1 of the Writing paper, you have to write an essay for your teacher in 140–190 words. You will be given a topic and a question, and some ideas to use. You must use these ideas in your essay, and also add one idea of your own.

Strategy:

- Read the task carefully.
- Think of ideas about the notes you are given. It may help to think of advantages and disadvantages of each one, with reasons for your opinions.
- Remember to think of another idea of your own, with a reason.
- Plan your answer so that you have an introduction and a conclusion that answer the question.
- Use a semi-formal style.
- It is important that you include all the ideas you are given in the notes as well as your own idea in your essay.

1 **Read the essay task and question below.**

> In your English class you have been talking about family life. Now your teacher has asked you to write an essay.
>
> Write an essay using all the notes and give reasons for your point of view.
>
>> Every family is different in size. Do you think it is better to grow up in a large family or a small one?
>> **Notes**
>> Write about:
>> 1 company
>> 2 support
>> 3 .... (your own idea)

2 **Choose the best linking words from the box to complete the sentences below. There is one word you don't need to use.**

while	as well as	in spite of	whereas
although	as	however	

1   It's great to have lots of brothers and sisters .... you always have someone to spend time with.

2   If you have cousins living near you .... friends, you can talk to them about problems.

3   I was always close to my sister .... the big age gap between us.

4   Parents can always give you support. ...., grandparents have more time to listen to you.

5   It's good to have younger siblings, ... they can also be annoying!

6   A big family can be very noisy, ... a small family may be much quieter.

3 **Look at the points a student wants to make in their essay. Which points are not relevant?**

> 1 company
> big family: always someone to talk to/competitive/play games
> small family: quiet/boring/internet
> 2 support
> big family: siblings listen to problems/parents pay for everything/don't need friends
> small family: more independent/can live in a flat/can spend more money
> 3 own point: grandparents
> you can find out about the old days/they have time to listen to you/they don't understand modern life

4 **Read the essay below. Underline the linking words the student uses to connect their points with their reasons.**

> Is it better to live in a large or small family?
> This is a difficult question to answer as we can't choose our family, and every family is different. We can only experience our own family! However, there are points I can make.
> In a big family with lots of siblings there is always someone to talk to and listen to your problems because they know you well and can really help you. On the other hand, siblings can also be very competitive, and that can cause problems.
> The problem with a small family is that life can be very quiet, and possibly boring, even though it does teach people to be independent, which is a good thing. Nevertheless, they need to make lots of friends outside their family.
> It is a great advantage when grandparents live in the family as well, since they can teach you about life in the past. They also have more time to listen to you as they don't go out to work like parents do, but sometimes they have problems understanding modern technology.
> On balance, it seems that there is no right answer, but there are more advantages than disadvantages to living in a bigger family.

5 **Read the task below. Decide which idea you agree with, and make notes about the points with your reasons. Then think of another idea of your own.**

> In your English class you have been talking about family relationships. Now your teacher has asked you to write an essay.
>
> Write an essay using all the points and give reasons for your point of view.
>
>> Is it better to be the oldest or the youngest in a family?
>> **Notes**
>> Write about:
>> 1 time parents have with you
>> 2 responsibilities you have
>> 3 .... (your own idea)

6 **Write your own answer to the task, using 140–190 words.**

Multiple-choice cloze (Part 1)

For questions 1–8, read the text below and decide which answer (A, B, C or D) best fits each gap. There is an example at the beginning (0).

Rock 'n' roll drummers are as fit as sports stars

Bands are (0) ...*A made up of*... talented people, each with their own (1) .... and status within the group. But drummers are different.

Doctors monitored drummers during rehearsals and (2) .... performances and their findings were surprising. Many drummers are as fit as (3) .... athletes. Good drumming requires a combination of physical and mental agility, and fitness is vital. (4) .... a performance a drummer can lose two litres of fluid and burn (5) .... hundreds of calories. One described it as having a three-hour workout every night. Modern drummers often follow a strict fitness regime, working with personal trainers and sticking to a special (6) .... Several hours before a performance, many start warming up by doing stretching exercises; like athletes, they eat bananas to (7) .... their energy levels and take specially prepared energy drinks with them (8) .... The comparison between drummers and sports stars seems fair.

0	**A** made up of	**B** put up with	**C** come up with	**D** done up of
1	**A** part	**B** purpose	**C** role	**D** section
2	**A** live	**B** realistic	**C** true	**D** authentic
3	**A** important	**B** special	**C** elite	**D** exclusive
4	**A** During	**B** While	**C** Through	**D** Whilst
5	**A** off	**B** out	**C** back	**D** in
6	**A** nutrition	**B** menu	**C** diet	**D** food
7	**A** keep up	**B** take up	**C** get up	**D** give up
8	**A** at stage	**B** on stage	**C** in stage	**D** by stage

Open cloze (Part 2)

For questions 9–16, read the text below and think of the word which best fits each gap. Use only one word in each gap. There is an example at the beginning (0).

Mother or father?

Are the roles of parents interchangeable? No – and (0) ...*they*... never will be, although both are crucial to a child's development. Surprisingly, even (9) .... women actually carry the babies, (10) .... art of parenting isn't necessarily instinctive. A child's relationship with his mother is different from the one he has with his father, but men can care for children every bit as much as women. Both men and women discover (11) .... to raise their children through a process of trial (12) .... error.

When children fail to achieve some goal they have set (13) .... or have arguments with their friends, it is often the mother (14) .... longs to make things right for them. The father is more likely (15) .... keep his distance and let the children fight (16) .... own battles in order to learn from them. But it is a matter of balance, and the equal involvement of both parents is becoming the pattern of modern life.

Word formation (Part 3)

For questions 17–24, read the text below. Use the word given in capitals at the end of some of the lines to form a word that fits the gap in the same line. There is an example at the beginning (0).

Music or architecture?

'Talking about music is like dancing about architecture.'

It is thought the **(0)** _composer_ Clara Schumann said this in 1846, although there's no conclusive **(17)** .... of that. But what did she mean? Let's think about it. Firstly, music sends its own message to its listeners, and so it may be **(18)** .... to talk about what it means. But it is not **(19)** .... to imagine a dance troupe doing an interesting and meaningful **(20)** .... with architecture as its topic. If so, Clara's **(21)** .... quote would be wrong and talking about music may be more **(22)** .... than she thought. People can hold their own **(23)** .... opinions about all forms of art, and the artist's own intention is not **(24)** .... any more valid than anyone else's interpretation of their work. So, let's keep talking about art, music and films. Wouldn't life be dull if no one wanted to share their opinion!

	COMPOSE
	PROVE
	POINT
	POSSIBLE
	PERFORM
	ORIGIN
	USE
	PERSON
	NECESSARY

Key word transformations (Part 4)

For questions 25–30, complete the second sentence so that it has a similar meaning to the first sentence, using the word given. Do not change the word given. You must use between two and five words, including the word given. Here is an example (0).

Example:

0 I am considering taking up golf.

OF

I am thinking of taking up golf.

25 She was watching television but turned it off when her son arrived.

STOPPED

She .... when her son arrived.

26 I was cleaning the cupboard when I found an old diary.

CAME

I .... when I was cleaning the cupboard.

27 When I was young I enjoyed listening to rock music but now I prefer classical.

LISTEN

When I was young .... to rock music but now I prefer classical.

28 I always went on holiday with my family to France every summer.

WOULD

I .... on holiday with my family to France every summer.

29 I'm still working on that report.

FINISHED

I .... that report yet.

30 There's a good chance that my team will win the cup this year.

VERY

It .... my team will win the cup this year.

Things that matter

Reading

Multiple choice (Part 5) ▶ CB page 26

1 You are going to read an article about singing and what it means to people. Read the article quickly and decide if the following statement is true or false.

All the people involved with Rock Choir are non-professionals.

2 Read the article again. For questions 1–6, choose the answer (A, B, C or D) which you think fits best according to the text.

1 What has Rock Choir meant for Nicholas Williamson?
  A It has allowed him to fulfil an ambition.
  B It has given him self-confidence.
  C It has given him and his girlfriend a chance to do something together.
  D It has made him aware of his musical ability.

2 Why did Caroline Redman Lusher decide to start Rock Choir?
  A She found it hard to make any money as a musician.
  B She was tired of teaching people who were not very talented.
  C She realised how much people enjoyed singing.
  D She knew this was what her parents wanted her to do.

3 Why do people like being in Rock Choir?
  A They meet people from many different walks of life.
  B There are always people of their own age in the choir.
  C No one judges the members' singing ability.
  D There are no members who can't sing in tune.

4 What does 'so' in line 36 refer to?
  A running Rock Choir
  B recruiting other instructors
  C being the only instructor
  D being in demand

5 In what way has Stef Conner benefited from being a Rock Choir instructor?
  A She has met new people.
  B She has learnt to compose pop songs.
  C She has been able to pay for her studies.
  D She has found an outlet for her personality.

6 How does Caroline Lusher see the future of Rock Choir?
  A She wants it to become even bigger.
  B She wants to fulfil members' aspirations.
  C She wants to set clear limits and not expand too quickly.
  D She wants to attract more publicity.

They will rock you: the rise of Rock Choir

With 7,500 members, Rock Choir has filled Wembley, signed a record deal and is now the subject of a TV show. Alice-Azania Jarvis meets the woman behind it.

Nicholas Williamson had never done anything like it. 'I've always liked music, but I'd never taken any opportunities,' explains the twenty-year-old student. 'I wasn't very confident.' But when his mother joined a local choir and his girlfriend expressed interest in doing the same, he decided to <u>give it a go</u>. Before long, the pair had signed up as members of Rock Choir, Glasgow City Centre. 'I wanted to be part of something big – and now I am.'

Rock Choir is, by all accounts, 'something big'. With 7,500 members <u>nationwide</u>, the choir has signed a three-album record deal and in May, filled out Wembley Arena to give a special performance to 3,500 spectators.

The whole thing is the <u>brainchild</u> of Caroline Redman Lusher. A professional singer from the age of fifteen, she studied contemporary music at Salford University before spending four years as a member of a band, entertaining guests at a top London hotel. 'I was lucky to make a living for so long,' she reflects. Eventually, though, she gave it up and took up a post as a teacher.

It was while she was teaching performing arts and music that the Rock Choir model began to take shape. 'I had all these students who wanted to sing, but hadn't necessarily had any training; it was about bridging the gap between amateur and professional.' What began as a small gathering of about twenty quickly <u>swelled</u> to a far more challenging 170. 'Before long, I had the mums and dads begging for their own version – that's when I realised that there was a market amongst the general public.'

And so it was that, in 2005, Lusher quit her job, borrowed £1,000 from her family and pinned a poster up in her local coffee shop. 'I was hoping for twenty people,' she says of her first choir practice. 'My dad and I laid out forty chairs. In the end, seventy turned up.' They were people of all ages, backgrounds and abilities; <u>crucial</u> to Rock Choir's appeal is the fact that there is no selection process, meaning that even the least confident, most inexperienced of singers can relax and enjoy themselves.

For the following three years, Lusher remained the only teacher at Rock Choir, but eventually demand became too much and she had to recruit *line 36* other instructors. Doing so was a risk since her <u>charisma</u> accounts for much of Rock Choir's success. She is energetic, enthusiastic and imaginative, playing the piano and calling out instructions into her microphone headset to choir members who learn only by repetition. Her teaching style combines professionalism with accessibility. Imitating it is certainly not easy.

Stef Conner had never heard of Rock Choir until she applied to be an instructor for a new group in Yorkshire. 'I was studying for a PhD in classical composition and I needed a job that I could do while I was studying.' With only a limited knowledge of pop music, working with the new style was a challenge for Stef – but one that has <u>paid off</u>. 'I spend a lot of time in isolation, composing. Rock Choir has opened up a whole new world to me: a new style of music, but also a place where I can go and be an extrovert.' Williamson feels the same way: 'You're part of a team having fun,' he reflects.

It's precisely this sort of experience – among both teachers and pupils – that accounts for the choir's rapid success. May's appearance at Wembley was typical of Rock Choir: over the years, it's <u>pulled off</u> a host of similar stunts – from flash mobs to Guinness World Records. The next project will be even bigger and better, says Lusher. 'One day I'd love to perform at the *Royal Variety Show*,' she says, 'and there's been some talk of the Olympics too. Ultimately, it's about what the members can say they've done. The sky's the limit.'

3 Match the underlined words in the article with definitions 1–8.

1 idea
2 succeeded in doing something difficult
3 try doing something
4 grew
5 been successful
6 very important
7 natural ability to make people like you
8 in every part of a country

Vocabulary

-*ed* adjectives and prepositions
▶ CB page 27

1 Find and correct the mistakes in sentences 1–6 below.

1 I get really annoyed of people talking loudly on their mobile phones during concerts.
2 I'm quite frightened with snakes, though I know it's stupid!
3 I worry a lot with the environment; we really have to do more to look after the planet.
4 My brother is really interested on sport – he loves it.
5 I get quite embarrassed of bad behaviour in sports events; I feel really bad about it.
6 We're going on holiday next week and I'm so excited with it!

2 Complete sentences 1–6 with the correct form of the words in the box.

excite	frustrate	annoy	embarrass
worry	interest		

1 I often go red and feel incredibly .... when people praise me.
2 It's quite .... when people talk loudly on their mobiles in quiet places.
3 I get very .... about holidays.
4 I was very .... about my sister recently when she had a wisdom tooth removed.
5 I find history very .... , particularly the sixteenth century.
6 I get very .... when people stop me doing what I want to do.

Grammar

present perfect and past simple ▶ CB page 28

1 **Underline the correct alternatives to complete the text.**

(1) I *have been/was* interested in photography all my life.

(2) I've *owned/owned* about ten different cameras over the years.

(3) I *started/'ve started* with quite a cheap camera that my parents

(4) *bought/have bought* me for my fifteenth birthday. **(5)** I *used to get/have got* the films developed at a local photography shop. Of course, **(6)** I *haven't had to/didn't have to* do that for a long time now. Digital photography **(7)** *has been/was* really bad for shops like that. Many of them **(8)** *have gone/went* out of business.

2 **Complete the text with the present perfect or continuous form of the verbs in brackets.**

Horse mad

Every Christmas and every birthday throughout my childhood I always put one thing and one thing only on the list of things I wanted: a horse. I **(0)** *have been* (*be*) mad about horses for almost as long as I can remember but it's only recently that I **(1)** _____ (*actually start*) learning to ride. Apparently, riding **(2)** _____ (*become*) popular with a lot of adults so I'm not alone. I **(3)** _____ (*have*) lessons at a local riding school for about two months now. I go twice a week so I **(4)** _____ (*have*) about fifteen lessons so far. I'm really impressed with the instructor and with my horse, Daisy. I **(5)** _____ (*learn*) so much from her. She's incredibly kind and patient with me though she **(6)** _____ (*get*) a little bit cross a couple of times. I **(7)** _____ (*read*) about the benefits of riding lately as well. Apart from all the physical benefits, riding improves self-confidence, helps you learn to face risks and makes you much more self-disciplined. Riding is more than just a hobby for me too. It **(8)** _____ (*give*) my life meaning.

Use of English

Open cloze (Part 2) ▶ CB page 29

About the exam:

In the Use of English paper, Part 2, you read a text with eight gaps. The missing words may be **grammatical**, e.g. parts of verbs, referents (*this, those*, etc.), connectors (*however, moreover*, etc.), *as* and *like*, or **vocabulary**, e.g. phrasal verbs or collocations such as *do your homework*.

Strategy:

• Read the title and the whole text to make sure you understand it.

• Look at the words on both sides of each gap.

• Decide what kind of word is missing.

---

1 **Complete sentences 1–6 with a grammatical word, collocation or phrasal verb.**

1 Some people find music can cheer them _____ when they feel low.

2 Make _____ you study hard before an exam.

3 I'm so busy that I don't know how I'm going to get _____ the amount of homework I have to do.

4 It's easy to _____ in touch with old friends from school on the internet.

5 I prefer doing sports _____ tennis to sitting reading.

6 I've always thought of you _____ my best friend.

2 **For questions 1–8, read the text below and think of the word which best fits each gap. Use only one word in each gap. There is an example at the beginning (0).**

Is that glass really half empty or half full?

What is really important in life? Sometimes it's good to sit back and think **(0)** *about* where you are right now and what you hope to be good **(1)** _____ in the future. Having aims and objectives is crucial, **(2)** _____ you must also appreciate what you have already and should be thankful for. Everybody has ups and downs, good days and bad days. Sometimes something **(3)** _____ may seem to be a huge problem one day can seem very insignificant the next. It's vital to **(4)** _____ things in perspective. Always believe that **(5)** _____ bad you may feel about something, there's always somebody out there who **(6)** _____ had a tougher or more difficult day than you. If you can't appreciate this fact, you're likely to feel more unhappy than you need to. Of **(7)** _____, that doesn't mean you can always be cheerful and smiling, but there are a lot of good things out there, so cheer **(8)** _____. People who say a half-full glass of water is half empty are considered to be pessimists – so try to see that glass of water as being half full! You'll feel much happier!

Vocabulary

money ▶ CB page 30

1 **Underline the correct alternatives to complete the sentences.**

1 It's a bad idea to lend money *to/for* a friend as it often causes problems.

2 It's nice when rich people give some money *away/back* to charity.

3 I'm always short *of/about* money at the end of the month.

4 It's important to try to live *within/about* your means and not borrow money from anyone.

5 I've just won a small amount of money and I feel as though I've got money *for/to* burn!

6 It's not easy to live *with/on* a tight budget but that's what students have to do.

2 **For questions 1–6, complete the second sentence so that it has a similar meaning to the first sentence, using the word given. Do not change the word given. You must use between two and five words, including the word given.**

1 She's incredibly rich so she can buy anything she likes.
   BURN
   She's _____ because she's incredibly rich and can buy anything she likes.

2 It's not a good idea to owe money to another person.
   IN
   It's not a good idea to _____ to another person.

3 I can't buy you everything you want because I just don't have enough money to do that!
   MADE
   I'm not _____ so I can't buy you everything you want.

4 I think that young people live better lives than their grandparents, financially.
   STANDARD
   I think that young people have _____ than their grandparents.

5 He's so rich – I can't imagine how much money he earns every week.
   FORTUNE
   He must be _____ because he earns so much money every week.

6 I haven't got much money at the moment, so I can't buy that new mobile phone yet.
   TIGHT
   Money _____ at the moment, so I can't buy that new mobile phone yet.

Listening

Sentence completion (Part 2) ▶ CB page 31

About the exam:
In the Listening paper, Part 2, you complete sentences with between one and four words. You must write the exact words you hear and the sentences come in the same order as on the recording.

Strategy:
• Read the instructions carefully and make sure you understand the context and who is speaking.
• Read the sentences and try to guess what kind of information you need to write, e.g. a job, a time, a month, and what part of speech it is.
• Listen and complete the sentences. If you miss an answer the first time, go on to the next sentence. You can complete any missed sentences when you listen for the second time.
• Check that your answers are grammatically correct and that you have not made any spelling mistakes.

1 ▶ 05 **You will hear a young naturalist called Steve Barnes talking to a group of students about his work and why it matters so much to him. For questions 1–10, listen and complete the sentences, using a word, a number or a short phrase.**

Steve first became interested in animals because he lived on a (**1**) _____ as a child.

Steve enjoyed collecting the (**2**) _____ after school.

Steve likes going (**3**) _____ and rock-climbing in his spare time.

Steve uses the word (**4**) _____ to describe the natural world he loves.

According to Steve, (**5**) _____ is the most important message of the programmes he makes.

Steve wants children to have a sense of (**6**) _____ with his programmes.

Steve gives the example of a time he was injured by falling over a (**7**) _____ to show how spontaneous his programmes are.

Steve is pleased with the way his programmes have made children more aware of ways in which changes in (**8**) _____ affect the natural world.

Some experts say that (**9**) _____ and media have a negative effect on children's connection with the natural world.

Steve feels proud of discovering the biggest species of (**10**) _____ on one of his expeditions.

Grammar

comparing ▶ CB page 32

1 Complete quiz questions 1–6 with the comparative or superlative form of the adjectives in brackets.

1 Which country has .... tourist industry? (*big*)

2 Where do you get .... weather all year round? (*sunny*)

3 Which city is .... – Melbourne or London? (*polluted*)

4 Which is .... mineral in the world? (*rare*)

5 Which country has .... students at maths? (*intelligent*)

6 Which country has .... record on environment protection? (*good*)

2 The answers (A–F) to the questions in Activity 1 contain mistakes with comparative and superlative forms. Correct the mistakes and match the answers with the questions.

A Fewest than two or three crystals of painite, which is said to be the rarest, are found each year.

B Switzerland, but my country, Australia, is much worser than I thought.

C Yuma in Arizona. The sun shines for more that 90 percent of the time.

D In Korea students get by far the high scores in maths tests but they're not as better at some other subjects.

E France has the more tourist visitors, but China is getting more and more popular.

F London, though they are trying to get lesser people to drive their cars in the centre of the city.

3 Underline the correct alternatives to complete the dialogue.

A: What do you like **(1)** *more/most* about the place you come from?

B: Well, there are some amazing buildings, but that's not nearly **(2)** *as important as/more important than* the people. They're great.

A: Would you like to move back to your home town when you finish studying or are you **(3)** *happier/happiest* here?

B: I'm **(4)** *just as happy/far happier* living here as I would be back home. This is **(5)** *the best/the better* place to live in the world, in my opinion.

Speaking

Long turn (Part 2) ▶ CB page 33

comparing similarities and differences

About the exam:
In the Speaking paper, Part 2, you have to compare two photographs and say something about them, according to the examiner's instructions.

Strategy:
Listen carefully to the examiner's instructions. If you are not sure what you are supposed to do, ask for clarification. Say something like: 'Excuse me. Could you explain again what I'm supposed to do?'

1 ▶ 06 Listen to the examiner giving a student some instructions and the student's response. Does she do what the examiner asks her to do?

2 Underline the correct alternatives to complete the extract from a speaking test. Then listen again and check your answer.

These photographs are similar because they both show groups of people but they are **(1)** *very different/more different* in other ways. The first photograph shows people on a beach, **(2)** *although/whereas* the people in the second photograph are probably in a city or town. In the first photograph, the people look **(3)** *as though/like* environmental activists protesting about some kind of problem. **(4)** *Although/Whereas* the people have signs, they look **(5)** *more relaxed/most relaxed* than the people in the other picture. In the second photograph, the people seem to be watching something happening in front of them. Most of them **(6)** *look/look like* excited so I think they might be watching a football match. Most of the people **(7)** *look as if/look* they are really upset about whatever has just happened, **(8)** *while/and* one man is clapping. Perhaps the other team has just scored a goal.

Writing
Article (Part 2) ▶ CB page 34

About the exam:
In Part 2 of the Writing paper, you choose from three options. One of these may be an article. The purpose of an article is to interest and engage the reader.

Strategy:
* Read the task carefully to identify what you must include in your article.
* Think of ways of interesting the reader, e.g. colourful language, rhetorical questions.
* Think of an interesting and memorable introduction and conclusion.

1 Read the task and then look at the ideas below that some students have had for their articles. Match activities 1–7 with the reasons they gave A–G.

> You see this advertisement on an English language website.
>
> ### Articles wanted
>
> **An activity I would never give up!**
>
> What is the best activity you do? Why is it important to you? Why wouldn't you want to give it up?
>
> Write us an article answering these questions.
>
> We will put the best article on our website.

Write your article. Write 140–190 words.

Activities
1 I know it sounds strange but I think I will go on studying throughout my life.
2 Something I would never give up is visiting my grandparents.
3 I've been meditating for about three years now and I could never do without it.
4 I would never give up playing tennis at our local club.
5 I just couldn't live without playing the guitar.
6 It doesn't matter how old I get, I will never stop surfing.
7 Working as a volunteer is more important to me than anything else I do.

Reasons
A The exhilaration you feel out there on your board is just incredible.
B There's always something new to learn.
C It helps me cope with stress and has really improved my concentration.
D I make new friends, meet old ones and it certainly keeps me fit.
E I love being able to make music for myself and for my friends.
F I know I'm using my time to make a difference and that's what matters.
G It really means a lot to them to see my cousins and me every weekend.

2 Look at the titles and opening paragraphs below. Which one is better?

A Something I would never give up: riding my quad bike

> I do a lot of different activities but the one I like most is riding my quad bike. I've only had the bike for a couple of months but I enjoy riding it so much, I don't think I will ever give it up. It is very important to me.

B Life just wouldn't be the same

> I enjoy a lot of the things I do but if you asked me if there was one activity I liked more than the others, my answer would have to be singing in a rock band. I honestly don't think I could ever willingly give it up. Let me tell you why.

3 Look at the conclusions to two more articles. Which one is better?

A

That is why I would never give up such an important activity. You should try it too. It's very good for you.

B

So, whatever people say, however old I get, whatever happens to me, I don't think I would ever give up doing martial arts. It's what keeps my body and soul together.

4 Write your article using the task information in Activity 1.

Battling nature

4

Listening

Multiple choice (Part 4) ▶ CB page 37

1 ▶ 07 **You will hear an interview with Alan Preston, a young man who sailed round the world alone at the age of sixteen. For questions 1–7, choose the best answer (A, B or C).**

1 How does Alan describe himself as a child?
  A keen to follow in his father's footsteps
  B interested in dangerous activities
  C willing to try anything new

2 Why does Alan say he started sailing seriously?
  A He wanted to please his parents.
  B He hoped to repeat a good experience.
  C He intended to follow his own ambitions.

3 How did Alan feel about preparing to sail round the world?
  A It was difficult getting financial help.
  B It was hard getting his whole family to agree.
  C It was tough dealing with personal criticism.

4 When he started the trip, Alan
  A found it too physically demanding.
  B was upset by difficulties with the boat.
  C worried about the prospect of loneliness.

5 Alan said that the worst moment of his trip
  A gave him confidence to cope with anything.
  B meant he had to use special equipment for the first time.
  C was challenging because of unexpected weather conditions.

6 Alan explains that he continues to sail because of
  A the feeling he gets from being at sea.
  B the competitive nature of the sport.
  C the things he sees while sailing.

7 What is Alan's most important advice for other young sailors?
  A Keep sailing in perspective.
  B Get the best advice you can.
  C Prepare differently for each trip.

Vocabulary

idioms: the body ▶ CB page 37

1 **Match 1–8 with A–H to make idioms connected with the body.**

1	get	**A**	.... a straight face about something
2	catch	**B**	.... cold feet about something
3	keep	**C**	.... your head around something
4	put	**D**	.... your foot down about something
5	come	**E**	.... eye to eye with someone about something
6	keep	**F**	.... someone's eye
7	see	**G**	.... face to face with something
8	get	**H**	.... an eye on something

2 **Replace the underlined words in sentences 1–8 with an idiom using the part(s) of the body given in brackets.**

Example: *I don't enjoy working with Josh – we never seem to* be able to agree *about anything.* (*eye*)

I don't enjoy working with Josh – we never seem to see eye to eye *about anything.*

1 That new car must have <u>been incredibly expensive</u>! (*arm, leg*)

2 I couldn't <u>stop myself laughing</u> when he wore those ridiculous clothes to the party. (*face*)

3 I'm <u>getting pretty nervous</u> about the meeting next week. (*feet*)

4 I feel really ill so I <u>don't feel like</u> going shopping this morning. (*face*)

5 I'm finding it hard <u>to understand</u> the new sickness policy at work. (*head*)

6 I'm sorry but I must <u>pay attention to</u> the time because I can't miss the bus. (*eye*)

7 I'm always scared of <u>saying the wrong thing</u> at work. (*foot*)

8 When I was shopping, that new camera really <u>attracted my attention</u> – I think I'll buy it next week. (*eye*)

Grammar

narrative forms ▶ CB page 38

1 **Find and correct the mistakes with narrative forms in sentences 1–10 below. There are mistakes in six of the sentences. Tick the sentences that are correct.**

1 I walked down the street when I saw my friend Brenda getting out of a sports car.

2 The man who was driving it was looking slightly familiar.

3 I was sure I had seen him somewhere before.

4 As he drove off, I was realising that I had met him at a party at Brenda's boyfriend's house.

5 He had been talking to my boyfriend just before we left the party.

6 Later that night, my boyfriend had told me that the man had been telling him a story about a friend who had disappeared.

7 Apparently this person was missing for several months before he was found living in France.

8 He had been working as a waiter in a restaurant and using a false name.

9 The man who told my boyfriend the story had had dinner in the restaurant and had recognised the missing man.

10 I still wonder what Brenda did getting out of his car that day.

2 **Complete the story with the correct form of the verbs in brackets: past simple, past continuous, past perfect or past perfect continuous.**

A would-be lifeguard

I **(1)** _____ (*jog*) along the beach with my boyfriend when I **(2)** _____ (*notice*) a man on a surfboard quite a long way out who **(3)** _____ (*wave*) his arms around frantically. I **(4)** _____ (*not stop*) to think and **(5)** _____ (*run*) into the water to try and save him. Only a month before I **(6)** _____ (*complete*) a special training programme for lifeguards and I **(7)** _____ (*want*) to try out what I **(8)** _____ (*learn*).

I **(9)** _____ (*swim*) as fast as I could to where I **(10)** _____ (*see*) the man on the surfboard but when I **(11)** _____ (*get*) there he **(12)** _____ (*disappear*) completely. I **(13)** _____ (*look*) around desperately but he **(14)** _____ (*be*) nowhere to be seen.

I **(15)** _____ (*feel*) really terrible. It **(16)** _____ (*be*) my first opportunity to rescue someone and I **(17)** _____ (*fail*) dismally. I **(18)** _____ (*walk*) sadly along the beach looking for my boyfriend when I **(19)** _____ (*see*) the man. He **(20)** _____ (*talk*) to my boyfriend and they **(21)** _____ (*laugh*)! It **(22)** _____ (*turn out*) that they **(23)** _____ (*know*) each other at university but **(24)** _____ (*lose*) contact. The man **(25)** _____ (*wave*) to attract my boyfriend's attention, not because he **(26)** _____ (*drown*).

Speaking

Collaborative task (Part 3)
▶ CB page 39

1 ▶ 08 **This is what two students said during a discussion about survival skills. Listen and complete their conversation.**

> I'd like you to imagine that you are going on a trip across the desert. Talk to each other about why these skills will be useful during your trip.

A: OK. Let's talk about what'd be useful on our trip. We have to eat so I reckon cooking **(1)** ....

B: I agree. The problem is, how would we do it? It'll be so hot we won't want a fire.

A: True, but we can cook at night when it's **(2)** .... – that'd be **(3)** .... in the daytime.

B: OK. I accept that. But what about fishing? That's **(4)** .... for anyone in the desert!

A: You mean because there's **(5)** .... anywhere else! I agree, that'd be pointless.

B: It's the **(6)** .... we'd need! Let's keep talking about other skills – there must be something more useful.

2 **Now decide which skills would be most useful.**

Reading

Multiple matching (Part 7) ▶ CB page 40

1 **You are going to read four texts about people from traditional societies and what they think about their environment. Read the texts quickly. Which of the following is <u>not</u> mentioned?**

tourists   animals   crime   families   sport

2 **Read the texts again more carefully. For questions 1–10, choose from the people (A–D).**

Which person

has experienced severe weather conditions?	1
dislikes the way other people live?	2
is worried about what will happen in the future?	3
could always find his way in the place where he lived?	4
talks about the role of the older generation?	5
had difficulty away from the place where he usually lived?	6
has seen a great change in the landscape?	7
made others appreciate the place he comes from?	8
has not given up an activity he did when he was younger?	9
has achieved something very difficult in a short time?	10

3 **Find words in the texts to match definitions 1–8 below. The words are in the same order in the texts and there are two words in each text.**

1 very famous and admired
2 not too expensive
3 say they have seen
4 the job that you do in order to earn money to live
5 playfully make fun of
6 changed direction
7 change the way you do things because of new conditions
8 seen something happen

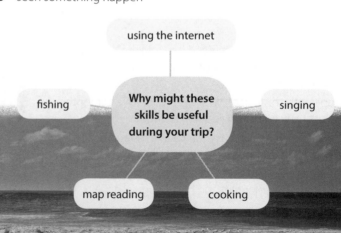

using the internet

fishing

Why might these skills be useful during your trip?

singing

map reading

cooking

In harmony with nature

**There are people who have a special relationship to their environment.
Celeste Weiss tells us about four such people.**

A Rabbit Kekai: Hawaii

Kekai is one of the legendary Hawaiian surfers who became known as the Waikiki Beachboys. The original Beachboys worked the beaches of Waikiki in the 1920s when it was just a tiny village. They taught wealthy visitors to Hawaii how to surf, catch waves in outrigger canoes and enjoy Hawaiian culture. Because the tourists usually spent long periods of time in Hawaii, the Beachboys often developed close friendships with them. Rabbit Kekai, for example, taught many Hollywood actors to surf. Like the other Beachboys, he was known for his charm and his love of Hawaii, which he instilled in the tourists he befriended. As air travel made access to Hawaii more affordable, more tourists came and stayed for shorter periods of time. These changes affected the relationships the Beachboys were able to cultivate with the tourists. Waikiki Beachboys still work the beaches but the film stars and wealthier tourists now stay away and life is very different. Rabbit still loves the beach and is still surfing, even at 91.

B Dawa Steven Sherpa: Nepal

Dawa was born in a village just twelve miles from Mount Everest over 1,000 metres above sea level. His father used to climb with famous British mountaineers and his grandfather, originally a yak herdsman, toured the world with Sir Edmund Hillary, the first man to reach the summit of Everest. All three generations of Dawa's family testify to major climate change taking place today. A glacier Dawa's grandfather used to cross while herding his yaks, the largest in Nepal, no longer exists. 'The whole thing has just melted,' says Dawa, who has climbed Everest twice since he took up climbing two years ago. Climate change has seriously affected local communities. Tourism is being hit because villages which once had a lot of water for trekkers now don't have any. 'Without the foreign trekkers these people will lose their livelihood,' says Dawa.

C Anaviapik: the Arctic

Anthropologist Hugh Brody describes the visit to London of Anaviapik, an Inuit who had never previously left the Arctic. Although he survived the several weeks he spent in the UK quite well, one thing he could never get used to was the buildings. Every day Brody would tease Anaviapik, challenging him to find his own way home from the local Tube station. Every day he got lost. 'How amazing that the white people live in cliffs,' he said to Brody. 'I would never be able to find my way here without you.' Back in the vast, white landscapes of the Arctic, Anaviapik had no such problems. On one occasion, Brody travelled with him hundreds of miles by dog sledge. On the way, Anaviapik diverted to a place he had not visited since 1938. 'How did you remember the way?' asked Brody. 'Inuit cannot get lost in our own land. If we have done a journey once we can always do it again.' This shows how different the attitudes of hunter-gatherers like Anaviapik are. To him, transformed landscapes like ours have no appeal or meaning.

D Dean Yibarbuk: Northern Australia

The Aboriginal people of Northern Australia do not necessarily see fire as bad and destructive. Dean Yibarbuk, secretary of a local land management agency, explains that traditionally, fire was seen as a way of bringing the land back to life. 'Unfortunately,' says Yibarbuk, 'this knowledge is being lost. To go forward, adults need to encourage children in the ways of the past. We have a great responsibility to ensure that these practices with fire are still used to keep our land alive and healthy.' Although climatic changes have always taken place, Yibarbuk's people were able to adapt easily. 'They were hunters and gatherers who looked for food and good places to live even in changed circumstances. When walking about, they would cover the whole area looking after our land according to our traditional land management practices.' The floods and violent storms that Yibarbuk has witnessed recently are not brought on by nature but by human behaviour. People no longer travel on foot and have stopped using fire in the traditional way.

Vocabulary

collocations and idioms: weather
▶ CB page 40

1 **Underline the correct alternatives to complete the sentences.**

1 When we went skiing, it was *absolutely/fairly/a bit* freezing.

2 I fell over in the snow so often my clothes were *absolutely/soaking/just* wet.

3 On the mountain there were often very *strong/torrential/hard* winds.

4 Sometimes there was also *hard/strong/dense* fog, which made it difficult to see anything.

5 At least there were two days with *hard/strong/thick* sun, which was lovely.

6 I was so *completely/freezing/absolutely* cold most of the time that I don't think I'll go skiing ever again!

7 There were no stars and so the night was *pitch/absolutely/strong* black.

8 There was a *freezing/hard/rough* frost last night; temperatures must have been really low.

Grammar

definite, indefinite and zero articles
▶ CB page 42

1 **Find and correct the mistakes with articles in sentences 1–10 below.**

1 That's a lovely house over there and it's got the beautiful garden.

2 We had dinner last night in a most expensive restaurant in town.

3 How often do you play the golf every month?

4 I had to go to dentist last week as my tooth was very painful!

5 Where did you have the lunch yesterday?

6 The most important thing we can all do for planet is to recycle more.

7 I'm staying at the home today.

8 I love a snow – it's great for skiing!

9 I could hear a rain beating on the roof of the tent all night.

10 I could see it was raining, so I just grabbed the umbrella from the collection in the cupboard.

2 **Complete the newspaper article with *a/an, the* or (–) for no article.**

Report from Antarctica

In March, I'm joining **(0)** ___–___ other scientists in Punta Arenas, **(1)** ___ southernmost town in **(2)** ___ Chile. We're departing on **(3)** ___ special research vessel heading for **(4)** ___ South Shetland Islands situated off **(5)** ___ Antarctic Peninsula for a thirty-two-day trip, and while we're at **(6)** ___ sea, we'll be collecting environmental data from **(7)** ___ waters surrounding **(8)** ___ islands. We're looking for any long-term trends and changes in **(9)** ___ Antarctic ecosystem. Antarctica is famous for having **(10)** ___ most treacherous seas on **(11)** ___ Earth, and during **(12)** ___ last trip we got hammered with **(13)** ___ bad weather. Not only does this make **(14)** ___ life on board pretty uncomfortable, but it also causes all sorts of sampling problems. **(15)** ___ last month, **(16)** ___ scientific team lost valuable and expensive gear. Of course, all this is normal when you're working in **(17)** ___ Antarctica and it's what makes **(18)** ___ Southern Ocean such an exciting environment to work in. Every year is **(19)** ___ new adventure and one I look forward to – even though **(20)** ___ dangers there are very real!

Use of English

Word formation (Part 3)   ▶ CB page 43

1 **Use the prefixes in box A to make the opposites of the adjectives and verbs in box B.**

A   un-   dis-   im-   mis-   ir-

B   successful   encouraged   healthy   fortunate
mature   responsible   understand   advantage
patient

0	*unsuccessful*	5	
1		6	
2		7	
3		8	
4			

2 **Complete sentences 1–4 with the correct form of the words in brackets. Add a negative prefix where necessary.**

1 The first expeditions to ascend Everest were _____ and several climbers died. (*success*)

2 I feel quite _____ if I'm criticised all the time. (*encourage*)

3 He's always having accidents. He's very _____. (*fortunate*)

4 Wait a minute! Don't be so _____! (*patient*)

3 **For questions 1–8 read the text below. Use the word given in capitals at the end of some of the lines to form a word that fits in the gap in the same line.**

Driven to extremes

People used to go on holiday for **(0)** *relaxation*. **RELAX**
Nowadays, however, there seems to be a real obsession with holidaying in a very different way – taking on extreme challenges. What began as a small number of people climbing Everest or crossing the Antarctic has developed into a **(1)** _____ industry. For those who choose to **SUCCESS**
undertake **(2)** _____ events such as a race across **COMPETE**
Death Valley, the enterprise can be dangerous and the chances of **(3)** _____ for those who are **SURVIVE**
(4) _____ in such conditions depends on experts making **EXPERIENCE**
sure they do not go **(5)** _____. Many do it because **PREPARE**
they find their everyday lives **(6)** _____ and so they **SATISFY**
dream of adventure. Instead of spending their time off in **(7)** _____ cafés enjoying glorious sunshine, **PLEASE**
people are suffering, attempting more and more outrageous things. Some people do it to raise money for charity but others want exciting and dangerous experiences, so they look for new and possibly **(8)** _____ challenges to face. **RESPONSIBLE**

Writing
Essay (Part 1) ▶ CB page 44

1 **Read the task below.**

In your English class you have been talking about the environment. Now your teacher has asked you to write an essay.

Write an essay using all the notes and give reasons for your point of view.

> What can we do as individuals to help the environment?
>
> **Notes**
> Write about:
> 1 recycling
> 2 transport
> 3 .... (your own idea)

2 **These sentences were written to answer the task in Activity 1. Complete the sentences with the best word or phrase from the box. There may be more than one possibility.**

apart from	as a result	as well as
because of this	in addition to	in my view
in order to	I believe	would lead to

1 ___I believe___, it is important for every individual to take responsibility for the environment.

2 People should use the same shopping bag over and over again, ___in order___ cut down on plastic.

3 It is easy to recycle paper, and this _____ fewer trees being cut down.

4 If we cycled everywhere, there would be fewer cars on the road and ___because___ there would be a decrease in fumes.

5 _____ cycling, people should also walk more; _____ saving energy the consequence would be that people would be healthier.

6 People should turn lights off when they leave a room; this would save energy ___as well as___ money.

7 ___in addition___ that if people didn't leave their computers on standby, they would save energy.

8 People use too much energy, and ___as a result___ the ozone layer is getting thinner.

3 **Which idea in the sentences in Activity 2 was not included in the task and was the student's own idea?**

a recycling   b transport   c saving energy

4 **Read this student's essay answering the task in Activity 1 and underline the correct linking words.**

Many people feel that it is not worth doing anything on their own to help the environment, since one individual cannot make a difference. **(1)** However / In addition, there are some things that **(2)** unless / if we all do them then we can improve the situation with the ozone layer. The first thing we can do is recycle our waste products. People should **(3)** also / too use the same shopping bag over and over again, **(4)** in order to / such as cut down on plastic.

Another idea is choosing the transport we use. **(5)** As well as / Instead of driving cars, if we all cycled everywhere this would mean that there were fewer cars on the road and **(6)** as a result / following there would be a decrease in fumes. This would also make people healthier.

I believe that saving energy is something that everyone can do, **(7)** and / since if people didn't leave their computers on standby, they would not use so much electricity and would save energy.

(8) While / What's more I agree that all of these things don't make a difference if only one person does them, if we all do them then we can start to look after our environment.

5 **Now write your own answer to the task below. Try to use linking words from Activities 2 and 4.**

In your English class you have been talking about the natural world. Now your teacher has asked you to write an essay.

Write an essay using all the notes and give reasons for your point of view.

> Is it important to have parks and green spaces in cities? Give your opinion.
>
> **Notes**
> Write about:
> 1 wildlife
> 2 beauty
> 3 .... (your own idea)

Multiple-choice cloze (Part 1)

For questions 1–8, read the text below and decide which answer (A, B, C or D) best fits each gap. There is an example at the beginning (0).

The science of happiness

Some scientists believe that asking people how happy they are is **(0)** _A similar to_ asking them about an event they've attended in the past – there's a lot they **(1)** .... no notice of during the experience, so how do they know? These scientists think that anyone studying happiness should pay more **(2)** .... to people's experiences at the time they occur, not afterwards.

Other scientists say that we are actually **(3)** .... up of our memories. They suggest that studying moment-to-moment experiences at the time **(4)** .... too much emphasis on temporary pleasures, and that happiness goes **(5)** .... than that. They identify three key **(6)** .... for happiness: pleasure, engagement (how involved we are with family, work, romance and hobbies) and meaning (how we use our personal strengths to achieve important **(7)** ....). It is interesting that, **(8)** .... to what might be expected, pleasure seems to play the smallest part in what makes us happy.

0	**A** similar to	**B** close to	**C** typical of	**D** consists of
1	**A** gave	**B** took	**C** got	**D** kept
2	**A** focus	**B** concentration	**C** attention	**D** regard
3	**A** made	**B** built	**C** created	**D** developed
4	**A** sets	**B** puts	**C** fixes	**D** rests
5	**A** stronger	**B** lower	**C** deeper	**D** greater
6	**A** ingredients	**B** parts	**C** factors	**D** items
7	**A** intentions	**B** plans	**C** marks	**D** goals
8	**A** against	**B** opposing	**C** contrary	**D** contrast

Open cloze (Part 2)

For questions 9–16, read the text below and think of the word which best fits each gap. Use only one word in each gap. There is an example at the beginning (0).

More than just a pretty face?

There are many stories of dolphins helping people in trouble, **(0)** _like_ saving swimmers from shark attacks by gathering round them or shepherding them to safety. **(9)** .... these stories are true, why do dolphins do it and **(10)** .... makes them behave in this way? Scientists **(11)** .... have studied them are not entirely sure. For dolphins to act together as a group to save humans implies that **(12)** .... is some sort of code of ethics among dolphins, but there is little evidence for that. The **(13)** .... likely explanation is that they instinctively respond to the appearance of predators like sharks by herding weaker members of their own group into **(14)** .... safe place – and there is proof that dolphins do cooperate with **(15)** .... other to ward off danger. Maybe they just mistake swimmers for part of their group, which would mean that dolphins don't have genuine feelings of kindness towards humans. **(16)** .... may be that their smiling appearance simply gives people the wrong idea.

Word formation (Part 3)

For questions 17–24, read the text below. Use the word given in capitals at the end of some of the lines to form a word that fits the gap in the same line. There is an example at the beginning (0).

The only way is down

The latest extreme sport has been attracting **(0)** *tourists* and risk-takers alike. It's a **(17)** .... ride called the 'fantasticable' which uses nothing but gravity. You're inside something which has been called a 'glorified baby carrier' attached to a metal wire which forms a **(18)** .... between one mountain summit and another. You then 'fly' across the deep valley below at **(19)** .... speeds of up to 110 kph. At the highest point this carrier can be as high as 400 metres off the ground. But isn't it rather **(20)** ....? Apparently not, as one ride in Italy started after local residents joked that it was a shame they could not fly across the deep valley that separated two villages as it would be a **(21)** .... way to visit neighbours! Now **(22)** .... rides are springing up in a variety of different **(23)** .... However, if you know you are a really **(24)** .... sort of person who worries about where the brakes are, this may not be the ride for you!

TOUR
FRIGHTEN

CONNECT

AMAZE

POINT

USE
COMMERCE

LOCATE
ADVENTURE

Key word transformations (Part 4)

For questions 25–30, complete the second sentence so that it has a similar meaning to the first sentence, using the word given. Do not change the word given. You must use between two and five words including the word given. Here is an example (0).

Example:

0 Please don't drive so fast – this is a dangerous road.

MORE

Please *drive more slowly* – this is a dangerous road.

25 Nothing irritates me more than getting hundreds of spam emails.

MORE

There is nothing .... getting hundreds of spam emails.

26 The tennis game was so exciting that the spectators cheered loudly at the end.

WERE

The spectators .... the tennis game that they cheered loudly at the end.

27 I'm very interested in learning about the culture of other countries.

IS

Learning about the culture of other countries .... me.

28 I find it very worrying if things go wrong on holiday.

GET

I .... things going wrong on holiday.

29 I get bored by people who talk too much.

FIND

I .... when people talk too much.

30 I had never seen a glacier before I went to Norway.

I

When I was in Norway .... the first time.

Eat your heart out!

5

Vocabulary
food and diet

1 Complete sentences 1–5 with the words in the box.

| high-fat | well-balanced | vegetarian | salt-free | vitamins |

1 I never eat meat – I follow a strict .... diet.
2 People who are overweight are rarely told to follow a .... diet.
3 It's good to give children a .... diet, including meat, fruit and sugar.
4 I love fruit, vegetables and so on; I know I'm getting a diet rich in ....
5 Older people may be advised to follow a .... diet for health reasons.

Grammar

countable and uncountable nouns and expressions of quantity ▶ CB page 47

1 Underline the correct alternatives to complete the sentences.

1 Would you like *some/a few* rice with your chicken?
2 I mustn't eat too *many/much* chocolate – it's bad for me!
3 People who eat too *much/many* salt can suffer from high blood pressure.
4 I drink *hardly any/a few* coffee; if I drink too *many/much* I can't sleep.
5 I buy very *few/little* eggs as I keep chickens, so I have new-laid eggs.
6 I eat *hardly any/a few* meat – I prefer vegetables!
7 There is always *many/a lot of* news about food scares these days.
8 There are *lots of/much* fantastic desserts at that new restaurant!
9 I try to eat *some/many* fruit every day.
10 There is a myth that if you eat *a few/a little* cheese in the evening you will have vivid dreams!
11 There are *no/any* sweets in my house!
12 I often eat *a bit of/a few* cake in the evening.

2 Complete sentences 1–8 with *few, a few, little* or *a little*.

1 I knew very .... people at the party, so I didn't stay long.
2 .... of us are going to have a barbecue in the garden tonight. Do you fancy coming?
3 Please could I have .... sugar – this coffee is rather strong.
4 I've got .... free time this week so I can do the work if you like.
5 I've eaten so many already that there are only .... chocolates left!
6 I knew very .... about Thai food so I bought a cookery book to learn more.
7 I know .... people who enjoy very spicy food, but not many.
8 People say that .... knowledge goes a long way!

Use of English

Open cloze (Part 2) ▶ CB page 48

1 Read the text below and think of the word which best fits each gap. Use only one word in each gap. There is an example at the beginning (0).

Food, glorious food

These days it's very hard to get people to agree **(0)** ___on___ anything. But there's one thing we can all accept – people like food! However, what makes good food is **(1)** _____ a universal concept – something considered repulsive in one part of the world is a delicious lunch in another. For example, many of us **(2)** _____ been brought up to believe that insects are for swatting rather **(3)** _____ eating, but in fact **(4)** _____ are an important part of the diet in many places and provide a valuable source of protein. Perhaps the problem really is that we have become too unadventurous – we are now so **(5)** _____ to vacuum-packed, tasteless ready-made meals that we are unwilling **(6)** _____ try anything unusual. Yet many less obvious combinations of food can change our tastes – simple touches **(7)** _____ combining carrots with sugar enhances their flavour – and how about trying strawberries with a bit **(8)** _____ pepper? There's food out there for everyone and if you look hard enough you are sure to find something you love.

2 Read the text again and underline an example of

1 a comparative.
2 a verb + preposition.
3 a quantifier.
4 a pronoun.
5 an auxiliary.
6 an uncountable noun.

Listening

Sentence completion (Part 2) ▶ CB page 49

1 Look at the text below and match the type of missing information, A–D, with sentences 1–5.

A adjective
B number
C noun (x2)
D noun – name of a subject

2 ▶ 09 You will hear a woman called Terri Preston talking about her unusual job. For questions 1–10, complete the sentences.

The horse nutritionist

Terri studied **(1)** _____ at university.

Terri takes part in **(2)** _____ to monitor the health of horses.

Terri was surprised to find that horses eat **(3)** _____ kilos of grass every day.

One day Terri monitored very **(4)** _____ horses which she found physically difficult.

Terri does not like doing **(5)** _____ very much.

Terri uses the word **(6)** _____ to describe how she feels about answering questions on the phone.

Terri is annoyed about the way **(7)** _____ is provided for her work.

Terri describes human nutrition as **(8)** _____ nowadays.

Terri says that the best approach for people to take to a diet is **(9)** _____ rather than reducing what they eat.

Terri uses the example of **(10)** _____ as something people should eat less of if they eat chocolate.

Reading

Multiple choice (Part 5) ▶ CB page 50

1 You are going to read an article about a teenager who runs his own chocolate-making business. Read the text once quickly and choose the best title.

1 With a little help from my friends
2 A talent for chocolate but no head for figures
3 Chocolate millionaire turns eighteen

2 Read the text again. For questions 1–6, choose the answer (A, B, C or D) which you think fits best according to the text.

Think teenagers, think couch potatoes eating pizzas out of the box or munching 99p burgers? Think again because there's a new teenager in town and he's on a chocolate-coated mission! Louis Barnett runs a rapidly-growing chocolate empire which counts among its customers the British supermarket chains Waitrose and Sainsbury's, as well as upmarket department stores in London, New York and as far away as Moscow. All this and Louis is still only eighteen.

But things weren't always that easy. Despite an IQ of 132, Louis dropped out of school when he was only eleven, frustrated and disheartened. 'It was terribly difficult for him,' his mother Mary explains. 'His handwriting was really bad and he struggled with spelling.' The problem was that Louis was, in his own words, 'dyslexic, dyspraxic and dyscalculic'. Nothing the school system had to offer made any sense to him.

So, with the help of his parents and a specialised tutor, Louis set about a vocational-based, home-study programme concentrating on the thing that he loved most: chocolate. 'I'd always been intrigued by it,' says Louis, who bought his first Belgian chocolates with his own pocket money when he was only nine. By the time he was thirteen he had already created his own line of specialist chocolates, a sample of which he sent to Waitrose head office.

'It was slightly bizarre,' admits Waitrose chocolate buyer, Greg Sehringer. 'One day a package arrived in reception addressed to the confectionary buyer. It spent a day or so in the post room before finding its way to me but as soon as I saw the product, I thought it was great. So we arranged to meet Louis and he arrived here a few days *line 33* later – with his parents. We didn't expect that.' But don't

think this is a case of pushy parents, Sehringer says. Louis did the talking.

The product Louis sent to Waitrose was a box made of chocolate. 'One Christmas I decided to make some chocolates for my family and friends to send as presents but when I looked into packaging I found that it was more expensive than the chocolate inside. So I thought, 'Why not make a chocolate box to put the chocolates in?'

He then gained a qualification in chocolate making from the prestigious Zurich-based Callebaut Academy, the youngest person ever to do so. They in fact sponsored the rest of his chocolate-making education. His grandparents also helped out, lending him the money for a special chocolate temperature-regulating machine. Once he had that, Louis was off and running. By the age of sixteen *line 48* he was selling chocolates to luxury department stores in both the UK and the USA. His company, called Chokolit because this is how Louis as a dyslexic spells chocolate, was very much on the map.

Louis calls himself an ethical chocolatier and includes pictures of endangered species on the packaging of his new range of palm oil-free chocolate bars, a percentage of the sales of which go to animal charities. Waitrose ordered 100,000 boxes of the bars in 2007 and Louis then had to move production from his parents' garage to a factory in the north of England. Louis still lives with his parents, both of whom work for his business, as does his girlfriend Sally, who is his PA. There have been a few problems finding the right staff, though, because some people are reluctant to take orders from a teenager.

As for dealing with the interest from the press and becoming a chocolate maker to the rich and famous, Louis is undaunted. 'What we've done so far is monumental,' he says, 'but I don't want to lose control of the business.' In fact, Louis is already thinking about how he can use the attention he is getting to encourage young people to get into cooking.

1 Why did Louis Barnett leave school?

    A He wanted to try something new.

    B The teachers didn't understand him.

    C He had special problems.

    D He kept failing spelling tests.

2 How did Louis's parents react to his problems?

    A They were very worried about their son.

    B They understood his needs.

    C They paid a private teacher to help him.

    D They blamed the school system for his failure.

3 What does *that* in line 33 refer to?

    A That they would receive a package in the post.

    B That they would actually meet Louis.

    C That Louis would be with his parents.

    D That Louis would arrive late.

4 What does the phrase *off and running* in line 48 mean?

    A trying to escape

    B competing in a race

    C moving quickly

    D progressing well

5 Why did Louis stop making his chocolates in his parents' garage?

    A The demand for his chocolates had grown.

    B He wanted to make chocolates using ethical principles.

    C He found it difficult to work with his parents.

    D He wanted to move in with his girlfriend.

6 How does Louis feel about his company?

    A He is proud of it but would not like anyone else to run it.

    B He would like to specialise in making chocolates for celebrities.

    C He is worried that it might be getting out of control.

    D He thinks it is not getting enough attention.

3 **Complete sentences 1–7 with the underlined words in the text. Sometimes you need to change the form of the word.**

1 I was .... to lend my sister my car. Last time she drove it she had an accident.

2 We went to a really .... restaurant where not a single thing on the menu cost less than €30.

3 I'm reading a really .... detective novel at the moment. I just can't work out who the killer is.

4 The prospect of getting up at 4a.m. to get to the airport seemed rather ....

5 We were .... to hear the good news about his successful hospital treatment.

6 Don't be so ....! Phoning up every day to see if you've got the job might make them decide to give it to someone else.

7 She had hoped to be able to sail around the world but couldn't find a ....

Vocabulary

phrasal verbs with *turn* ▶ CB page 50

1 **Underline the correct prepositions to complete the sentences.**

1 I get completely turned *up/off* a restaurant if it is not clean.

2 I had so much to do that I turned *out/down* the chance to go out with friends.

3 She was so angry that her dinner was undercooked that she turned *in/on* the poor waitress.

4 My parents had no idea I was going to see them – I just turned *off/up*.

5 My birthday party turned *down/out* to be the best evening ever!

6 I was turned *off/away* from the restaurant on Saturday night because it was full.

2 **Rewrite the underlined part of the sentences using the words in brackets.**

1 So many friends <u>came</u> to the party that we had to go and buy extra food. (*up*)

2 I <u>refused</u> the offer of a job as a waitress as I preferred to work in an office. (*down*)

3 My son got really upset when the other children <u>got angry with</u> him for no reason. (*on*)

4 I wanted to go to the concert but I was <u>refused entry</u> because I didn't have a ticket. (*away*)

Grammar
passive forms ▶ CB page 52

1 **Find and correct the mistakes with passive forms in sentences 1–10.**

1 Rice is always serve with your meal so there's no need to order it separately.

2 Are you been picked up at the station or shall I meet you there?

3 Turkey are eaten every year at Christmas in the UK.

4 The cookery book was wrote by a famous television chef.

5 In the past, women was expected to do all the cooking.

6 Too much fast food are eaten nowadays – people should be educated about healthy eating.

7 It is believe that people should be educated about the health benefits of regular exercise.

8 People are expected throw their litter in the bins, not on the pavement.

9 Orders for our special banquet menu must placed at least two days in advance.

10 She was always being ask to prepare the food for parties since everyone knew she was such a good cook.

2 **Complete the email with the correct active or passive forms of the verbs in brackets.**

Dear Julia,

You'll never guess what **(1)** .... (*happen*). Our lovely new car **(2)** .... (*steal*)!

One day last week Jack went out to the beach for a swim and as usual he **(3)** .... (*hide*) the car keys in the toe of his shoe. When he came out of the water, he **(4)** .... (*not notice*) anything suspicious. It didn't look as if his clothes **(5)** .... (*touch*). When he started to put them on, however, he realised that the keys **(6)** .... (*take*) and when he got to the car park, of course, the car was gone too.

The police say there is a gang of car thieves who **(7)** .... (*know*) to be operating in the area. They think Jack **(8)** .... (*watch*) as he arrived at the beach. The thieves saw where he had parked the car and then where the keys **(9)** .... (*hide*).

It was almost two weeks ago now and although we hope it **(10)** .... (*find*), we're beginning to think we might never see it again.

Well, that's all from me. Write soon and tell me all your news.

Love,

Raquel

3 **Complete the second sentence so that it has a similar meaning to the first sentence, using the word given. Do not change the word given. You must use between two and five words, including the word given.**

1 The chef gave him the recipe.

WAS

He .... the chef.

2 The discussion about food raised many interesting issues.

BROUGHT

Many interesting issues .... the discussion about food.

3 Mary baked the cake using six eggs.

BAKED

The cake ...., who used six eggs.

4 You can't smoke anywhere in the restaurant.

PERMITTED

Smoking .... anywhere in the restaurant.

5 Please check that someone has washed up before you leave!

DONE

Please check that the .... before you leave.

6 Jo had opened the restaurant by himself before Rafa joined him as his business partner.

HAD

The restaurant .... Jo before Rafa joined him as his business partner.

Speaking
Long turn (Part 2) ▶ CB page 53
comparing and giving a reaction

About the exam:

In the Speaking exam, Part 2, each candidate is asked to compare two photographs and give a reaction of some kind in response to the examiner's question. The candidate talks about the photographs for about a minute, pointing out the similarities and differences between the photographs, and then answers the examiner's question.

Strategy:

Make sure you leave enough time to give your reaction after comparing the photographs.

1 ▶ **10 Listen to the instruction an examiner gives to a candidate. What does the examiner ask the candidate to do?**

1 Compare the pictures and say how the people are feeling about being together.

2 Compare the photographs and say what the people are enjoying about eating in different places.

2 Complete the candidate's comparison of the two photographs with the words in the box.

clear	similar	see	both	of
shows	looks	seems	obviously	if

Both these photographs are of people eating together. The first one **(1)** _____ a barbecue. There are quite a lot of people so I think there must be more than one family involved. It **(2)** _____ to be somewhere like the USA. There are a lot of trees in the background, and green grass. Everyone **(3)** _____ as if they are really enjoying the barbecue and the pleasant landscape. There is a woman who is giving out food to the rest of her family and they are all smiling and laughing. There are baskets full of food and jugs of juice in the foreground of the photo. In the background I can **(4)** _____ men who are standing around the barbecue, so I think they are still cooking. They're **(5)** _____ just about to eat. The other photograph is **(6)** _____ a family having breakfast. It's **(7)** _____ to the first photograph in that everyone looks very happy and as **(8)** _____ they are really enjoying being together. The older child is sitting down at a table and the younger child is sitting on her mother's lap. The mother and father are **(9)** _____ looking at their children, who are eating fruit, breakfast cereal and biscuits, and drinking milk. They are all sitting at one end of the table, which seems to make it easier for everyone to talk together and it's **(10)** _____ that they are really enjoying that.

3 ▶ 11 Listen to a candidate giving her response to the photographs and complete her comments.

I think we all like joining our friends and family for meals **(1)** _____ in the photos. It's particularly enjoyable to eat in the open air but even an ordinary meal **(2)** _____ in the kitchen is a good time for the family to get together and talk before the beginning of a busy working day or at the weekends **(3)** _____ .

Writing
Review (Part 2) ▶ CB page 54

About the exam:
In Part 2 of the Writing paper, you choose between various options. One of these options might be a review.

Strategy:
• Balance your review by writing positive and negative comments on whatever you are asked to review.
• You can organise your comments into separate paragraphs (one for positive comments and one for negative) or combine them into one paragraph using linking words.

1 Look at this task and the points two students (A and B) plan to include. Which student's ideas will make a more interesting answer?

> You have been given this task by your English teacher.
>
> ***Can you be our café critic?***
> Have you tried a new café near your school recently? We'd like to know about the food, the place itself and the cost. Tell us whether you would recommend it to other students.
>
> The best review will be published in the school newsletter.

A Chill Out Natural Burger Bar
  - serves burgers and fruit juices
  - open every day
  - prices vary
  - only opened about six months ago
  - not popular with all my friends
  - cheap lunch

B Gloria's Global Salad Bar
  - wide range of healthy options with vegetarian options
  - bright colours and posters on the walls
  - very busy so there can be queues – but worth it
  - friendly helpful staff
  - rather loud music
  - some meals expensive, but there are cheap sandwiches and interesting salads

2 A review should include positive and negative points, although it should always give a final opinion. Which points in list B are negative?

3 Write your own review of Gloria's Salad Bar, using the points given. Decide whether your review is generally positive, and whether you would recommend the bar. Write 140–190 words.

On camera

6

Speaking

Discussion (Part 4) ▶ CB pages 58–59

About the exam:

In the Speaking exam, Part 4, you have a discussion with the other candidate in response to the examiner's questions.

Strategy:

• Make sure you include the other candidate in the discussion and listen to what he or she says.

---

1 ▶ 12 **Listen to two exam interviews and decide if statements 1–8 are true (T) or false (F).**

1 The examiner in the first interview asks Ana about the difficulties of being a famous actor or musician.

2 Ana tries to include Mario in the discussion.

3 Mario summarises what Ana has said.

4 Ana does not accept Mario's argument.

5 The examiner in the second interview asks Celina for her opinions about the *Eurovision Song Contest*.

6 Celina tries to get Gabriel to express an opinion.

7 Gabriel summarises what Celina has said.

8 Gabriel agrees completely with Celina's opinion of the *Eurovision Song Contest*.

2 **Listen again and tick the phrases that you hear the candidates use.**

1 I think …

2 I see what you mean but …

3 Is that what you think too?

4 Would you agree?

5 In my opinion …

6 Well, I suppose you're right up to a point.

7 The point you're trying to make is …

8 I'm not sure about that.

9 What you're saying is …

10 As far as I'm concerned …

3 **Complete the table with the phrases from Activity 2.**

Expressing an opinion	Asking for the other candidate's opinion	Tentatively disagreeing with the other candidate	Summarising what the other candidate has said
(1) .... (2) .... (3)	(4) .... (5)	(6) .... (7) .... (8)	(9) .... (10) ....

Vocabulary

the arts ▶ CB page 59

1 **Put the nouns in the box into the correct column. Some may go in more than one column.**

costumes   production   exhibition
set   premiere   painting   actors
conductor   screenplay   performances
scenery   gallery   stage   play
director   location   critics   review

Film	Art	Theatre	Musical

2 **Complete sentences 1–8 with words from Activity 1.**

1 Have you seen the .... of the film online? The .... have been very complimentary about it.

2 I loved the film in general but the .... was very unnatural – the .... seemed to have difficulty saying the words.

3 The film was beautiful to look at – they filmed it on .... in the mountains.

4 That .... at the local art gallery is brilliant and there are some amazing paintings!

5 Last time I went to the theatre my seat was so far away from the .... I could hardly see what was happening! It was very cheap though.

6 I went to stand outside the cinema at the .... of the latest blockbuster film and I saw all the stars arriving, including the .... of the film.

7 I love musicals, but it's important to have a live orchestra – the .... makes such a difference to the way the music is played.

8 The last .... I saw in the theatre was by Shakespeare and the .... the actors wore were very traditional and from the right period so they looked great.

Listening

Multiple choice (Part 1) ▶ CB page 60

About the exam:

In the Listening exam, Part 1, you hear eight unrelated extracts. You answer one question about each extract by choosing from three options. You hear all the extracts twice.

Strategy:

- Read the question and all the options before you listen.
- After you have heard the extract, choose your answer, then move on to the next question.
- If you are not sure of an answer, don't worry about it – choose an option and move on.

1 ▶ **13 You will hear people talking in eight different situations. For questions 1–8, choose the best answer (A, B or C).**

1 You overhear two people talking in a coffee shop. What are they talking about?
   A a film
   B a musical
   C a live performance

2 You hear a man talking about his choice of career. How does he feel about it?
   A sure that it is right for him
   B pleased to be following his parents' example
   C concerned that his friends don't like what he does

3 You overhear a couple talking at a bus stop. How does the woman feel about something she's done?
   A irritated   B worried   C frustrated

4 You hear part of a radio phone-in programme. Why has the man called the programme?
   A to complain about something
   B to clarify some facts
   C to make a suggestion

5 You overhear a woman speaking to a receptionist on a mobile phone. Where is the receptionist?
   A in a gym   B in a hotel   C in a college

6 You hear two friends talking about a film. What do they agree about?
   A The standard of acting was poor.
   B The special effects were disappointing.
   C The film was not as good as they'd expected.

7 You overhear two people talking. What is the relationship of the woman to the man?
   A line manager   B wife   C colleague

8 You hear a woman talking to a friend. What is she doing?
   A disagreeing with a point of view
   B recommending a solution to a situation
   C expressing regret about a mistake

Grammar

future forms ▶ CB page 61

1 Complete sentences 1–8 with the correct future form of the verbs in brackets.

1 I .... (meet) Jo outside the cinema at six – we arranged it this morning.

2 The plane .... (leave) at six, so I .... (get) a taxi to the airport at four probably.

3 That sounds like the postman; I .... (check) if he's left any post for you.

4 I'm not sure who'll win the gold medal; it .... (be) Magnus this year.

5 That new stadium is almost built – it's definitely .... (finished) next month.

6 I expect that the banks .... (raise) interest rates soon – that's what the papers say.

7 As soon as the programme .... (end), I'm going to bed.

8 We'll have dinner when Joe .... (arrive).

2 Underline the correct alternatives to complete the dialogues.

Dialogue 1

A: What **(1)** *are you doing/will you do* next year?

B: **(2)** I*'m studying/could study* acting at the Royal Academy of Dramatic Arts in London. I did an audition a while ago and I got an email to tell me I'd been accepted yesterday.

A: So you **(3)** *are going to live/live* in London?

B: Yes, **(4)** *I will/I am.* **(5)** *I'll probably share/I probably share* a flat with other students.

A: When **(6)** *does/will* the course start?

B: In mid-September but there **(7)** *will be/is going to be* an orientation week first.

A: Good luck with the course. I'm sure you **(8)** *will really enjoy/are really going to enjoy* it.

Dialogue 2

A: In what ways do you think the entertainment industry **(1)** *changes/will change* over the next few years?

B: Well, one thing I'm certain of is that things like CDs and DVDs **(2)** *are disappearing/will disappear* altogether. **(3)** *We'll download/We download* all of our music, movies and TV series directly from the internet.

C: Well, I agree that CDs **(4)** *are probably not going to be/are probably not* around for very much longer but I think the DVD boxed sets of TV series **(5)** *will still be/are still* popular, even if we can download everything we want. People find them very attractive. Some people are going back to vinyl LPs as well, so maybe **(6)** *there is/there'll be* a return to the good old days.

B: You could have a point there. Some people say that in fifty years' time no one **(7)** *will even remember/is remembering* what a printed book looks like and everyone **(8)** *reads/will read* on e-book readers or smartphones. But a lot of people like to hold a book in their hands and turn the pages.

Reading

Gapped text (Part 6) ▶ CB page 62

1 You are going to read an article about two young actors who are identical twins. Read the article and the sentences that have been removed. Decide if the statements are true (T) or false (F).

1 The fact that they are twins is what has made them successful as actors.

2 They really like being twins.

2 Read the article and the sentences again. Six sentences have been removed from the text. Choose from sentences A–G the one which fits each gap (1–6). There is one extra sentence which you do not need to use.

A Now they were known as the twins again, this time on a global scale.

B James shares this view.

C But even their closest friends can't tell them apart.

D 'Not especially,' they say.

E Even when it came to casting them, there seems to have been a temptation to see them as one unit.

F They seem to have fallen into acting by accident, rather than it being a burning passion.

G They admit it is something they have to battle against.

3 Find words in the article connected with film and theatre to match definitions 1–6.

1 the words of a speech, play or film that have been written down

2 the part of a particular actor in a play or film

3 gave a short performance to see if they were good enough to act in the film

4 something built and provided with furniture, scenery, etc., to represent the scene of part of a film or play

5 the person responsible for choosing the actors for a play or film

6 repeatedly be given the same kind of parts in plays or films

Life after Harry Potter

James and Oliver Phelps play the Weasley twins, Fred and George, in the *Harry Potter* films. Emine Saner meets them.

As Fred and George Weasley, respectively, Ron Weasley's mischievous older twin brothers in the *Harry Potter* films, James and Oliver Phelps must be one of the most famous sets of twins in the world. They were fourteen when they auditioned for the role and had no acting experience other than a bit of drama at school. **1** 'I felt like I wasn't a proper actor for about three or four years,' says James, who still occasionally takes acting lessons. 'I'm very aware that I'm lucky to call it my job.'

Though quick to express their gratitude for their parts in the films they admit that going on set as 'the twins' felt like a step backwards. They had spent the last few years at secondary school carefully carving out their own identities and making their own friends. **2** For one thing, they had to look the same, something they had always fought against. 'I did cringe a bit,' says Oliver. 'In certain bits, they are dressed differently but the argument was made to us that Fred and George dressed the same to be mischievous, so it made sense.'

3 At the first read-through of the script on set, James and Oliver still didn't know which Weasley they would be. 'The casting director went over to speak to the director and JK Rowling. She came back in less than a minute and said, "James, you're Fred; Oliver, you're George."'

Were James and Oliver Phelps very conscious that they were twins as children? **4** Their parents would dress them in different clothes, mainly to tell them apart but also because the family were involved in the Twins and Multiple Births Association, which has always stressed encouraging children's individuality. 'If anyone referred to us as "the twins", the temptation was to ignore them,' says James. 'I know people don't mean to be insulting, and I know that some twins enjoy being seen as twins, but we're at the other end of the scale.'

The trick now for the Phelps twins is to stop being the Phelps twins and, after ten years of the *Harry Potter* safety net, start to forge their own careers. Is there a danger that they will be typecast as a twosome? **5** 'We want to continue acting but not necessarily together,' says James. 'We've had a few meetings with agents in the States but there is a perception that we come as two. I said I want to do individual stuff and one guy just said, "Oh no, I don't see that happening." I shut off as soon as he said that. I wasn't interested.'

What if one finds huge success while the other's career doesn't quite work out? Would a change in their respective fortunes affect their relationship? 'Not particularly,' says Oliver. 'We've always said we're both actors, so obviously we're competing against each other in one way but we're also brothers, so we want the other to do just as well.'

6 'Family means more than the job,' he says. 'If we were both successful, that would be fantastic, but I think you just have to ride the highs and the lows. If he was ahead of me, or I was ahead of him, it would push us even more. He would probably take being considered less successful better than I would. I might find it hard,' he says with a smile, 'if people start asking me if I'm Oliver Phelps.'

4 Complete the tables with words from the article.

Adjective	Noun
(1)	mischief
(2)	luck
(3)	insult
grateful	(4) ....
safe	(5) ....

Verb	Noun
argue	(6) ....
perceive	(7) ....
succeed	(8) ....
(9)	ignorance
tempt	(10) ....

5 Complete sentences 1–5 with words from Activity 4.

1 To be a really .... actor, you have to find a balance between being yourself and acting a part.

2 We didn't have any .... getting tickets for the show. They were all sold out when we got there.

3 I'm so .... to you for telling me about the auditions for the play. I've been given one of the main parts.

4 The children got up to all sorts of .... while we were out. The kitchen was in a terrible mess.

5 My parents didn't want me to be an actor. Their main .... against it was that you could never rely on being able to earn a living.

Grammar

future perfect and continuous
▶ CB page 64

1 There are words missing in some of the sentences below. Insert the words in the correct place. Tick the sentences that are correct.

1 Directors will started to make most of their films in places other than Hollywood.

2 All video clubs have closed down. Everyone will be able to watch whatever they want via the internet.

3 People won't have stopped going to big music festivals like Glastonbury and Benicassim every summer. They'll still be very popular.

4 Many people will have stopped using mobile phones as a result of all the health warnings.

5 People will have using smartphone applications for so long that they'll have got bored with them.

6 Webcams will have become 3D so that it will really feel as if the person you are talking to is in the room with you.

7 A lot of record companies will have gone out of business because most people have started to make their own music and upload it to the internet.

8 People will got used to paying for music and will accept this as only right and fair since the money will go directly to the performer.

Use of English

Multiple-choice cloze (Part 1)
▶ CB page 65

1 Match questions 1–6 with answers A–F.

1 Is there anything you don't get about the homework?

2 Can you get your parents to do whatever you want?

3 When did you last get really angry?

4 How do you get to school every day?

5 How many cups of coffee do you get through in a day?

6 How tired do you get at the end of the day?

A Oh yes – I just have to be nice to them.

B I'm not sure about the writing task.

C Not very – I often go to the gym then.

D I'm actually trying to cut down!

E By bus, unless Dad takes me in the car.

F It must have been when my mobile phone was stolen.

2 Underline the correct prepositions to complete the sentences.

1 It took me ages to get *over/through* that virus but I'm better now.

2 I can't come out tonight because I've got too much work to get *off/through*.

3 Bad weather always gets me *under/down*; I feel much happier when the sun shines!

4 I hate ironing so I just leave it and never get *round to/in to* doing it.

5 My boss is really tough so I never get *over with/ away with* poor quality work.

6 I really got *into/up* skiing last winter; I loved it and want to go again!

7 I love chocolate but I'm trying to cut *down/off* on the amount I eat every day, otherwise I'll get fat!

8 I work hard so holidays are important to me – I try to get *away/through* at least twice a year.

3 For questions 1–8, read the text and decide which word (A, B, C or D) best fits each gap.

To be a star or not to be a star?

If you're longing to lead a film star lifestyle, join the queue of hundreds of would-be actors streaming into Hollywood, **(0)** _D heading_ for the movie studios where they think their dreams will come **(1)** .... But it goes without **(2)** .... that virtually none of these hopefuls will go straight into major roles in mainstream films. Most find temporary jobs to pay the rent, waiting for the **(3)** .... break they think will come eventually – though the **(4)** .... are heavily stacked against them. It isn't easy to get yourself invited to any kind of **(5)** .... Even if you do, being rejected is part of the process – you have to get **(6)** .... it and keep on trying. Never let it get you **(7)** .... – that way you will never succeed. Having said that, you should have an alternative plan just in case you don't **(8)** .... it to the top. If you have to accept that your dreams are just that, and do something completely different, it may actually turn out to be ultimately more satisfying.

0	**A** going	**B** getting	**C** setting	**D** heading
1	**A** true	**B** correct	**C** right	**D** real
2	**A** speaking	**B** saying	**C** talking	**D** expressing
3	**A** huge	**B** big	**C** enormous	**D** massive
4	**A** chances	**B** opportunities	**C** odds	**D** gains
5	**A** audition	**B** rehearsal	**C** practice	**D** interview
6	**A** to	**B** under	**C** through	**D** over
7	**A** down	**B** off	**C** on	**D** in
8	**A** succeed	**B** make	**C** get	**D** pass

Writing
Report (Part 2) ▶ CB page 66

About the exam:
In Part 2 of the Writing paper, you may have the opportunity to write a report. You will be given some information and ideas about what to write.

Strategy:
Read the instructions and the whole task very carefully. Identify:
• the purpose of your report
• what you have to write about.
You should evaluate your ideas and make recommendations or give your opinion at the end.
Use a semi-formal style.

1 You see this announcement on your school noticeboard.

We want your ideas!
We are planning to set up a performing arts club for students, which will include a choir, dance group or theatre group.

Which of these ideas would students like most? How can we improve the facilities that are already there?

Send us a report and we will make a decision.

2 Look at the DOs and DON'Ts and the report a student wrote. Put a cross (✗) next to advice he has ignored and a tick (✓) next to advice he has followed.

1 ☐ **DO** give your report a heading.
2 ☐ **DON'T** begin 'Dear Sir or Madam'.
3 ☐ **DO** divide your report into clear sections.
4 ☐ **DO** use headings which link to the task.
5 ☐ **DON'T** give your opinion at the beginning.
6 ☐ **DON'T** use very informal language.
7 ☐ **DO** use an impersonal style, e.g. the passive and reporting verbs (*it was suggested/claimed/believed*).
8 ☐ **DO** use expressions of purpose, linkers and quantity expressions such as *quite a few, several*.
9 ☐ **DO** check spelling carefully.
10 ☐ **DO** make recommendations.

This report is to sugest ways in wich we could establish a performing arts club in our school. I intervewed a number of students about this issue and the following were there oppinions. Most students were in favour of forming a choir. It was felt that almost everyone would enjoy this. Although it was acknowledged that singing ability varies, it was generally aggreed that in a large group individual talent was not a problem. Another opinion that was shared among the students was that the music chosen should be mostly rock or pop music rather than clasical. Beatles songs were often mentioned in the survey as were Abba and Take That. Finally, a number of students raised the issue of reharsal space and equipment. Although the common room is the obvious place to rehearse, it was pointed out that the piano needs to be repaired. In my opinion a choir offers students an excellent way of taking part in performing arts, and the piano should be repaird.

3 Write the report out again following the advice in Activity 2 that the student ignored.

4 Now write your own answer to the task.

Multiple-choice cloze (Part 1)

For questions 1–8, read the text below and decide which answer (A, B, C or D) best fits each gap. There is an example at the beginning (0).

Do men really cook better than women?

Are women better cooks than men because they have a natural love for food and don't show **(0)** _B off_ ? Or are men better because they **(1)** .... cooking more seriously? Maybe it has **(2)** .... to do with ability – women may be more instinctive, have a better **(3)** .... of smell and a greater understanding of food. **(4)** ...., there are other things to take into account when considering cooking as a career.

Restaurant kitchens are a man's world, because men can carry heavy pans and often work longer hours. Yet, **(5)** .... the fact that the work is physical and stressful, women are calmer in the kitchen, and often have a different attitude; they cook to show they care about others. As one said, '**(6)** .... I'd love to run my own restaurant, but I'd **(7)** .... teach people to be good home cooks. I know it's controversial, but I believe a woman's **(8)** .... is cooking at home.'

0	**A** out	**B** off	**C** in	**D** up
1	**A** take	**B** hold	**C** think	**D** have
2	**A** nothing	**B** something	**C** anything	**D** none
3	**A** instinct	**B** feeling	**C** sense	**D** touch
4	**A** Moreover	**B** In addition	**C** Also	**D** However
5	**A** in spite	**B** though	**C** despite	**D** whether
6	**A** Conversely	**B** Fortunately	**C** Naturally	**D** Hopefully
7	**A** prefer	**B** better	**C** rather	**D** fairly
8	**A** place	**B** job	**C** post	**D** opportunity

Open cloze (Part 2)

For questions 9–16, read the text below and think of the word which best fits each gap. Use only one word in each gap. There is an example at the beginning (0).

A good show? Really?

I love going to the theatre but I am often disappointed **(0)** _by_ the show itself, which fails to live **(9)** .... to my expectations. So what's the best way to **(10)** .... out whether a particular production is worth seeing? Some people read the critical reviews, but **(11)** .... far can they be trusted? There are always glowing tributes outside theatres promising a 'thrilling' evening, or a 'sensational' show, but many theatre managers choose these advertising quotations **(12)** .... great care. This is because they want to **(13)** .... theatre-goers the impression that the reviews were **(14)** .... positive than they might have been. One musical was advertised with the words 'the songs remind you of how fabulous the band were', but more negative comments were left **(15)** .... So maybe what we have to do **(16)** .... read the reviews carefully, but then trust our own judgement about whether we should pay good money to go and see the show.

Word formation (Part 3)

For questions 17–24, read the text below. Use the word given in capitals at the end of some of the lines to form a word that fits the gap in the same line. There is an example at the beginning (0).

Lose your bottle!

There have been many food fads over the years driven by **(0)** _snobbery_ or supermarket advertising campaigns. But promoting bottled water is probably the most **(17)** .... of all. Although they have cheap, clean cold water on tap, many people choose instead to pay vast sums for water **(18)** .... taken from Hawaiian springs or Icelandic glaciers, which is then shipped thousands of miles in tiny plastic bottles to supermarket shelves. Apart from the **(19)** .... damage that all those journeys must do to the planet, I wonder how many of the advertised health benefits **(20)** .... remain after the water has been standing in those plastic bottles for months before a **(21)** .... goes into a shop and buys it? **(22)** .... it would be better if, instead of being drawn into this trend that many might regard as **(23)** .... as well as stupid, we simply aimed at providing clean **(24)** .... water for everyone?

	SNOB
	RIDICULE
	ALLEGE
	ECOLOGY
	ACTUAL
	CUSTOM
	SURE
	MORAL
	DRINK

Key word transformations (Part 4)

For questions 25–30, complete the second sentence so that it has a similar meaning to the first sentence, using the word given. Do not change the word given. You must use between two and five words, including the word given. Here is an example (0).

Example:

0 A very kind friend took us home after the party.

 TAKEN

 After the party, we _were taken home by_ a very kind friend.

25 I couldn't wait to see my friend again after her long trip abroad.

 LOOKING

 I .... my friend again after her long trip abroad.

26 The last time Joe saw Carlos was the day they both graduated from university.

 SEEN

 Carlos .... the day they both graduated from university.

27 'You must do your homework, Tom,' said Carol.

 REMINDED

 Carol .... his homework.

28 I never seem to find the time to read newspapers these days.

 ROUND

 I never seem to .... newspapers these days.

29 Nothing irritates me as much as getting piles of junk mail through the post.

 MORE

 There is nothing .... getting piles of junk mail through the post.

30 The idea of flying is very frightening for some people.

 ARE

 Some people .... the idea of flying.

A home from home

Vocabulary

expressions with *home*

1 **Complete the sentences with the expressions in the box.**

feel at home	home town	holiday home	stay at home
at home	home from home		

1 I was born and brought up in Paris – that's my ....

2 George is a very good host – he makes everyone .... in his house.

3 I'm saving to buy a ....; somewhere I can go to every summer.

4 I can't afford to go away this summer – I'm going to ....

5 Oh no – I haven't got my wallet with me. I must have left it ....

6 Every time I go to Barcelona I stay with my friends Eva and Josep. Their house has become a real .... for me.

Reading

Multiple choice (Part 5) ▶ CB page 69

1 **You are going to read a story about a man who lives a long way from his family. Read the story once quickly and decide if the following statement is true or false.**

The story is about a strange coincidence.

2 **Read the story again. For questions 1–6, choose the answer (A, B, C or D) which you think fits best according to the text.**

1 Why did the writer decide not to go to his grandfather's funeral?
   A His mother did not want him to go.
   B He didn't have enough money to pay for an airline ticket.
   C He didn't want to go on such a long journey.
   D He realised he would probably not arrive soon enough.

2 What was the writer thinking about as he sat on the balcony?
   A How much he would like to see his grandfather and George again.
   B How well his grandfather had looked after his garden.
   C How depressing and dark it was outside in the street.
   D How difficult it was to see properly.

3 What was peculiar about the old man's hat?
   A It was like the one the writer's grandfather wore.
   B It was a strange hat to wear on a day like that.
   C It had not been well looked after.
   D It was an unusual style that was difficult to find.

4 Why didn't the writer follow the man and the dog?
   A He was convinced he hadn't really seen them.
   B He knew he would never be able to catch up with them.
   C He didn't want to have his suspicions confirmed.
   D He was afraid they might turn out to be real.

Too far from home

It was the day after I received the news of my grandfather's death that I first saw the man and the dog. My mother had phoned with the sad news a little before midnight. We discussed all the possibilities but I came to the conclusion that it was completely <u>unrealistic</u> for me to attempt to travel from one side of the world to the other. It would cost a fortune and it was unlikely I would make it in time for the funeral even if I did manage to find a ticket. I knew this but I still wished there was some way I could be there. I barely slept that night and when I did <u>drift off</u>, I was disturbed by dreams that my grandfather was in fact still alive and asking my mother where I was.

At dawn, I gave up even trying to rest and took a cup of tea out onto the little balcony. The street below was deserted. On a normal Sunday a few people might have ventured out even at such an early hour but this was a dark, rather <u>forbidding</u> day. I sat staring into the street but the images that filled my mind were of my grandfather <u>dozing</u> in a wicker chair in the overgrown garden of his house, an old straw hat shielding his face from the sun, his dog George asleep at his feet. I would have given anything to walk again towards those two sleepers, gently wake them and set out with them on a long walk through the country lanes.

Something in the street snapped me out of my <u>reverie</u>, though I did think at first that I was in fact dreaming. An old man was walking along the pavement directly opposite my house. With him there was a small black dog. Oddly, for the time of day and the wintry weather, the man was wearing a panama hat, much like my grandfather's though in slightly better condition. Stranger still, the dog, little more than a pup, was <u>uncannily</u> like George. I closed my eyes and shook my head expecting when I opened them again to see the street as devoid of life as it had been earlier. But the man and the dog were still there. When they reached the corner, the man looked back towards me and leant down to unclip the dog's leash, just as my grandfather had always done when he and George got to the garden gate. Then both man and dog vanished.

At first, I thought that it had almost certainly been a hallucination brought on by sleeplessness and <u>grief</u>. And yet there had been something so real about the two that the vision, if that was what it was, would not let go of me. As the months passed, I thought I saw them disappearing round a corner once or twice but was reluctant to try and follow them. If they were nothing more than a figment of my imagination, I preferred not to know. Believing they existed somehow kept my grandfather present. It was as if he and George had come all this way to watch over me even if I never caught more than an occasional <u>glimpse</u> of them.

But then, one afternoon, I did. I stepped out of my _line 58_ front door and found the man and the dog right in front of me. The man was not as much like my grandfather as I had thought but the dog, though younger than poor old George had been the last time I saw him, was in every other respect a <u>carbon copy</u>. I realised the man was looking at me as if he expected some kind of explanation. 'I'm looking at your dog,' I said. 'My grandfather had one just like him when I was a child.' The man <u>chuckled</u>. 'Have him if you like,' he said. 'No, no. Of course not. I can see he's very fond of you and you of him.' I leant down to pat the dog's glossy head. 'What's his name?' I asked. 'George,' said the man. What else would it be, I thought. 'It's good to see you again, George,' I whispered. The dog looked up at me as if in recognition.

5 What does 'did' in line 58 refer to?
  A prefer to know
  B catch more than a glimpse
  C believe they existed
  D keep my grandfather present

6 At the end of the story what impression are we left with?
  A The man did not want his dog any more.
  B The man did not like the writer patting his dog.
  C The writer would like to have a dog of his own.
  D The writer suspected the dog would be called George.

Vocabulary

deducing meaning
▶ CB page 69

1 **Look at the underlined words and expressions in the story on page 49 and decide which of the two alternatives, A or B, is closest to the meaning in context.**

1 unrealistic
   A impractical
   B fantastic

2 drift off
   A fall asleep
   B float away

3 forbidding
   A prohibiting
   B unpleasant

4 dozing
   A reading
   B sleeping

5 reverie
   A daydream
   B light sleep

6 uncannily
   A not very
   B remarkably

7 grief
   A trouble
   B sadness

8 glimpse
   A view
   B understanding

9 carbon copy
   A a copy made with carbon paper
   B an exact likeness

10 chuckled
   A laughed
   B frowned

Grammar

modal verbs: possibility and certainty ▶ CB page 70

1 **Complete sentences 1–6 with the correct form of the modal verbs in the box. You may need to make other changes to the sentence.**

must	can	could	may	might

1 The test wasn't so bad – it .... a lot worse!

2 I haven't seen her today so she .... ill, though it's unlikely.

3 Sue hasn't replied to my email which is not like her; she .... received it.

4 He .... here because he sent me a text to tell me he'd arrived in the building.

5 I didn't hear the postman knock because I .... asleep.

6 I drove to work but I can't find my car keys now. I .... left them in my coat pocket – I often do!

2 **Write sentences similar in meaning to sentences 1–6. Use one of the modal verbs in brackets to replace the underlined words and phrases.**

1 I don't know why I can't contact her – it's possible her mobile phone is switched off. (*must/could*)

2 He has his own webpage, I'm pretty sure. (*may/must*)

3 It's impossible for them to be eating outside because it's raining! (*can't/mustn't*)

4 It's possible that John is arriving tonight. (*might/must*)

5 It's impossible for us to leave because it's too early. (*couldn't/can't*)

6 I'm not sure, but I think that the new student is from Germany. (*could/must*)

Speaking

Long turn (Part 2) ▶ CB page 71

1 ▶ 14 **Listen to an examiner giving a candidate instructions about the two photographs. What does the examiner ask the candidate to do?**

1 Compare the photographs and say why people choose to celebrate their weddings in situations like these.

2 Compare the photographs and say which of the weddings would be more difficult to organise.

2 **Decide whether phrases 1–10 express certainty (C), probability (P) or doubt (D).**

1 They seem/appear (to be) …

2 It looks like/as if (they are) …

3 It/They must be/have done …

4 It/They could/may be/have done …

5 It/They can't be/have done …

6 I imagine (that they are) …

7 I'm fairly/absolutely certain (they are) …

8 As far as I can see, (they are) …

9 I suppose (they are) …

10 They are definitely …

3 ▶ 15 **Listen to what a candidate said about the photos in Activity 1 and complete the text.**

Well, the first couple have chosen to have a cycling wedding. **(1)** .... they are on their way to the reception in the photograph and that the wedding ceremony itself **(2)** .... already taken place. **(3)** .... very happy about it, and the other members of the wedding party **(4)** .... they are enjoying it too. The other couple have decided to have one of their wedding photos taken under water. **(5)** .... have had the actual wedding there. **(6)** .... of that.

The first couple **(7)** .... cycling fanatics. **(8)** .... really love the sport if they have chosen to cycle to the reception. The other couple **(9)** .... just wanted an unusual wedding photograph for their wedding album. **(10)** .... an underwater photograph would be rather difficult to organise but it **(11)** .... be fun. **(12)** .... there's nobody else in the photo, so **(13)** .... it was also taken after the wedding itself. **(14)** .... been taken the day after. It wouldn't be much fun sitting through the reception in a wet wedding dress!

Listening

Multiple choice (Part 4) ▶ CB page 73

1 **The words in the box are used to describe places. Which two are positive?**

characterless   desolate   empty
grandeur   remarkable   weird

2 ▶ 16 **You will hear a radio interview with a musician and photographer called Karen Wilson. For questions 1–7, choose the best answer (A, B or C).**

1 What does Karen say about her teachers at school?
   A They developed her interest in music.
   B They enabled her to improve her artistic talent.
   C They followed old-fashioned methods of teaching.

2 How did Karen feel when she was asked to write a travel book?
   A concerned about other people seeing her pictures
   B pleased to be able to demonstrate her individuality
   C surprised that a publisher was interested in her

3 In her books, Karen's main aim is
   A to encourage more people to travel.
   B to help people enjoy their own travel experiences.
   C to make people think more deeply about what they see.

4 Karen says that what she finds fascinating about places is
   A the mismatch between appearance and reality.
   B the different types of place she has to go to.
   C the people she meets on her travels.

5 What did Karen enjoy most about her trip to Argentina?
   A seeing unusual wildlife
   B giving successful concerts
   C being alone in the natural landscape

6 What does Karen say she has learned from travelling?
   A It may be helpful to be a tourist in some places.
   B It's sometimes necessary to accept places for what they are.
   C It improves the travel experience if you try to understand a place.

7 What does Karen say has contributed most to her success?
   A having a lot of luck in life
   B responding to a challenge
   C getting support from others

Vocabulary

travel ▶ CB page 73

1 **Complete the sentences using words from the box.**

guided tour	return ticket	business trip
sightseeing tour	package holiday
camping trip	season ticket	domestic flights

1 I'm looking forward to the _____ of the city – it's the best way to see a lot of places in a short time.

2 Buy a _____ for the train because two singles are much more expensive.

3 I'm going on a _____ in the mountains with friends – it's great to live rough!

4 People who commute to the city from the country buy an annual _____ on the train.

5 _____ within a country are usually cheaper than international flights.

6 My husband is going on a _____ to Germany, but I'm not going because he'll be working all the time.

7 I went on a _____ of Windsor Castle and learned so much about the history of the place from the expert who showed us round.

8 When you book a _____ everything is organised including accommodation and travel.

Grammar

relative clauses ▶ CB page 74

1 **Underline the correct relative pronouns in sentences 1–10.**

1 I don't enjoy stories *that/who* have sad endings.

2 The island, *which/that* is smaller than Wales, is very beautiful.

3 The city, *who's/whose* main industry is tourism, is growing bigger every year.

4 Most tourists *which/who* come to the island choose the summer months.

5 It's July and August *when/where* the temperatures are warmest.

6 The place *that/where* you can see a glorious sunset is on the beach.

7 Tourists often want to visit the caves, in *where/which* you can see amazing wall paintings.

8 All the tourist guides, *who/that* speak many languages, are extremely good.

9 It's the food they cook on the barbecue *where/that* is my favourite.

10 I'm not sure *whose/who's* coming to the party but I know there will be a lot of people.

2 **Mark the sentences in Activity 1 as defining (D) or non-defining (ND) relative clauses.**

3 **Put five missing commas where necessary in the text.**

The island of Saint Brendon which is situated in the northwest is the largest in the area. To the east is La Esperanza which is slightly smaller and from which there are breathtaking views of all the surrounding islands. Saint Brendon has a population which exceeds six million people, who all speak English. The island whose climate is mild but changeable has lush green vegetation which may be a result of the frequent showers of rain! However, this is what makes it so beautiful, and a place where tourists love to spend some time.

Use of English

Key word transformations (Part 4)
▶ CB page 75

1 **Complete the second sentence so that it has a similar meaning to the first sentence, using the word given. Do not change the word given. You must use between two and five words, including the word given. Here is an example (0).**

0 It seems as though they have cancelled the meeting.
LIKE
It *looks like the meeting* has been cancelled.

1 I think I'm too impatient to be a teacher.
ENOUGH
I don't think _____ to be a teacher.

2 Because I was really enjoying the trip I didn't want it to end.
MUCH
I was enjoying the trip _____ I didn't want it to end.

3 I couldn't understand the lecture because it was so technical.
FOR
The lecture was _____ to understand.

4 It was the most exciting film I have ever seen.
NEVER
I have _____ exciting film.

5 It's possible that you met him at the party but it seems unlikely.
COULD
You _____ at the party but it seems unlikely.

6 I think she is definitely telling us the truth.
LYING
She _____ to us.

Writing
Essay (Part 1) ▶ CB page 76

1 Read the exam task below.

In your English class you have been talking about why people choose to travel abroad. Now your teacher has asked you to write an essay.

> There is no need for people to travel to find out about the world when they can see it all on the internet. What's your opinion?
>
> **Notes**
> Write about:
> 1 personal experience
> 2 languages
> 3 .... (your own idea)

2 Read the essay below and match paragraphs 2, 3 and 4 to the topics in the task in Activity 1.

People travel abroad for many reasons, but <u>the most likely</u> reason is for a holiday. However, is this really necessary now that we can all see everything about the world through the internet?

.... <u>I believe that</u> there is nothing better than personal experience. People can see a beautiful place on their computer, <u>but</u> they can't hear the birds, smell the flowers or get a true feeling about it.

.... <u>Another factor is</u> being able to speak to local people in their own language. <u>Of course</u> it's possible to learn other languages in your own country, and even on the internet itself, but if you can speak to people in their own country, it gives you confidence and you find out more about them. It can also be great fun.

.... <u>Finally</u>, and <u>to put a different point of view</u>, I would say that using the internet is the best way of finding a lot of information about a place if you can't visit it yourself, and it's certainly true that it is much cheaper than actually travelling.

<u>However</u>, there is no doubt that travelling is the best thing and everyone should do it.

3 What are the reasons the writer gives for their opinions? Tick those that are mentioned.

Paragraph 2
☐ having a real experience
☐ not being able to see everything
☐ not seeing wildlife

Paragraph 3
☐ being able to learn
☐ having fun
☐ meeting other people

Paragraph 4
☐ finding facts
☐ saving time
☐ cost

4 In which paragraph could the following reasons also be included?

a .... being able to take photographs
b .... convenience
c .... helping with future job prospects
d .... having memories
e .... getting more independent
f .... helping the environment

5 Look at paragraphs 1 and 5 in the essay in Activity 2. Match them to the functions below.

a .... to introduce the general topic
b .... to give the writer's own opinion
c .... to give reasons for the writer's opinion

6 Tick the words and phrases below that could be used instead of the underlined words in the essay in Activity 2.

1 I believe that
   a In my opinion   b It is common knowledge
   c It's often said
2 the most likely
   a possibly   b conversely   c probably
3 but   a since   b although   c unless
4 Another factor is
   a However   b In addition   c Nevertheless
5 Of course   a Clearly   b Really   c Actually
6 Finally   a At last   b In the end   c Lastly
7 to put a different point of view
   a in contrast   b the opposite   c on the other hand
8 However   a Moreover   b Well   c To sum up

7 Now write your own answer to the exam task below. Remember to think of good reasons for your opinions and to use a variety of linking words. Write 140–190 words.

In your English class you have been talking about working in another country. Now your teacher has asked you to write an essay.

> Is it a good idea for young people to spend a short time working or studying abroad?
>
> **Notes**
> Write about:
> 1 personal experience
> 2 languages
> 3 .... (your own idea)

Moving on

8

Listening

Multiple matching (Part 3)   ▶ CB page 78

1 Match expressions 1–5 with meanings A–E.

1	be top of my list	**A**	start something
2	take the first steps	**B**	relax
3	earn big money	**C**	investigate
4	go into something	**D**	have a good salary
5	chill (with friends)	**E**	be most important

2 ▶ 17 **You will hear five different people talking about jobs they plan to do in the future. Choose from the list (A–H) the reason each speaker gives for wanting to do the job. There are three extra letters which you do not need to use.**

A the influence of friends
B following a parent's example
C pursuing a dream
D the salary
E a desire to travel
F good prospects for promotion
G wanting to combine a hobby with work
H the chance to meet people

Speaker 1 [   ]
Speaker 2 [   ]
Speaker 3 [   ]
Speaker 4 [   ]
Speaker 5 [   ]

Vocabulary

collocations and phrasal verbs with *work*
▶ CB page 79

1 **Complete the sentences and do the crossword.**

Across

2 Nursing used to be considered a female …

4 work out (in a gym)

6 He got his job through an employment …

7 She was not allowed to … medicine when she first arrived in Australia.

9 There are a lot of … opportunities in engineering.

Down

1 worked up (about an upsetting incident)

3 work out (the cost of something)

5 Acting is great but there's no job …

8 We managed to work around the …

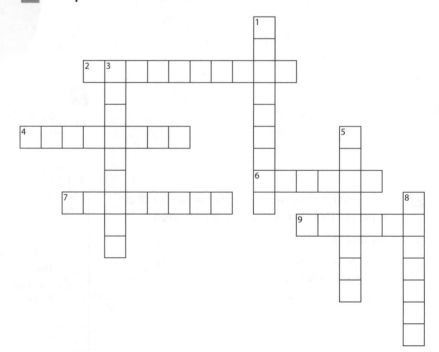

Speaking

Collaborative task (Part 3)
▶ CB page 80

agreeing and disagreeing

1 **Look at the speaking task and the discussion that two students had about it. Complete the discussion with the words in the box.**

> Here are some things that people often think are important when they work from home. Talk together about why these things might be important for people who work from home.

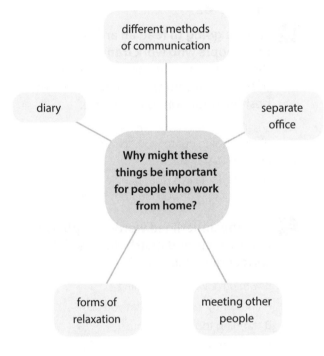

self-disciplined   distraction   deadlines
desktop   colleagues   concentrate
desk   landline

A = Ana, **M** = Marek, **E** = Examiner

A: Well, if you work at home <u>I think</u> it is important to have contact with other people.

M: <u>I suppose so</u>. If you don't have any **(1)** .... to talk to you need other people around.

A: It's good to have a bit of company but the trouble with friends and relatives in the house is that they can be a bit of a **(2)** ....

M: I think you need a separate office though. After all, if you're working you need to be able to **(3)** .... I know I'd be tempted to sit on the sofa!

A: <u>That's just what I was going to say</u>. I'd probably convince myself I could work lying down on the sofa. I know what you mean about the TV being unnecessary.

M: <u>So would you agree that</u> the computer is absolutely essential though?

A: I would, but <u>actually I'm not sure that it's necessary</u> to have a **(4)** .... computer. Maybe a laptop would be better. Then you can work anywhere – even in the garden.

M: <u>Yes, that's true</u> but I'm not very **(5)** .... and on sunny days I'd probably be out in the garden rather than getting my work done.

A: Ah, but <u>that's why it would be important</u> to have a diary to keep track of your **(6)** ....

M: Yes, absolutely. <u>What about communication?</u> I wouldn't actually want a telephone on my **(7)** .... if I was working at home. There'd be too many interruptions that weren't related to work.

A: <u>I agree up to a point</u>. You probably don't need a **(8)** .... if you've got a mobile, but <u>you certainly need an internet connection</u>.

2 **Now decide which one is not important.**

3 **Look at the underlined expressions in the discussion in Activity 2 and put them into the correct section.**

Agreeing
(1) ....
(2) ....
(3) ....
(4) ....

Asking for an opinion
(5) ....
(6) ....

Expressing opinions
(7) ....
(8) ....
(9) ....
(10) ....

Grammar

reporting verbs ▶ CB page 81

1 **There are mistakes in some of the sentences below. Find and correct the mistakes and tick the sentences that are correct.**

0 Andrew asked me whether I ~~will~~ **would** finish the report by Friday.

1 Carlos told that he would meet us at the cinema.

2 Harry offered giving me a lift to the station.

3 Joe reminded me to call the hotel to cancel the reservation.

4 The boss accused me using the internet at work.

5 We warned him to avoid the traffic jam in Port Street.

6 Sue suggested us to take the bus because the trains were running late.

7 Juan explained that the computer system had crashed so emails weren't getting through.

8 Peter refused apologising to Mary.

2 **For questions 1–6, complete the second sentence so that it has a similar meaning to the first sentence, using the word given. Do not change the word given. You must use between two and five words, including the word given.**

0 'Can you lend me your car, Lee?' asked Chris.

BORROW

Chris asked _Lee if he could borrow_ his car.

1 'I don't think you should go out without an umbrella,' said Jaime.

ADVISED

Jaime .... go out without an umbrella.

2 'I didn't write that bad report,' he said.

DENIED

He .... that bad report.

3 'Send Bob a card – it's his birthday on Friday,' said Mum.

REMINDED

Mum .... a card because it was his birthday on Friday.

4 'Don't forget to lock up before you leave,' the boss told us.

WARNED

The boss .... before we left.

5 'You should take more exercise,' said the doctor.

RECOMMENDED

The doctor .... more exercise.

6 'I'll help you with that report,' said Karen.

OFFERED

Karen .... with the report.

Reading

Multiple matching (Part 7) ▶ CB page 82

1 **You are going to read an article about four people who work from home. Read the article once quickly and decide which of these two sentences would make the best introduction to the article.**

A Susan Taylor tells us about four people who disliked going out to work so much that they decided to stay at home.

B Susan Taylor talks to four people about the disadvantages of working from home.

2 **Find the underlined words and phrases in the article and match them with the correct meaning, A or B.**

1 *breathing down your neck* (line 3)

A constantly watching what you do

B standing too close to you

2 *lifeline* (line 13)

A a kind of telephone line

B something that makes it possible for you to survive

3 *established* (line 16)

A recognised and accepted

B conservative

4 *squished* (line 21)

A seated on soft cushions

B between people who are pushing against you

5 *switch off* (line 24)

A stop a machine working

B stop thinking about work

6 *ungodly* (line 30)

A very early **B** not religious

7 *dodgy* (line 53)

A exciting **B** low quality

When you don't go out to work

A Max: language tutor

My work involves teaching people English via the internet. The best thing about working from home is not having anyone <u>breathing down your neck</u> or telling you what to do and being able to work in your own time. I teach people in other time zones

5 **so** a lot of my classes are in the evenings or early mornings. The negative points have to be when an unexpected caller insists on ringing the doorbell when I'm working or when it's a very hot, sunny day and you'd rather be out in the sunshine but have to put in your hours. At the beginning, I was putting in far too

10 many hours, actually. That was before I started using a diary. I make a note of all my appointments and classes, personal and professional alike. I don't think I could manage without it. It's my <u>lifeline</u>. I have one unbreakable rule: I always keep Sunday free for myself.

B Peter: historian

15 I have always been home-based. Soon after university I started work as a researcher for an <u>established</u> writer on archaeology and then I started writing my own books. Of course, I have had other jobs. As a kid I used to help in my parents' shop and I had a few holiday office jobs as a student **as well**. I learnt from the

20 office jobs that I never wanted to do that sort of thing again! I feel sorry for those people who spend two hours a day <u>squished</u> in a Tube train breathing in bad air and then have to work in places like that. My office at home, the largest room in the house, has a sofa, TV and radio. I think it is important to be able to <u>switch</u>

25 <u>off</u> occasionally and watch the news or whatever. Apart from not having to commute, you can also do two things at the same time, like monitoring the washing machine while getting on with work.

C Mervin: musical supplier

I supply music rolls for mechanical organs. For me working from home has all the usual advantages like not having to get up at some <u>ungodly</u> hour to go out to work, especially when it's freezing 30 outside; no office politics, no boss looking over my shoulder and I can sit in the garden with my wife when the sun comes out. I can't think of any disadvantages **but** there are some things to take into account. Firstly, a home-based business sometimes has less credibility than a 'proper' one. It's generally not a good 35 idea to let new customers know that you are working from home until you can show them that you are serious about what you do. **Another thing is that** sometimes it is illegal to run a business from your premises unless you get planning permission, especially if your work involves extra traffic, either deliveries or 40 people, activity or noise.

D Gary: magazine journalist

I was injured in a car crash and was stuck in the house with nothing to do. I did a lot of thinking about things and realised that I hated my job so much that it was making me miserable. **Despite** having wanted to be a journalist since I was a kid, I'd 45 never really tried to get into it. It seemed a good time to change that, so I decided to contact a magazine with some story ideas. I ended up with my first commission and had enough work to go self-employed within six months. I need to do things pretty much the minute I get the commission. I don't mind, **though**. I like 50 the pressure. I do find that without it, I just don't work. I need to have a bit of a crisis mentality. That's where I get the motivation from. Without it I end up watching <u>dodgy</u> television programmes instead of working.

---

3 Read the article again. For questions 1–10, choose from the people A–D.

Which person

offers some advice to others planning to work from home? `1`

finds it annoying when others interrupt his work? `2`

had to control the amount of time he was spending on work? `3`

sometimes finds self-discipline a problem? `4`

regards taking breaks and relaxing as a good thing? `5`

likes to spend longer in bed in the mornings? `6`

resists the temptation to go and sit outside? `7`

realised early on that he could not do some sorts of work? `8`

has managed to fulfil an ambition? `9`

is sympathetic with other workers and what they have to put up with? `10`

4 Complete the paragraph with the words and phrases in bold in the article in Activity 2.

I work in the evenings from five to ten. I don't mind **(1)** .... It means I don't have to get up early in the morning. **(2)** .... if I have to do something like go to the bank or the dentist, I don't have to take time off work. I can do all my shopping in the mornings **(3)** .... My girlfriend is a student and her classes are in the mornings **(4)** .... we don't get to see much of each other during the week. That's a pity **(5)** .... it can't be helped. **(6)** .... not getting home until about 10.30, I usually manage to be in bed by eleven. I like to meet up with friends for a drink or to go to the cinema but I need my sleep too.

Grammar

reported statements ▶ CB page 84

1 Look at the answers a candidate gave in an interview and complete the report the interviewer wrote below.

I studied English and history but I also took modules in French and Italian.

I'm working with an advertising company now and I worked in London before that.

I've been working with the company for two years.

I earn around £24,000.

I really enjoy the teamwork in my current job because I'm a team player.

I prefer to stay where I am at the moment – I don't want to move to London because it's only an hour on the train and there are regular services.

I am not being stretched in my current job and I need a challenge.

I have good communication skills; I don't have any weaknesses.

I will bring a fresh and different approach to the work – and I'm enthusiastic.

She said that she **(1)** .... English and history at university but also she **(2)** .... modules in French and Italian. She said currently she **(3)** .... with an advertising company, and **(4)** .... in London before that. She **(5)** .... with her present company for two years. She told me that her current salary was £24,000 and that what she enjoyed about her current job **(6)** .... the teamwork – she explained that she was a team player. When I asked whether she **(7)** .... to London, she replied that she **(8)** .... to stay where she was because it **(9)** .... only an hour on the train and there **(10)** .... regular services. She said that she wanted the job because she **(11)** .... stretched and that she **(12)** .... a challenge. She said that she had good communication skills, and **(13)** .... any weaknesses and that she **(14)** .... bring a fresh and different approach to her work. She **(15)** .... also enthusiastic. I liked her and would recommend her for the job.

Use of English

Word formation (Part 3) ▶ CB page 85

1 Add the suffixes from the box to the correct words below to make nouns. There is one you do not need to use.

-iour -ant -er -or -ative -ment -ism

1 tourist
2 application
3 representation
4 improve
5 employment
6 behave

2 For questions 1–8, read the text below. Use the word given in capitals at the end of some of the lines to form a word that fits in the gap in the same line. There is an example at the beginning (0).

What NOT to do at a job interview!

People often feel **(0)** *extremely* nervous before they go for a job interview and are worried about how to make a good first **(1)** .... on a potential **(2)** .... There is lots of advice on the internet about what job **(3)** .... should do to increase their chances of having a successful interview, so here are some hot tips on what to avoid. Number one is dress **(4)** .... If you turn up for an office job wearing casual clothes you will be off to a very bad start. Secondly, avoid too much **(5)** .... – I don't mean with your interviewers who **(6)** .... will expect you to talk to them, but with your friends, who may call you at the most **(7)** .... moment on your mobile phone. Finally, even if you don't get the job, don't take it **(8)** .... Learn from the experience and any mistakes you may have made. Move on to the next opportunity – it will almost certainly be better!

EXTREME
IMPRESS
EMPLOY
APPLY

APPROPRIATE

COMMUNICATE
NATURAL

CONVENIENT

PERSONAL

Writing
Letter of application (Part 2)
▶ CB page 86

About the exam:
In Part 2 of the Writing paper, you may have the opportunity to write a letter of application for a job, course, etc.

Strategy:
- Read the task carefully and underline the key words and phrases.
- Use a formal style and include the following information in this order:
  1 Why you are writing, where you saw the advertisement and which position you are applying for.
  2 Why you are a suitable candidate (your skills and qualifications).
  3 When you will be available and how you can be contacted.

1 Look at this task and the letter of application a student wrote. Put the sentences in the correct order.

You see this advertisement in an international newspaper.

Trainee Journalist

We are looking for an enthusiastic and creative person with a good knowledge of student life and young people's interests to work as a trainee journalist on our most recently launched magazine, *Actualise it!*

We offer flexible working hours and conditions, training on the job and intensive courses in Chinese or English.

Send a letter of application to:

Mark Ellington
Editor
Actualise it!
37 Westwick Gardens
London

Write your letter of application in 140–190 words.

Dear Mr Ellington,

.... I can be contacted by telephone on 01094893214 or by email at SamRuffolo@ymail.com.

.... Also, would it be possible to learn both the languages you mention in your advertisement? I have a good knowledge of English, but can certainly improve and I have always wanted to study Chinese.

.... Firstly, I would like to know whether it would be possible to work from home.

.... I am writing in reply to your advertisement in Tuesday's Global News.

.... I would like to ask some questions about the position.

.... I would like to apply for the position of trainee journalist on *Actualise it!* magazine.

2 Now look at these DOs and DON'Ts for job applications and the letter in Activity 1. Tick (✓) the advice the student has followed.

1 ☐ **DO** say which job you are applying for, and where and when you saw it advertised. Invent a newspaper and date if you need to.
2 ☐ **DO** mention each of the areas in the advertisement when you write your application.
3 ☐ **DO** say how you can be contacted.
4 ☐ **DON'T** forget to mention why you would be suitable.
5 ☐ **DO** begin and end your letter as you would other formal letters.

3 Read the task in Activity 1 again. Rewrite the student's letter, adding in all the information required. Remember to divide your letter into paragraphs.

Multiple-choice cloze (Part 1)

For questions 1–8, read the text below and decide which answer (A, B, C or D) best fits each gap. There is an example at the beginning (0).

A review of a collection of short stories

This collection of short stories is not an optimistic read in which good conquers evil; **(0)** _A instead_ it explores the idea that horror and evil live inside us all.

The first story concerns the psychological **(1)** _____ that occur after a man persuades his own son to help him murder his wife. The reader is left to **(2)** _____ his own mind about whether the supernatural is involved, though I suspect in this **(3)** _____ it isn't.

The second story is based on the **(4)** _____ of revenge. It follows the victim of a crime, and the cold-blooded way in which she **(5)** _____ the situation. Although she is cruel, we feel genuine **(6)** _____ for her problems.

Finally, there is an exciting account of what would happen if, after many years of marriage, you **(7)** _____ your spouse was a serial killer – and he knew that you knew.

Overall, **(8)** _____ some flaws, this is generally a satisfying collection of stories, which I recommend.

0	**A** instead	**B** and	**C** despite	**D** though
1	**A** ends	**B** significances	**C** consequences	**D** summaries
2	**A** make over	**B** make out	**C** make up	**D** make for
3	**A** moment	**B** time	**C** place	**D** case
4	**A** movement	**B** argument	**C** sense	**D** theme
5	**A** gets up to	**B** deals with	**C** comes up to	**D** goes with
6	**A** sympathy	**B** identity	**C** sensitivity	**D** consideration
7	**A** found out	**B** looked for	**C** went through	**D** got from
8	**A** since	**B** although	**C** in spite of	**D** as

Open cloze (Part 2)

For questions 9–16, read the text below and think of the word which best fits each gap. Use only one word in each gap. There is an example at the beginning (0).

Not ideal – but good enough!

I fell into my first job **(0)** _by_ chance. I'd graduated with a reasonable degree, but I was at **(9)** _____ loss to know what to do next. I had no money, but **(10)** _____ this I had unrealistic dreams of being able to travel the world. **(11)** _____ the end what happened was a happy coincidence. An uncle of mine had set **(12)** _____ a language school in the Caribbean, and needed someone to help him run the office. I jumped at the chance, **(13)** _____ at the time I had no idea that it would turn out to be a real challenge. There were **(14)** _____ many problems to deal with that I couldn't cope, **(15)** _____ there were times when I felt overwhelmed. The advantages included good money and fantastic weather, but finally the pressure became too great so I quit. **(16)** _____ , working in a school helped me realise that was what I really wanted to do, and now I'm a teacher!

Word formation (Part 3)

For questions 17–24, read the text below. Use the word given in capitals at the end of some of the lines to form a word that fits in the gap in the same line. There is an example at the beginning (0).

The perfect horror novel

What is the most important **(0)** _factor_ in creating a perfect horror novel? The most **FACT**

(17) .... horror novelists realise that **SUCCESS**
simply delivering cheap shocks through
descriptions of violence is not the best
way to do it. **(18)** .... writers appeal **PROFESSION**
to the reader's feelings by creating
(19) .... characters, and are also **BELIEVE**
able to produce extremely powerful
images that stay in the reader's mind for
a long time. They understand that the
most **(20)** .... things are in our own **SCARE**
imaginations, not what we actually read
on the page.

Of course their novels also work up
to a very intense climax, but perfect
horror novels involve the reader at an
(21) .... level and often don't end **EMOTION**
with any kind of clear **(22)** .... This **RESOLVE**
leaves the reader in a state of suspense.
They can suggest that there are many
(23) .... realities that exist beyond **DIFFER**
the one we live in, and this creates
(24) .... possibilities for their **AMAZE**
readers.

Key word transformations (Part 4)

For questions 25–30, complete the second sentence so that it has a similar meaning to the first sentence, using the word given. Do not change the word given. You must use between two and five words, including the word given. Here is an example (0).

Example:

0 'Why don't you stay to dinner, Jo?' asked Peter.

   INVITED

   Peter _invited Jo to stay_ to dinner.

25 'Don't open your present until your birthday,' Carol told Sue.

   NOT

   Carol told Sue .... until her birthday.

26 'I'm sorry I was late for the meeting,' said Carlo.

   APOLOGISED

   Carlo .... late for the meeting.

27 I become very upset if I have any pressure at work.

   WORKED

   I .... if I have any pressure at work.

28 How is your relationship with Mike these days?

   GETTING

   How .... with Mike these days?

29 You were wrong to tell Jim about the surprise party.

   SHOULD

   You .... Jim about the surprise party.

30 It rains so much that everyone carries an umbrella.

   SUCH

   It .... that everyone carries an umbrella.

Lucky break?

9

Vocabulary

sport and competition

1 **Complete the text with the words in the box. There are some words you do not need to use.**

charm	opponents	mascot	stamina	rivals	medallist
laid-back	coach	referee	scuba diving	gymnast	
athlete	track	training	championships	competitive	

I started doing rhythmic gymnastics when I was a small girl. I suppose you could say I'm a fairly good **(1)** .... now. I've taken part in the national **(2)** .... though I've never won a medal or anything like that. My sister, on the other hand, is a really world-class **(3)** .... She specialises in **(4)** .... events like the 800 metres and was a silver **(5)** .... at the last Olympics. Her **(6)** .... says she's just more **(7)** .... than some of her **(8)** .... When she's not **(9)** .... or competing she's actually pretty **(10)** ...., especially when we're on holiday. We usually go to Tenerife and we both love **(11)** .... off Octopus Cove there. Naturally, we take our Yorkshire terrier, Tiger, with us. He comes along when we compete too. We wouldn't be able to do it without him. He's our lucky **(12)** ....!

Reading

Gapped text (Part 6)   ▶ CB page 88

1 **You are going to read an article from a sports science magazine. Six sentences have been removed from the text. Read the article and the sentences quickly and choose the best title.**

1 What it takes to win a race

2 Why athletes get tired

3 Mind over matter is the key to success

2 **Read the article and the sentences again. Choose from sentences A–G the one which fits each gap. There is one extra sentence which you do not need to use.**

A If you did accumulate too many chemicals in your muscles that too would be very dangerous.

B What they will tell you is that athletes tire when something in their physiology fails, causing them to stop or slow down.

C That simplifies things far too much.

D But there is another theory which gives the brain a much greater role.

E Everyone who has ever run in the heat will tell you that you actually start more slowly.

F We still don't have an answer to that question.

G How is this possible?

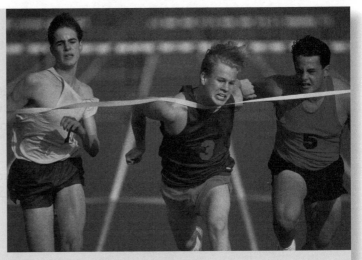

We've all seen it: a runner or cyclist looks <u>exhausted</u>, he seems to be struggling to even get to the end of the race, his face a mask of agony. And then suddenly he speeds up in the final 400 metres, sprints to the finish line and wins. [1] And if the runner or cyclist had that 'reserve capacity' all along, why did he not speed up 800 metres before the end? Why not two kilometres? Why didn't he maintain that speed throughout the race?

Conventional theories can't really answer these questions. [2] The failure can be a failure to supply enough oxygen to the muscles, failure to keep levels of 'poisonous' chemicals down or a failure to <u>lose</u> heat, causing the body temperature to rise too high. Once this failure point is reached, the athlete must slow down or stop altogether. The key point is that the origins of fatigue lie in the muscles.

[3] Called the 'Central Governor' theory, the idea is that during exercise, the brain regulates performance to balance all the body's physiological systems. Fatigue, or the slowing down in pace, is the result of this regulation, which happens before any physiological 'failure' can occur. Therefore, rather than slowing down as a result of lack of oxygen, high body temperatures, high chemical levels and so on, you slow down in order to <u>prevent</u> them.

In this alternative theory, performance and fatigue are regulated to prevent the potentially <u>harmful</u> limits from being reached. If your body temperature rises above 41 degrees, you'd stop and be in serious trouble. [4] But when exercise takes place, neither of these things happen because the brain is in control, and it regulates the body specifically to protect against that damage.

This theory is controversial but there is evidence to support it. Let's say you run a 10 km race at sea-level and in cool temperatures. Your time is forty minutes, giving you a speed of four minutes per kilometre. But if I put you in Beijing in the summer time, where it's 35 degrees, and humidity is 60 percent and I make you run that same 10 km race, immediately your time of forty minutes is under <u>threat</u>. You might be lucky to do forty-two minutes in these 'extreme' conditions.

The important question, however, is: when do you first slow down? [5] In fact, it takes less than twenty seconds for your body to 'decide' to run more slowly than usual. It happens so early that nothing is different, except for your sensation that it's hotter. That sensation, then, seems to be key. But it can't be that you are already overheating within the first thirty seconds, or even two minutes of your run. So how, then, do you 'decide' to slow down? The answer is that your brain tells you to.

So is fatigue all in the mind then? [6] Mental strength and willpower are part of the answer, but they never beat physiology. You cannot commit suicide by holding your breath, and the same goes for exercise: physiology wins the day, every day, but with the help of the brain.

---

3 **Complete sentences 1–6 with the correct form of the words underlined in the article.**

1 The referee .... to send her off in the second half of the match but in the end he only gave her a yellow card.

2 He was suffering from heat .... and had to abandon the race.

3 He regretted his .... to retire from professional tennis and made a come-back last year.

4 The team suffered so many disastrous .... that a lot of their fans stopped going to see them play.

5 Many sports stars took drugs they believed were .... only to discover later that they had done permanent damage to their health.

6 When it comes to sports injuries, ... is always much better than cure.

Vocabulary

collocations: success
▶ CB page 89

1 **Cross out the word or phrase that does <u>not</u> collocate with the verbs in bold.**

1 **have** *a bad day/a vicious streak/a brilliant sporting career/an enormous effort*

2 **fulfil** *a lifelong ambition/ her early potential/an important obligation/a good deed*

3 **set** *a strong demand/ a reasonable target/a high standard/a clear limit*

4 **make** *a go of something/ a good try/a favourable impression/a serious attempt*

5 **overcome** *considerable obstacles/anxiety/a sporting rival/a difficult past*

2 **Underline the correct alternatives to complete the sentences.**

1 In sport it's vital to know how to cope *with/for/to* success as well as failure.

2 She just couldn't face *out/up/on* to the fact that her sporting career was over.

3 He's taken *in/on/after* some new challenges and has really improved his game.

4 She decided to focus *at/in/on* improving her serve and backhand.

5 Our national team are going *for/at/to* three gold medals in the athletics at the next Olympics.

6 He was so exhausted he gave *in/on/over* to an overwhelming urge to stop and rest.

Speaking

Discussion (Part 4): compensation strategies
▶ CB page 90

1 **Look at compensation strategies 1 and 2. Would you use them to a) give you time to think or b) stop the other candidate from interrupting you?**

1 Well, it's difficult to say …   2 OK, let me see …

2 ▶ 18 **Two students are discussing some questions in Paper 4, Part 4. Listen and complete their conversation.**

E = Examiner, **D** = David, **S** = Sara

E: Do you think luck is important in life?

D: (1) .... Well, I always wish my friends good luck before an exam or job interview so I suppose that does mean I believe in it to some extent. What about you?

S: Me too – and I really believe it makes a difference. I always carry a – I'm not sure how to say this in English – it's <u>a little thing that is supposed to be lucky</u>. It's a silver bead that my grandmother gave me. If I did an exam without it, I know I would fail.

D: (2) .... that you actually think it affects your success in the exam?

S: Well, yes. I do.

D: Well, I suppose I do too now I come to think of it. I have things I always do like wearing the same socks and walking on the same side of the street on the way to the exam.

E: How much does luck contribute to success in sporting events?

D: (3) .... but not so much, in my opinion. **(4)** .... other things are more important like – I can't remember the word – <u>how well you can do things</u> like hit the ball or passing in football.

S: But in tennis, for example, you often see that for one player the ball hits the top of the – what's it called? – you know, <u>the long thing that divides the court into two halves</u> – and the ball doesn't go over. That's to do with luck if you ask me.

D: So you think luck is more important?

S: No, not always. **(5)** .... that in some sports it can play quite an important role. I'm very superstitious. There are a lot of things that I avoid doing, like stepping on the lines on the pavement or walking under <u>those things that you use to climb up to paint the house</u> – and if I do my English friends tell me to say 'bread and butter'!

D: Why?

S: (6) .... it's supposed to stop anything terrible happening to you.

D: But perhaps some superstitions are logical.

S: What do you mean?

D: (7) .... that sometimes there really is a danger. For example, the painter could drop something and it could fall on you and cause some kind of <u>harm or damage to you physically</u>.

E: Do superstitions ever stop people doing things they might enjoy or benefit from?

D: (8) .... enjoy?

E: Yes.

D: (9) .... I suppose they do but I would never decide not to go on a trip or something because it was on the thirteenth of the month.

S: (10) .... that if you go to the airport and the airline gave you seat 13D on the plane you would still go?

D: Well, I might feel a bit … <u>not exactly afraid but kind of a bit worried and uncomfortable</u> but it wouldn't stop me flying.

3 **Match the underlined paraphrases the students used in Activity 2 with words 1–6.**

1 ladders   **2** skill   **3** uneasy   **4** injury   **5** good luck charm   **6** net

Grammar

conditional forms (1) ▶ CB page 91

1 **Match sentence beginnings 1–6 with endings A–I. There are some endings that you do not need to use.**

1 If I play tennis with you on Saturday afternoon,
2 If I spend too much money every month,
3 If I moved to live in another country,
4 If I drink too much coffee,
5 If I go to the disco on Saturday night,
6 If I walked under a ladder,

A I find it difficult to sleep.
B I would have a lot of bad luck.
C I am not able to pay my credit card bill.
D I will get a job more easily.
E I would be able to go out with my friends.
F I would miss my family a lot.
G I will probably meet a lot of my friends there.
H I can't have a good time.
I I will not have time to go out in the evening.

2 **For questions 1–6, complete the second sentence so that it has a similar meaning to the first sentence, using the word given. Do not change the word given. You must use between two and five words, including the word given.**

1 You can't smoke in restaurants without getting into trouble.
SMOKE
If you .... get into trouble.

2 The only thing stopping me doing my homework is that I don't have my dictionary here.
IF
I .... I had my dictionary here.

3 It's going to rain so you are sure to get wet.
IT
If .... get wet.

4 I am not very good at typing but it would be useful for my job if I could do it.
WERE
It would be useful for my job if .... at typing.

5 People often find it difficult to concentrate in noisy places.
THEY
When .... people often find it difficult to concentrate.

6 I refused to swim when the sea was rough.
NOT
If the sea was rough I .... swimming.

Listening

Multiple choice (Part 4) ▶ CB page 92

1 ▶ **19** **You will hear a radio interview with Carol Johnson, a successful young racing cyclist. For questions 1–7, choose the best answer (A, B or C).**

1 Why did Carol start cycling?
A Her parents encouraged her.
B A younger person made her jealous.
C She wanted to do something better than her friend.

2 How does Carol describe herself?
A too competitive
B very quiet when she's working
C different from some other athletes

3 Carol thinks that her training programme is
A hard and not very enjoyable.
B the key to winning all the time.
C important for the right mental attitude.

4 What does Carol say about the attitude of other sportspeople?
A They are less confident than they appear.
B They are often self-centred.
C They are driven to succeed.

5 What is Carol's attitude to luck?
A It's more important than anything else.
B It's balanced by practical techniques.
C It's limited to certain aspects of racing.

6 How does Carol feel about the media?
A It is an unnecessary part of her sport.
B It is difficult to deal with sometimes.
C It stops her getting financial support.

7 What advice does Carol have for young cyclists?
A Keep things in perspective.
B Plan for life after sport.
C Enjoy your success.

2 **Match 1–6 with A–F to make collocations.**

1 ride   A about an achievement
2 boast   B a goal
3 take up   C a bike
4 keep   D your best
5 achieve   E your mouth shut
6 do   F a new sport

Use of English
Word formation (Part 3)
▶ CB page 93

1 Use forms of the word *compete* to complete sentences 1–4.

1 Sandra is a fantastic .... She never gives up.

2 He won an underwater photography .... The prize was a scuba-diving holiday in Thailand.

3 Denise says that she isn't a .... person but she hates to lose.

4 Those new exercise machines are quite .... priced. I think I might get one.

2 For questions 1–8, read the text below. Use the word given in capitals at the end of some of the lines to form a word that fits in the gap in the same line.

Do we make our own luck?

We all rely on an element of luck to get by, but where does it come from and why do some people appear to be **(0)** *consistently* lucky or unlucky? — **CONSISTENT**

Richard has spent years investigating this and says it's not **(1)** .... or psychic ability that matters but a person's approach to life. He has some advice for people seeking an **(2)** .... in their luck. — **INTELLIGENT** / **IMPROVE**

'If you expect to be **(3)** ...., then sadly you often will be. Accept that bad luck will happen but turn it around by imagining how things could have been worse and looking for **(4)** .... to a problem.' — **FORTUNE** / **SOLVE**

So the secret is learning to look at life **(5)** .... Richard now runs courses, helping people to change their mindset. Trish says that before attending the course she was prone to **(6)** .... in her personal life. Now she has a more positive outlook. Since changing her **(7)** ...., by not looking for bad luck, she feels luckier. — **DIFFERENT** / **HAPPY** / **BEHAVE**

So those **(8)** .... people who keep telling us to cheer up and look on the bright side may be right after all! — **ANNOY**

Grammar
third conditional ▶ CB page 95

1 Complete sentences 1–8 with the correct form of the words in the box. There is one word you do not need to use.

| win | give | know | go out | buy | make | be | see | meet |

1 You .... the match easily if you had practised hard enough.

2 If I .... how much fun surfing is, I'd have started doing it years ago.

3 If you had bought a laptop from that store in town, they .... you a free smartphone.

4 If I'd realised the film was on television last night, I .... with friends.

5 If I hadn't gone on holiday to France last year, I .... Sue.

6 If I .... more money when I was younger, I would have been able to buy a house by now.

7 I .... Mike at the party if I had arrived earlier but I'm not sure whether he was there.

8 I .... the car if it had been cheaper, though I'm not sure.

2 For questions 1–6, complete the second sentence so that it has a similar meaning to the first sentence, using the word given. Do not change the word given. You must use between two and five words, including the word given.

1 Given more time, I'd have been able to finish all the work.
   HAD
   If I ...., I'd have been able to finish all the work.

2 Jo would have been very upset if he hadn't had an invitation to our party.
   NOT
   If we .... to the party, Jo would have been very upset.

3 George turned up late for the meeting because his alarm didn't go off.
   IF
   George would not have been late for the meeting .... off.

4 It's very unfortunate that the referee didn't give a penalty as the team would have won the game.
   LOST
   It's very unfortunate; if the referee had given a penalty, the team .... the game.

5 It's lucky that I have got a car otherwise I'd have to use the bus.
   GOT
   If .... a car I'd have to use the bus.

6 I didn't have the right tools to finish the job, so I had to leave it.
   HAD
   If I'd had the right tools to finish the job, I .... leave it.

Writing

Essay (Part I) ▶ CB page 96

1 Look at the task below and read the plans (A and B) two students wrote. Which plan matches the essay?

> In your English class you have been talking about how luck influences success in sport. Now your English teacher has asked you to write an essay.
>
> > In many sports, luck is sometimes more important than skill or physical fitness. Do you agree with this?
> >
> > **Notes**
> > Write about:
> > 1 luck
> > 2 skill
> > 3 .... (your own idea)

A

> Introduction: repeat the statement in the title in different words
> Paragraph 2: luck is more important (example)
> Paragraph 3: skill is more important (example)
> Paragraph 4: motivation plays an equal part (example)
> Conclusion: summarise main points and give my opinion

B

> Introduction: Say whether I agree or disagree with the statement in my own words.
> Paragraph 2: Arguments to support my point of view with examples.
> Paragraph 3: Arguments to support the opposite point of view with examples.
> Paragraph 3: Arguments to assess both points of view.
> Conclusion: Sum up and repeat my point of view in different words.

2 Choose phrases from the box to substitute underlined words in the essay. There is one extra phrase you do not need.

many people claim that	we can easily see
this can be said of	nevertheless
in conclusion	it is my view that
in contrast	as an illustration of this point

3 Put the instructions for planning and writing an essay A–E into the correct order.

A Check carefully for mistakes with spelling and grammar, especially verbs and conditionals.

B Choose one of the plans from Activity 1 (they are both good plans).

C Write your essay.

D Make notes of ideas and reasons for the ideas in the task.

E Think of your own ideas.

4 Read the task below and write your answer. Use 140–190 words.

> In your English class you have been talking about sport in school. Now your English teacher has asked you to write an essay.
>
> > Not all schools have sport as a compulsory subject. Do you think this is a good thing?
> > **Notes**
> > Write about:
> > 1 health
> > 2 new interests
> > 3 .... (your own idea)

(1) <u>It is often said that</u> luck is the most important factor in sporting success and it has more influence than physical fitness and skill.

There are aspects of sport where luck plays a part. Let's take a penalty kick in football **(2)** <u>as an example</u>. A goalkeeper who moves in the same direction as the ball and stops it going into the goal has probably just been lucky rather than skilful.

(3) <u>It is clear</u>, **(4)** <u>on the other hand</u>, that skill and fitness contribute most to success in many other circumstances. **(5)** <u>This is true of</u> tennis, for example. If a ball hits the net, is it because a player is unlucky? The player himself would probably say he had made a mistake and his skill was not good enough.

The last factor in success is motivation; a runner who is really determined to win trains harder and then tries harder than other competitors, and so wins races.

(6) <u>To sum up</u>, although luck does occasionally influence the outcome in some sports, **(7)** <u>in my opinion</u>, there is simply no substitute for skill, fitness and determination.

Virtual friends

Vocabulary

friendship

1 Complete the text about friendship with the correct form of the words in brackets.

> **68   WHAT IS A FRIEND?**
>
> True **(1)** .... (*friend*) is a unique blend of **(2)** .... (*affect*), **(3)** .... (*loyal*), love and fun. Friends often share similar interests but always have mutual respect and a strong sense of **(4)** .... (*connect*). It means not having to think about what you say because someone knows you better than you do yourself, and is **(5)** .... (*sense*) to your moods and **(6)** .... (*support*) of you in every **(7)** .... (*emotion*) crisis. It is a sense of trust and **(8)** .... (*companion*).

Listening

Multiple matching (Part 3)   ▶ CB page 99

1 ▶ 20   You will hear five people talking about friendship. For questions 1–5, choose from the list (A–H) what each speaker says is most important to them in a friendship. Use each letter only once. There are three extra letters which you do not need to use.

A frequent contact

B mutual trust

C shared interests

D good manners

E emotional support

F similar personalities

G a sense of humour

H some experience of school

Speaker 1 [   ]
Speaker 2 [   ]
Speaker 3 [   ]
Speaker 4 [   ]
Speaker 5 [   ]

Grammar

conditionals: alternatives to *if*   ▶ CB page 100

1 Underline the correct alternatives to complete the sentences.

1 It's very easy for friends to keep in contact *unless/as long as* they use Facebook or Twitter.

2 I always try to phone my friend every evening *unless/whether* I know she's out.

3 It's good to keep in touch with friends *otherwise/even if* it can be a hassle sometimes.

4 Whenever I travel I send everyone a postcard, *whether/otherwise* they miss me.

5 I take an umbrella with me when I go out, *even if/whether* it's not raining.

6 It's a good idea to make plans, *otherwise/unless* things can go wrong.

7 My friend always comes shopping with me *whether/even if* I don't want her to.

8 You'll pass the exam *unless/provided that* you work hard.

9 You can borrow my laptop *as long as/even if* you promise to take care of it.

10 I want to go for a walk with my friend on Saturday *provided that/unless* she's too busy.

11 I don't know *whether/as long as* it's a good idea to call him.

12 I'll call you tonight *unless/otherwise* I hear from you first.

2 Complete sentences 1–5 with the correct form of the verbs in the box.

learn	buy	stand	argue	cook

1 You won't be able to live in Italy unless you .... speak Italian.

2 Even if you .... your new television on the internet, you wouldn't have got a better deal.

3 I'll help you with your work this evening as long as you .... the meal.

4 He'll give you a lift to work provided that you .... at the corner of the street at 8a.m.

5 We never talk about politics, otherwise we .... all the time.

3 For questions 1–6, complete the second sentence so that it has a similar meaning to the first sentence, using the word given. Do not change the word given. You must use between two and five words, including the word given.

1 Without using a dictionary, I'm sure I won't understand the article.

UNLESS

I'm sure I won't understand the article .... a dictionary.

2 I won't help you unless you agree to come out tomorrow.

LONG

I will only .... you agree to come out tomorrow.

3 I clean my teeth every night so that they won't decay.

OTHERWISE

I clean my teeth every night, ... decay.

4 I'll finish the report if they give me enough time to do it.

THAT

I'll finish the report .... enough time to do it.

5 I found the job rather boring but at least the salary was good.

EVEN

The salary was good .... was rather boring.

6 Have you decided to invite Joe to the party?

WHETHER

Have you decided .... Joe to the party?

Use of English

Multiple-choice cloze (Part 1) ▶ CB page 101

1 Underline the correct alternatives to complete the sentences.

1 That painting is totally *particular/unique*. It's one of a kind.

2 I'm worried about Harry – he's not as cheerful as *typical/usual*.

3 It's easier to learn if you get *individual/unique* attention.

4 Arguments don't *affect/effect* me; I never get upset.

5 That restaurant has a *special/particular* menu at lunchtime.

6 I'm sorry I don't know the *actual/present* truth about the affair.

2 For questions 1–8, read the text below and decide which word (A, B, C or D) best fits each gap. There is an example at the beginning (0).

To twitter or not to twitter?

Some people claim social networking sites have a negative impact on people's ability to make friends in **(0)** *real* life. There has been a **(1)** .... deal of speculation about the long-term impact of their use on people's social lives and much of it has **(2)** .... on the possibility that these sites are **(3)** .... users' relationships, pushing them away from participating in the offline world. Twitter 'friends' may become more important than neighbours. However, **(4)** .... to such fears, recent research suggests that people who use such sites actually have a higher **(5)** .... of close relationships and are more **(6)** .... to be involved in civic and political activities than those who don't. Social networking sites help people with busy lives find ways of **(7)** .... in touch and providing regular updates The world of networked individuals will certainly **(8)** .... evolving, so who knows what the future holds for our personal relationships?

0	**A** actual	**B** true	**C** right	**D** real
1	**A** big	**B** great	**C** huge	**D** large
2	**A** centred	**B** looked	**C** examined	**D** investigated
3	**A** cutting	**B** wounding	**C** injuring	**D** damaging
4	**A** opposing	**B** contrary	**C** opposite	**D** contrasting
5	**A** collection	**B** amount	**C** number	**D** group
6	**A** likely	**B** probable	**C** possible	**D** expected
7	**A** holding	**B** staying	**C** continuing	**D** maintaining
8	**A** turn up	**B** get through	**C** carry on	**D** make out

---

Reading

Multiple choice (Part 5)
▶ CB page 103

1 **You are going to read an article giving advice about how to end a friendship. Read the article once quickly and say which of the points 1–4 below are <u>not</u> mentioned.**

1 breaking up with someone you've been going out with

2 'unfriending' someone on a social networking site

3 having an argument with an old friend

4 how women regard friendship

2 **Read the article again. For questions 1–6, choose the answer (A, B, C or D) which you think fits best according to the text.**

1 Why, according to the author, is it sometimes easier to end a romantic relationship?
A Your friends comfort you more.
B You can blame your ex-partner for what happened.
C You can get specialised advice about what to do.
D You and your partner understand that a change has taken place.

2 What can go wrong with the 'slow fade out' approach?
A You may lose all the friends you have in common.
B You might keep running into the friend you want to lose.
C Your friend might not notice what you are doing.
D Your friend might realise you actually want to end the friendship.

How to lose friends

I should have seen it coming. There was no big betrayal, no rows about money but the spark had gone. The end, when it came, was swift: 'We may as well call it a day,' I was told. In shock, I called my sister and told her the news. 'Oh no, you've been <u>dumped</u>,' she said. And indeed I had, but not by a boyfriend or lover. By a friend.

When a romantic relationship ends, things are relatively simple. There are broken hearts, recriminations. Mutual friends choose sides. No matter how upsetting, at least it's clear: you were a couple and now you're not. When a friendship <u>cools</u>, it's seldom so straightforward. The experts, however, are on hand to offer help. As far as they're concerned there are two possible ways to end it.

First we have what I call 'the slow fade out'. Irene Levine, Professor of Psychiatry at New York University and author of a book on the subject explains: 'Sometimes it's possible to downgrade the relationship by seeing the person less or to <u>dilute</u> it by seeing the person with a group.' If you have a lot of mutual friends, or are likely still to see each other, 'downgrading' makes things less awkward, but if the friend is too naive or self-absorbed to read the signals, or just really persistent, it may not be enough. Eventually you may need to do the decent thing and dump them properly.

It's then that you need the other method where you actually tell the person that the friendship is over, and that takes courage and honesty. It doesn't have to be cruel but it does mean telling someone you were once close to why you feel they are no longer worthy of your time. No one likes to hear that, so you need to <u>tread</u> carefully, warns Jodyne L Speyer, author of another book on dealing with this problem.

Speyer suggests giving a warning: 'If you tell me something's wrong, maybe I can fix it, and if I can't,

then at least I knew this was coming, so it prepares me. And be kind about it, say, "Here's what's not working." I don't need 100 reasons, but let me know what the problem is, so I can have that information and move on. I don't have to agree with it but at least I have something.' This is difficult to do, of course, but according to Speyer it gets easier with practice: 'When you're clear about your feelings, other people respond to that. You may think you're doing someone a favour by not telling them you don't want to continue with the friendship but in the long run it can make it worse.'

Even so, however gently you break the news, chances are someone will feel hurt and resist. 'Most friendships, even very good ones, don't last for ever,' Levine says. 'Yet women particularly are brought up to believe the romanticised notion of "best friends forever". In our culture, we are judged by our ability to make and keep friends, so we have a hard time getting over the loss of a best friend and see it as a personal failure.' Things are made worse by the fact that many end so slowly. 'When friendships <u>drift</u>, we rarely discuss it,' says relationship psychotherapist Paula Hall. 'Because they usually don't end in conflict, there is no closure. You don't feel you're better off without each other, it just stops, so there can be feelings of loss.' *line 63*

Joseph Epstein, another friendship expert, compares today's friendships to the seating in a sports stadium: your closest friends sit with you in the box seats, secondary friends are in the grandstand seats and the rest are in the stands. But, according to Epstein, there is hope, even in the cheap seats, because friendships aren't static, so people can move from one area of the stadium to another. Someone who starts out in the stands – perhaps a classmate or neighbour – can be promoted via the grandstand to the box seats. Sadly, the <u>reverse</u> is also true and that's when we need to know how to end it all.

3 How, according to Jodyne L Speyer, should you tell your friend that it's over?

  A You should be unkind if necessary.

  B You should say you never want to see them again.

  C You should give them as many reasons as possible for ending the friendship.

  D You should explain your position clearly and tactfully.

4 Why do people often feel they have failed when a friendship ends?

  A The process has taken too long.

  B Others admire us less if we don't have many friends.

  C It is natural to think that friendships last for ever.

  D They have false expectations of friendship.

5 What does the word *they* in line 63 refer to?

  A friends

  B things

  C friendships

  D women

6 How does the author feel about the break-up of friendships?

  A accepting of the fact that they happen

  B cynical about the way they often end

  C critical of people who end them

  D optimistic about relationships in general

3 **Match the underlined words in the article with meanings 1–6.**

1 make less intense   **4** becomes less close

2 rejected   **5** opposite

3 communicate   **6** pointlessly continue

4 **Complete the sentences with the correct form of the underlined words and phrases in the article.**

1 The boat broke loose from its mooring and .... out to sea.

2 The fruit juice was very sweet so we .... it with water.

3 They were fined for .... their old fridge in the street.

4 He put the car into .... and backed into the parking space.

5 I'm always accidentally .... on my cat's tail.

6 Wait till the soup .... a bit. It's too hot to eat.

Vocabulary

compound adjectives: personality
▶ CB page 103

1 **Cross out the adjective in each list which cannot form a compound adjective with the word in bold.**

1 even/hot/cross/quick   **-tempered**

2 empty/hard/level/heavy   **-headed**

3 **self-** absorbed/demanding/confident/conscious

4 warm/hot/cold/kind   **-hearted**

2 **Use one adjective from each list in Activity 1 to complete the description.**

I've always been quite an (1) .... person. Nothing much makes me lose my cool, including my younger brother, who can be very irritating. I'm quite (2) .... as well. I mean I don't get over-excited about things. I just weigh up all the advantages and disadvantages and reach a decision. Sometimes people say I'm a bit (3) .... I suppose they mean that I don't really notice what other people are thinking and feeling all the time but I'm not (4) .... I really feel for my friends, especially when they're having problems.

3 **Underline the correct alternatives to complete the sentences.**

1 When I was younger, I was very self-*conscious/confident*. I imagined that everyone was looking at me and criticising me.

2 Be careful what you say to Sandra this morning. She's always very *quick/even*-tempered when she's had a late night.

3 I really think Tina's one of the most self-*centred/critical* people I've ever met. She never seems to think about what anyone else might want or need.

4 Tim is completely *empty/hard*-headed. I don't think I've ever heard him talk about anything serious or express an opinion about things that matter.

5 Leo is one of the most *kind/cold*-hearted people I know. He always sees the best in people and wants to help them.

Grammar

participles (-ing and -ed)
▶ CB page 104

1 **Change the participle clauses into relative clauses in sentences 1–8 below.**

0 There is a shop selling bread near my house.
There is a shop which sells bread near my house.

1 There was a steel box in the cupboard containing lots of old photographs.

....

2 That new shop opening in the High Street on Saturday looks like it'll be really good.

....

3 There is a path leading down to the sea from our hotel.

....

4 She found the camera belonging to my sister.

....

5 All those wishing to buy a ticket should queue up near the Box Office.

....

6 My best friend is a lively person bursting with energy.

....

7 I'd love to get a job in film involving set design.

....

8 My friend gave me a beautiful photograph taken by her brother.

....

2 **Find and correct the mistakes in sentences 1–10 below.**

1 I remember meet my friend for the first time – I didn't like him at first!

2 He introduced himself by say 'Howdie!'

3 Once we became friends we didn't stop to talk.

4 We were both interesting in playing football.

5 People said we would end up play professionally together, though sadly that didn't happen.

6 When he moved to another town I missed to speak to him every day.

7 After have been so close, it was hard at first.

8 Now we share our experiences on Facebook and that's fascinated.

9 He's good at take photographs, so I like looking at them on the computer.

10 I hope that we'll carry on be friends for the rest of our lives.

Speaking

Collaborative task (Part 3)
▶ CB page 105

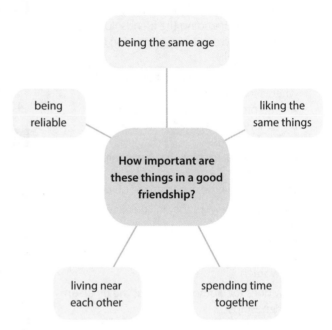

1 ▶ 21 **Look at the task and listen to the examiner's instructions to the two candidates. Decide if this statement is true (T) or false (F).**

Each candidate is supposed to choose the most important item.

2 **Now decide which one is <u>not</u> important.**

3 **Look at some of the things that candidates said in response to the instructions and match them to items 1–6.**

1 starting a discussion

2 encouraging the other person to say something

3 asking the other candidate to repeat what they said

4 showing that you share the other candidate's opinion

5 raising an objection to what the other candidate has said

6 explaining something

A What I mean is, trust is crucial.

B I've always said that friends need an interest in common. Would you agree with that?

C Well, that's certainly true in my case.

D Shall we start?

E Sorry. I interrupted you. What were you saying?

F No, I suppose not but what if you were a vegetarian and your friends kept inviting you to barbecues?

4 Use the words in the box to complete these ways of saying that things are important or unimportant in choosing friends. You need to use some of the words more than once.

matters   vital   influence   factors

1 I don't think having the same musical tastes .... much.

2 Going to the same school or college has a big .... on who you end up being friends with.

3 Knowing that my friends have the same values really .... to me.

4 In my opinion liking the same foods really isn't all that ....

5 For me it's really .... that the person likes animals as much as I do.

6 Sharing a hobby or interest is probably one of the most significant ....

Writing

Article (Part 2)   ▶ CB page 106

1 Look at the task below and the points a student noted down to include in their article. Cross out the points that are not relevant.

> You see this advertisement on an English language website.
>
> ### Articles wanted!
> **A great place for meeting friends!**
>
> Where do you meet them? Why is it such a good place? How could it be improved?
>
> Write us an article answering these questions. We will publish the best articles on our website.

1 reasons young people want to meet friends
2 what parents think about the place
3 how people get there
4 the need for parking
5 what we do there
6 what makes the place special
7 a description of my friends
8 other places to meet friends

2 Look at the opening paragraphs (A and B) of two different answers to the task in Activity 1. Which one is more interesting?

A

Where I meet my friends
It's important to meet friends. My friends like getting together at the weekend so we meet either on Friday night or Saturday morning. One nice place is the café in the town centre, which has tables and chairs outside and cheap cakes. We have a nice time together talking.

B

A fantastic place to meet!
It's great if there is a place where young people can meet to relax, chat and have a good time. There's an amazing café in my town, which has live music; not only can we hang out there, but there's a really fun atmosphere as well.

3 Now read the main part of the article. Replace the underlined words with more interesting adjectives from the box.

exciting   live   interesting   quiet
convenient   challenging

It's a really **(1)** nice place in the evenings because it is busy. There is always something happening and you can even dance to the **(2)** nice music. Sometimes there are **(3)** nice games or quizzes, which are fun to do with friends and you learn something, even if they're hard! It's **(4)** nice to meet new people, too, although if the music is loud it can be difficult to talk to them because you can't hear what they're saying. It would be much better if there were a **(5)** nice room somewhere so that people can just talk to each other there. It would also be **(6)** nice if the space at the back could have a bike rack so that we can leave our bikes there. That would be much better because at the moment we have to get there on the bus.

4 Choose the best ending for the article.

A To sum up, this is a very good place to meet friends.

B All in all, just imagine what a great time you'd have if you were able to come and join us!

C It's the coolest place I know.

5 Now write your own answer to the task in Activity 1.

Multiple-choice cloze (Part 1)

For questions 1–8, read the text below and decide which answer (A, B, C or D) best fits each gap. There is an example at the beginning (0).

Silly – or the key to success?

We've all seen athletes working **(0)** ...*A through*... the same series of movements before each competition and heard stories about a player wearing lucky socks or **(1)** .... on using a favourite racquet. To a lot of **(2)** .... it may all seem rather silly, but **(3)** .... , for some people these things may actually influence their performance on the sports field. Whether an athlete wins or loses, he tries to establish 'cause and effect' by reviewing the events of the day, **(4)** .... in his mind things like what he ate or was wearing. If he performed really well he then **(5)** .... that down to that particular set of circumstances, and **(6)** .... tries to recreate them before every competition. However, the true value of such behaviour may be the increased confidence and **(7)** .... of control it can give an athlete. After all, if anyone believes that **(8)** .... a specific action or ritual will make them achieve more, it probably will.

0	**A** through	**B** over	**C** with	**D** out
1	**A** demanding	**B** insisting	**C** emphasising	**D** urging
2	**A** audience	**B** viewers	**C** witnesses	**D** spectators
3	**A** absolutely	**B** at the end	**C** in fact	**D** finally
4	**A** keeping on	**B** looking up	**C** taking up	**D** going over
5	**A** sets	**B** puts	**C** places	**D** brings
6	**A** after	**B** following	**C** therefore	**D** consequent
7	**A** sense	**B** consciousness	**C** implication	**D** prediction
8	**A** doing	**B** making	**C** producing	**D** preparing

Open cloze (Part 2)

For questions 9–16, read the text below and think of the word which best fits each gap. Use only one word in each gap. There is an example at the beginning (0).

Motivation, motivation, motivation

It is a well-known fact **(0)** ...*that*... success in sport requires a great deal **(9)** .... patience, hard work and motivation.

But **(10)** .... is this best achieved? There are two kinds of motivation. The first is called extrinsic motivation and it comes **(11)** .... external influences such as money or social recognition. The second kind of motivation is intrinsic, **(12)** .... means it is generated by the individual alone who does things because they want to. But **(13)** .... does this mean for athletes? A highly motivated person would clearly be keener to perform better than a lower motivated one. On the **(14)** .... hand, someone with greater motivation can train hard and beat another more talented athlete who lacks that driving force.

However, being motivated does **(15)** .... automatically mean that people perform better. Surprisingly, athletes can fail because they are over motivated – they may be **(16)** .... keen to perform well that they mentally go beyond their physical limits.

Word formation (Part 3)

For questions 17–24, read the text below. Use the word given in capitals at the end of some of the lines to form a word that fits in the gap in the same line. There is an example at the beginning (0).

How to be a better friend	
How good a friend are you **(0)** _really_ ? And could you be a better one?	**REAL**
The best kind of friends are good **(17)** _____. That means resisting every urge to butt in, and holding back your opinion until it's needed, even if you don't agree with what your friend says or does. Try to be as	**LISTEN**
(18) _____ as possible – asking for help is hard for anyone, so be the first	**SYMPATHY**
to offer **(19)** _____. If your friend	**ASSIST**
takes you up on it they'll love you for being **(20)** _____ – and even if they	**SUPPORT**
don't you will certainly have made a good **(21)** _____ on them! But be	**IMPRESS**
careful what you say – everyone loves gossiping, but only when negative or **(22)** _____ comments are not aimed	**PLEASE**
at them. Be patient. Don't expect your advice to be taken at that moment, or your **(23)** _____ friend to be cheered	**HAPPY**
up **(24)** _____. Remember, true	**INSTANT**
friends are in a relationship for the long haul.	

Key word transformations (Part 4)

For questions 25–30, complete the second sentence so that it has a similar meaning to the first sentence, using the word given. Do not change the word given. You must use between two and five words, including the word given. Here is an example (0).

Example:

0 I don't mind going to a party on my own if I know other people who will be there.

PROVIDED

I don't mind going to a party on my own _provided that there will be_ other people there who I know.

25 In the event of heavy snow, we will cancel the game.

IT

If _____, we will cancel the game.

26 If you don't do any practice, you won't get any better.

UNLESS

You won't get any better _____ practice.

27 We should get to the airport on time if there isn't any heavy traffic on the motorway.

AS

We should get to the airport in time _____ no heavy traffic on the motorway.

28 You missed the plane because you didn't check in on time.

CAUGHT

If you had checked in on time _____ the plane.

29 I want to go to Australia but I don't have enough money.

HAD

If I _____ go to Australia.

30 The man living next door always sings loudly in the morning.

WHO

The man _____ always sings loudly in the morning.

Living on the edge

Vocabulary

risk and adventure

1 **Match 1–8 with A–H to make collocations related to risk and adventure.**

1	lone		**A**	clothing
2	risk		**B**	yachtswoman
3	roller		**C**	boarding
4	snow		**D**	diving
5	safety		**E**	coaster
6	sky		**F**	helmet
7	protective		**G**	driving
8	reckless		**H**	taker

Reading

Gapped text (Part 6) ▶ CB page 110

1 **You are going to read an article about someone who is a leading figure in an extreme sport. Six sentences have been removed from the article. Read the article and the sentences below and decide if statements 1–3 are true (T) or false (F).**

1 .... It is the mental challenge that motivates Johnny.

2 .... Johnny is worried that he might not be strong enough.

3 .... Johnny is only doing this because he wants to become famous.

2 **Read the article and the sentences again. Choose from the sentences A–G the one that best fits each gap (1–6). There is one extra sentence which you do not need to use.**

A Then last autumn, without telling his friends where he was going or what he was planning, he cancelled all his engagements.

B Naturally, this involves a lot of repetition.

C Johnny isn't worried about that.

D He is, though, somewhat fitter.

E If he makes it back by early afternoon, he turns round and does it all over again.

F It's an odd admission for someone who has spent the past six months running up and down the Welsh mountains every day, and even stranger when you know why.

G They invited him to take their physical fitness tests.

A SHORT HOP TO PARIS

Johnny Budden hates running. 'It's so boring,' he complains. [1] Beginning on 1 April, Budden plans to run from John O'Groats to Paris – a total of 1,000 miles – in a month, averaging more than a marathon every day.

Budden has no background in endurance sports. Going by the name 'Sticky', he is one of the world's foremost practitioners of parkour, the sport in which extremely agile people treat city landscapes as their obstacle course and throw themselves across railings, walls and rooftops.

Having helped found the UK freerunning scene in his teens, Sticky was flown around the world to appear in advertising campaigns and teach movie stars stuntwork. [2] He retreated to North Wales with a secret mission: to become the first person to freerun over 1,000 miles, camping out each night in the countryside and performing parkour when he arrives in the cities.

'Freerunning involves working out the most efficient way of going from point A to point B through a process of trial and error,' says Budden. [3] 'You do some cool stuff over 20 metres and then you go back and do the same thing again. I wanted to push it to the next level. It's about overcoming obstacles in my head.'

One particular incident last year confirmed that he was ready for the challenge. He had been running workshops for the Royal Marines, who want to use freerunning techniques in combat situations. [4] 'It normally takes sixteen weeks to train up for it,' says Budden, 'and I did them first time. That's when I realised I had potential I wasn't yet using.'

There's also something monastic about his life up here in the hills that wouldn't be out of place in a martial arts movie. The cottage he has been lent has no heating, just a fire for which he must chop wood. Every day he rises at 7a.m., chooses a nearby mountain, and runs to the top. [5] Some days he sets himself extra tasks – 1,000 squats, 200 chin-ups, or, if it has snowed overnight, to complete his run barefoot. But there's no hint of ego or vanity in his manner. He's far more interested in talking about the charity he's running for – the Motor Neurone Disease Association – than himself.

His girlfriend is very worried about his plan to attempt his run without a support vehicle and carrying a one-man tent on his back. 'She keeps saying, "You can't do it! You need a shower every night!"' [6] 'I'll just use the rivers,' he says. 'I still believe that to do freerunning you only need a pair of trainers and an open mind.'

3 Complete sentences 1–6 with the underlined words from the article in Activity 2. Sometimes you need to change the form of the word.

1 There are several marathon runners who train ....
2 One of the cyclists was actually knocked off his bike by his own ....
3 When passing in football, ... is just as important as speed.
4 ...., the ability to do an activity for a long time, is developed by training.
5 She had to .... her own fears before attempting to swim the English Channel.
6 She .... one of the players from the men's tour to see if he could beat her.

Vocabulary

using prefixes to work out meaning
▶ CB page 110

1 Match prefixes 1–10 with meanings A–J.

1 im-   A .... again
2 hyper- B .... three
3 over-   C .... between
4 inter- D .... more than usual
5 tri-   E .... a negative idea
6 pre-   F .... badly, wrongly
7 re-   G .... before
8 dis-   H .... words beginning with 'm' or 'p'
9 mis-   I .... in favour of
10 pro-   J .... too much

2 Complete sentences 1–8 with prefixes from Activity 1.

1 I'm trying to diet – I feel as though I'm just a bit ....weight.
2 The team has just set off to play in the ....national competition in the USA.
3 I've already read the book three times but I love it so much I'm going to ....read it.
4 My new car has a great radio with loads of ....set stations already in place.
5 Unfortunately I'm very ....organised – my flat is in a real mess!
6 My friend is a ....-athlete – he runs, swims and cycles long distances in the same race.
7 My nephew is ....active because he just rushes around all the time and I can't cope!
8 I'm sorry I went to the wrong place – I must have ....understood your message.

Grammar

mixed conditionals
▶ CB page 112

1 **Tick all the possible options to complete sentences 1–4.**

1 He would not be famous
   A if he were a typical sportsman.
   B if he had been a typical sportsman.
   C if he must have been a typical sportsman.

2 Please ask the teacher for our homework books
   A if you happened to see her.
   B if you will see her.
   C if you see her.

3 If I had seen the review in the newspaper earlier,
   A I would have gone to see the play.
   B I will go to see the play.
   C I would be at the play now.

4 If I'd left the party earlier
   A I wouldn't be tired now.
   B I won't be tired now.
   C I wouldn't have been so tired now.

2 **Complete sentences 1–8 with the most suitable form of the verbs in brackets. There may be more than one possible answer.**

1 If she only got on the plane an hour ago, she .... (not be) in Rome yet.

2 If I hadn't stayed out in the sun so long I .... (not be) so burnt today.

3 I would have moved to Italy if I .... (speak) good Italian.

4 I'd feel much happier now if I .... (meet) Sue to discuss the problem yesterday.

5 If I'd started playing tennis when I was younger, I .... (be) a much better player now.

6 If you .... (not come) over tonight, we .... (help) each other with our homework now.

7 If you .... (plan) to withdraw a lot of money from the bank at one time, you .... (need) to notify them in advance.

8 If I ever .... (want) someone to talk to, he .... (always be) there for me.

3 **Find and correct the mistakes in mixed conditional sentences 1–6 below.**

1 If I didn't spend so much money last Saturday, I would have more in my bank account now.

2 If I had been able to find a job in London, I wouldn't have lived in Paris now.

3 If I hadn't studied German for six years at school I'm not so good at it now.

4 If I had worked harder I was in a higher position in the company now.

5 If I could choose my name when I was born I would be called Chloe now.

6 If I would win the lottery, I would give all the money away.

Vocabulary

verbs, nouns and adjectives ▶ CB page 113

1 **Write the verb and adjective forms of nouns 1–8 below.**

0	decision	_decide_	_decisive_
1	intention	....	....
2	separation	....	....
3	threat	....	....
4	experience	....	....
5	support	....	....
6	weight	....	....
7	strength	....	....
8	terror	....	....

2 **Complete sentences 1–6 with the correct form of the words in brackets.**

1 She's a very .... (decide) person because she makes her mind up very quickly.

2 The film was .... (terror) and lots of the audience left before the end.

3 The man looked quite .... (threat) but in fact he was not really dangerous.

4 My parents are always .... (support) – I know I can rely on them.

5 Male dancers develop their upper-body .... (strong) so they can lift their partners.

6 Before you go to the airport, make sure your hand luggage doesn't .... (weight) too much.

Use of English
Word formation (Part 3)
▶ CB page 113

1 For questions 1–8, read the text below. Use the word given in capitals at the end of some of the lines to form a word that fits in the gap in the same line. There is an example at the beginning (0).

A risk worth taking?

Are people going too far seeking new challenges to test their physical and mental **(0)** _capabilities_? One extreme sport is described as 'entering an exciting world of **(1)** .... beauty by sliding through rapids, jumping off waterfalls and abseiling down cliffs'. But are such sports too dangerous? It's the danger that attracts thrill-seekers and their **(2)** .... is that it's human nature to want to push back the boundaries of achievement.

Not everyone agrees. **(3)** .... have called for tighter controls on such sports, to avoid situations where **(4)** .... have to go to the aid of those who get injured. However, one man who went on an adventure trip has no regrets.

'Our **(5)** .... was of the utmost importance for those in charge. Luckily I also know my limitations. If I climbed more aggressively than I should have, it was my own **(6)** .... I believe it's far too easy to get housebound with all the home **(7)** .... available. An increase in extreme sports is **(8)** .... to people turning into handset control freaks!'

CAPABLE

SPOIL

ARGUE

CRITIC

RESCUE

SAFE

CHOOSE

ENTERTAIN

PREFER

Listening
Sentence completion (Part 2) ▶ CB page 114

1 ▶ 22 You will hear a young man called Pete Williams talking to a group of people who are about to set off on a cycling expedition. For questions 1–10, complete the sentences.

Meeting the challenge

Pete says that **(0)** _preparation_ is the key to having a successful cycling expedition.

According to Pete, getting all the **(1)** .... in place is the first practical thing to sort out.

Pete advises other cyclists to have **(2)** .... when trying to speak to people who might support them.

Pete says that the best advice he was given was not to change the **(3)** .... of departure.

During his trip, Pete found it interesting that people told him about their ambitions and **(4)** ....

Pete uses the word **(5)** .... to describe how he thinks about the experience of his trip.

Pete says that people on expeditions should accept any **(6)** .... they get from local people.

Pete found that the most difficult thing for him was **(7)** .... during his trip.

Pete was very interested by the **(8)** .... he saw on the trip.

Pete enjoyed keeping his **(9)** .... up-to-date during the trip.

Pete plans to become a **(10)** .... once he gives up his expeditions.

Vocabulary
adjectives and verbs with prepositions
▶ CB page 115

1 Complete sentences 1–6 with the correct form of the verbs in the box.

wear	cut	call	tell	see	put

1 The whole expedition was .... off because of the blizzard.

2 The heavy snow on the road meant that the village was completely .... off.

3 The expedition leader was furious when I got lost and .... me off in front of the others.

4 When we left for Everest, all my friends came to .... me off at the airport.

5 I need to be fit for the next trip but I find it difficult to do the training and I keep .... it off until later!

6 Doing challenging things can be terrifying at first but the fear usually .... off as you get used to it.

2 Complete the text with suitable prepositions.

A great experience

I never thought I'd have the chance to go on an expedition to the North Pole – but I did, and although I was worried **(1)** ...... the cold before I went it turned out to be a great experience. I was thrilled **(2)** ...... having the chance to go, and I was determined **(3)** ...... do well. The expedition was intended **(4)** ...... people in good physical shape, and keen **(5)** ...... pushing themselves physically and mentally – great, but it meant I had to be confident **(6)** ...... my own level of fitness. I did a whole lot of training! We had to rely **(7)** ...... cross-country skiing to cross the difficult terrain, which was very demanding, and we also needed to be able **(8)** ...... pull a heavy sled (between 30 and 40 kilos) for several hours at a time. Towards the end of each day when we stopped skiing, it was critical that we had enough energy **(9)** ...... set up camp, melt snow for hot tea or cocoa, and make dinner. The expedition leaders insisted **(10)** ...... maintaining a spirit of support and teamwork, as dealing **(11)** ...... such difficult weather conditions is very challenging. We didn't need to be world-class athletes to participate **(12)** ...... this expedition but it was certainly challenging and my friends were very impressed **(13)** ...... my achievement when I got back! This is an experience that will stay with me for the rest of my life and I'd love to be involved **(14)** ...... another one before too long!

Blog

Grammar

hypothetical meaning ▶ CB page 116

1 Underline the correct alternatives to complete sentences 1–8.

1 Tim really wishes he *runs/would have run/could run* in the next London Marathon but the doctor says he is not able to.

2 If only I *hadn't bet/wouldn't have bet/didn't bet* all my money on that horse winning the race.

3 I wish you *would take up/would have taken up/had taken up* a safer sport than parkour now that you are getting older.

4 If only your grandfather *would be/has been/were* alive to see you win the cup.

5 Don't you wish that you *had never started/would not start/did not start* this project?

6 I really wish I *could improve/improved/have improved* my agility and muscle endurance.

7 If only I *didn't live/wouldn't live/haven't lived* so far from the sea.

8 Eleanor wished she *has/would have/could have* joined the expedition to the Arctic Circle but her parents wouldn't let her go.

2 Find and correct the mistakes in sentences 1–4.

1 The film was so well made I felt as if I have actually climbed Mount Everest myself.

2 I'd rather you don't invite Jamie to the party. He doesn't get on very well with Max.

3 It's high time we had left for the station. We'll be lucky to catch the 9.30 train.

4 It was very silly of you to go out on your bike without a helmet. Suppose you fell off and hit your head?

Speaking

Long turn (Part 2) ▶ CB page 117

1 ▶ 23 Listen to the examiner's instructions and what one candidate said. Has he followed the instructions?

2 Look at the examiner's question to some other candidates. Match responses 1–4 with the examiner's comments A–D.

Examiner: Which of these two trips would you prefer to go on?

1 The second one.

2 I would prefer to be the person on the bicycle. I would love to travel alone like that.

3 No, I haven't but I'd like to.

4 I can see many nice things in these photographs. For example, the plane looks fun to fly in and I think the bicycle looks like a very expensive one and very fast.

A Misunderstood the question.
B Answer far too brief.
C Response too long and irrelevant.
D Good clear response.

Writing
Review (Part 2) ▶ CB page 118

1 Read the task below.

> You see this announcement in an English language magazine.
>
> **Reviews of computer games wanted!**
>
> Have you played a computer game recently that you really liked?
>
> Write a review, describing the game and explaining what you liked about it. Tell us whether or not you would recommend it to other people of your age.

2 In a review you use functions (describe, explain, give an opinion and recommend). Look at the words and phrases below and decide which functions each one is.

1 In my view … ....
2 What I mean is … ....
3 What happens is … ....
4 It seems to me that … ....
5 It's a fast-moving game with lots of action. ....
6 I enjoyed the speed of the game. ....
7 I can only suggest that you try it yourself. ....
8 It's not to be missed! ....

3 Read the review below. Which functions (describe, explain, give an opinion, recommend) does the writer use in each paragraph?

I've been playing 'Demon warriors' for the last few months, and it's pretty awesome. It's a game with different levels, and you have to collect special tokens as you play so that you can progress to the next level. There are some great sets, which are very colourful, thrilling music and, of course, there are lots of things like monsters to stop you getting there!

What I like about it is the variety. Although some people could get irritated if they can't move on, it is designed in such a way as to be challenging. This means that when you do well it makes you feel really good. You can also play it with friends, so there's a competitive element to it.

It's not a cheap game, which might put some people off. But in my view it's worth the money, as it gives you hours of fun. I would certainly suggest that you try it yourself!

4 Find words in the review in Activity 3 that mean the same as these words.

1 fantastic ....
2 move up ....
3 exciting ....
4 annoyed ....
5 planned ....
6 factor ....

5 Now write your own answer to the task in Activity 1. Try to use a variety of interesting language. Write 140–190 words.

Crime scene

Listening

Sentence completion (Part 2)   ▶ CB page 120

1 **Underline the correct alternatives to complete sentences 1–6.**

1 I read crime novels because I love *solving/working* problems.
2 It's important to *make/do* research before writing a book.
3 It's useful when tips are *passed on/given on* by successful writers.
4 People love *going through/getting out* clues to a crime.
5 Writers can waste a lot of time waiting for inspiration to *hit/strike*.
6 A good cover will *grab/take* people's attention and make them pick up the book.

2 ▶ 24 **You will hear a young crime writer called Carrie Thomas talking to a group of students about her life and work. For questions 1–10, complete the sentences.**

Carrie believes that writing crime fiction is a (**1**) .... that anyone can learn.

Carrie uses the word (**2**) .... to describe writer's block.

Carrie advises would-be crime writers to be sure of their personal (**3**) .... for wanting to be a writer.

Before she started writing, Carrie spent a lot of time finding out about police (**4**) .... and how they work.

Carrie suggests analysing other writers' books to see what makes their books (**5**) .... and why they make money.

Carrie thinks that crime novels are popular because readers like working out the answer to a (**6**) .... before anyone else.

Carrie appreciated being told not to forget to conform to the conventions and (**7**) .... of crime writing.

Carrie emphasises the importance of taking the advice of your (**8**) .... when writing.

Carrie says that the synopsis of the book on the dust jacket must be interesting but (**9**) .... as well.

According to Carrie, writers must be good at (**10**) .... as well as telling stories.

Vocabulary

crime

1 **Complete the text with the words in the box.**

defendants	trial	police	evidence
facts	sentences	court	innocent

After the riots were over **(1)** .... spoke to witnesses to establish the **(2)** .... of the situation and collect proof of wrong-doing. Having collected all the **(3)** .... they needed, they arrested many people, who then appeared in **(4)** .... After each **(5)** .... had finished, the judge considered the case, decided whether the **(6)** .... were guilty or **(7)** .... and gave those who had caused criminal damage long prison **(8)** ....

2 **Cross out the alternative that does not collocate in sentences 1–6.**

1 The police *interviewed/arrested/sentenced* the suspect.

2 The woman was *accused/suspected/fined* of stealing the car.

3 The robber was given a big *fine/sentence/punishment* by the judge.

4 The woman *caught/got/had* a glimpse of the burglar on the roof.

5 A jury often finds it hard to *reach/come to/decide* an agreement on their verdict.

6 The man was *caught/seen/got* in the act of breaking into the car.

Grammar

modal verbs ▶ CB page 122

1 **Underline the correct alternatives to complete the sentences.**

1 He *shouldn't/mustn't* have told John about the misunderstanding because it just caused trouble.

2 You *needn't/mustn't* drive me to the station as it's only a five-minute walk.

3 You *need/must* read that new crime thriller – it's really good.

4 We're not *allowed to/supposed to* speak to the newspapers about the case, though it's not actually illegal if we do.

5 I *need/must* to go to the dentist this afternoon, so I'll have to miss the meeting.

6 You *mustn't/don't have to* say anything if you're arrested.

2 **Find and correct the mistakes in sentences 1–8. Tick the sentences that are correct.**

Did you have
0 ~~Had you~~ to give evidence to the police after the accident?

1 She had leave home early to make sure she didn't miss the meeting.

2 The teacher told me I needn't do the test again because my marks were good enough.

3 You are not allowed driving at over 100 mph on the motorway.

4 You must to try not to get depressed – we know you're innocent.

5 Witnesses may think they don't have to telling the truth to the judge, but they do.

6 You are not allowed to drink and drive – it's illegal.

7 You mustn't do the washing-up; it's not necessary because I can do it later.

8 You shouldn't smoke anywhere in public buildings.

3 **For questions 1–6, complete the second sentence so that it has a similar meaning to the first sentence, using the word given. Do not change the word given. You must use between two and five words, including the word given.**

1 It's all right if members bring guests to the gym on Monday evenings.

ALLOWED

Members .... guests to the gym on Monday evenings.

2 The police insisted that he paid the fine on time.

HAD

He .... the fine on time because the police insisted.

3 The robber was not obliged to meet his victim to apologise, but he did.

NEED

The robber .... meet his victim to apologise, but he did.

4 Is it really necessary for me to make a statement now?

HAVE

Do .... make a statement now?

5 I'm working late tonight as they've asked me if I can hand in this report tomorrow.

SUPPOSED

I'm working late tonight as .... hand in this report tomorrow.

6 They say I'm not allowed to smoke anywhere in the building.

MUST

They say .... anywhere in the building.

Speaking

Discussion (Part 4) ▶ CB page 123

1 **Read what students said in answer to a discussion question. Underline where the student**

1 gives examples. (find four examples)

2 tries to include the other candidate in the discussion. (find three examples)

3 uses phrases for agreeing and disagreeing. (find three examples)

E = Examiner, **G** = Günther, **M** = Manoela

E: How has the public's awareness of cyber crime changed?

G: I think people are far more conscious of the risks than they were a few years ago. For example, if they're shopping online and need to pay for something with a credit card, most people know they should only do this if it's a site they can trust. Otherwise, they run the risk of identity theft. Would you agree?

M: I certainly would, particularly after what happened to my mother. She's a bit careless about things like that. A couple of weeks ago she had a problem because someone had got hold of her credit card details and had tried to book a train ticket somewhere in France. Has anything like that ever happened to you?

G: No, fortunately. But sometimes I wonder if there is such a thing as a secure site. After all, we're constantly hearing that confidential information has been leaked from a site because of hacking. Even mobile phones aren't safe.

M: No, they're not. I get a lot of unwanted messages on mine. But what about social networking sites? I think they can be very risky. Something really horrible happened to a friend of mine, for instance. Another boy created a page using his name and said all sorts of terrible things about him and his friends.

G: If he managed to find out who it was he could sue him for libel.

M: It was someone in our class at school who was always insulting my friend and calling him names. It turned out he'd posted pictures of another friend of ours without asking her permission and also tried to get a lot of people to put insulting comments on her wall. He's a real cyber-bully. My friend was partly to blame, though. She should have checked the privacy settings on the site so that people who were not her friends wouldn't have access. Everyone should do that, don't you think?

G: Yes and no. I mean, it's also quite good if old friends can find you and get in touch.

Reading

Multiple choice (Part 5) ▶ CB page 124

1 **You are going to read an article about a stolen bicycle. Read the article once and decide if the following statement is true or false.**

The woman took the bicycle because she believed it was hers.

2 **Read the article again. For questions 1–6, choose the answer (A, B, C or D) which you think fits best according to the text.**

1 What made it easier for the thieves to steal the writer's bike?

A They knew it had been left unlocked.

B They knew no one would see them.

C They had a special tool.

D They had plenty of time.

2 Why was the writer frustrated with the response from the police?

A She thought it was their duty to go with her to the market.

B She didn't think they believed she could find her bike there.

C She didn't think they had given her good advice.

D She thought they were being deliberately uncooperative.

3 How did the writer feel when she realised her bike was not in the white van?

A Relieved because she would not have been brave enough to speak to the man.

B Afraid because the man might have seen her watching him.

C Worried because she didn't know where else her bike could be.

D Hopeful because she thought she might find it in another van.

4 The writer thinks the boy gave her the bike because

A he saw how angry she was.

B he knew it was stolen.

C he thought she was going to pay him.

D he realised she was bigger than him.

5 What does *there* in line 38 refer to?

A standing in the crowds.

B between the stalls.

C with the boy.

D just behind the writer.

6 How does the writer feel now?

A annoyed about having to repair her bike.

B sorry for having made a mistake.

C relieved to have her bike back.

D guilty about what she did.

THE DAY I STOLE A BICYCLE

It was my first brand new bike. Nothing fancy – the cheapest Ridgeback on the market – but I was really proud of it and I loved it.

Two months later, on a sunny Saturday afternoon, I locked it up on Whitechapel High Street in London. There were lots of people about. I felt sure it would be fine, but two hours later, it was gone. The lock was lying on the pavement. It had been cut straight through with a pair of bolt cutters. I was <u>gutted</u>.

I felt sure it would turn up at Brick Lane Market the next day and tried to arrange to meet the police there so that we could look for it together and reclaim it, but they told me that they couldn't go along with me. They were very sympathetic and said that if I was to find my bike I should ring 999 and they'd <u>be straight over</u>. I didn't want to argue but I couldn't see how that was going to help. The market would be crowded and my bike would <u>be long gone</u> in the time it took them to reach me.

I got to the market early. At the far end of the street a particularly <u>scary-looking</u> man was directing two others who were unloading bikes from a white van. He had his back to me and he was shaven-headed and absolutely huge. I knew if my bike came out the back of that van I'd be going home to save up for another one without saying a word, but I watched anyway. I was almost glad that my silver Ridgeback didn't appear, though lots of other bikes did. There were other vans but my bike didn't come out of those either.

By ten o'clock I'd been at the market for over two hours and it was getting crowded. The white vans had stopped coming but bikes were still arriving ridden by teenagers. This is where I saw my bike – my <u>pristine</u>, two-month-old silver ladies' Ridgeback – except now it had a <u>buckled</u> front wheel and it was missing a seat post. I couldn't tell how old the boy holding it was but I was relieved that he was smaller than me. I was scared but angry enough to go ahead and speak to him. I asked him how much he wanted. He said £90. I told him that it was my bike and he could either give it to me or he could wait for the police to arrive and I would show them my receipt. He gave it to me, turned around and walked away.

I took a deep breath and started to wheel my unrideable bike through what were now thick crowds between the stalls. When I had confronted the boy I had noticed a man watching us from the other side of the narrow street. The boy had walked off in his direction. As I looked over my shoulder, I could see this man was now behind me in the crowds. I kept walking but every time I looked over my shoulder the man was still there. We both knew that he was going to <u>catch up with</u> me as soon as I crossed the road. I couldn't see that there was anything else for me to do. I got on the bike and rode it, with its <u>wobbly</u> wheel and no seat post – but I didn't care. I just needed to get away from this man who I believed was intent on doing me harm. I made eye contact with the man chasing me once more as I clanked away down the street. He had stopped following me. He took one good sour look at my face and turned around to walk back into the market.

I made it home <u>in one piece</u> and, after a deep breath and a cup of tea, flipped my bike over to remove the buckled front wheel. Here comes the <u>shameful</u> part. This is when I checked the serial number against my receipt and realised that this wasn't my bike after all. It was the same make and colour but it wasn't mine. I kept it anyway.

38

3 Match the underlined words and phrases in the article in Activity 2 with definitions 1–10.

1 undamaged and clean
2 moving from side to side in an unsteady way
3 have disappeared a long time before
4 very upset and disappointed
5 deserving blame
6 come immediately
7 with a frightening appearance
8 bent
9 unhurt
10 reach

Vocabulary
phrasal verbs ▶ CB page 125

1 **Find phrasal verbs in the text and use them to replace the underlined words and phrases in these sentences.**

1 I thought someone in the office must have taken my favourite pen but it suddenly <u>appeared</u> in my coat pocket.
2 Susan saw a boy take my wallet out of my bag but he managed to <u>escape</u> before we could stop him.
3 The police are still <u>searching for</u> clues in the hope of finding out what happened in the hours before the girl disappeared.
4 Most young offenders ask a parent to <u>accompany</u> them when they have to appear in court.
5 The detective walked as fast as he could and managed to <u>reach</u> the woman he was following as she got into the lift.
6 Even though she knew there would be serious consequences she decided to <u>proceed</u> with her decision to admit that she had forged his signature.

Grammar

have/get something done
▶ CB page 126

1 Complete the conversation with the prompts in brackets. Make sure you use the correct tense of the verbs.

J = José, **K** = Karin

J: Why is Elena looking so worried?

K: She **(1)** .... (*bicycle, steal*) last week when she went to the market.

J: Oh, no! What's she going to do about it?

K: Well, amazingly enough she **(2)** .... (*it, return*) to her already. She found it outside her house this morning, or at least she thought it was her bicycle.

J: What do you mean?

K: There's a problem. It's the same make but it's a different colour. She thought the thieves **(3)** .... (*it, repaint*) so that it would be more difficult to identify.

J: So is she **(4)** .... (*it, painted*) silver like it used to be?

K: She was, but then she discovered that one of the wheels was buckled and she took it to the bike shop to **(5)** .... (*it, repair*).

J: What happened?

K: Well, in the bike shop they asked to see her receipt and when they checked the serial number on the receipt and compared it to the one on the bike, they didn't match. She **(6)** .... (*it, fix*) anyway but she took it to the police station.

Use of English

Open cloze (Part 2) ▶ CB page 127

1 Read crime stories 1–2. A student has made mistakes filling in some of the gaps. Find the mistakes and correct them.

1 Bungling Burglar
A burglar was caught after he fell **(1)** down a chimney while trying to climb over the roof of a house he had just **(2)** breaked into. Police arrested the 33-year-old after **(3)** been called out by the house owners who heard his calls **(4)** for help. The man had tried to escape out of a window in the roof with his booty of cash and jewellery, but tumbled in the dark and **(5)** get stuck inside the chimney.

2 Forgetful robber
A man went into a drug store, pulled **(6)** up a gun from his pocket and announced that the store was **(7)** being robbed. He pulled a paper bag over his head **(8)** as a face mask. He immediately realised that he'd forgotten to cut eyeholes in the bag and so he couldn't see anything. He **(9)** had arrested by security men that he hadn't seen standing **(10)** on the corner of the room.

2 For questions 1–8, read the text below and think of the word which best fits each gap. Use only one word in each gap. There is an example at the beginning (0).

Are you helping criminals?

We all send them, thinking that we **(0)** *need* to keep others in touch with our movements. But **(1)** .... much might we actually be revealing in our Out-of-Office email messages? A careless, frivolous message conveys a sloppy, unprofessional image. But **(2)** .... you think that's bad, think again. Let me give you **(3)** .... example. Last week I got 135 automatic emails. Of these, twenty gave away information about clients and projects and twenty-seven were insecure, leaving the sender open to cyber crime.

How does it work? Apparently **(4)** .... cyber criminals do is send thousands of emails completely **(5)** .... random. Once they get your automatic response, they can find out personal details, even possibly **(6)** .... you live, by cross-referencing the information. An automatic message can alert thieves to the fact that you are away, and the chance of someone breaking **(7)** .... your house in your absence is increased.

So include the minimum of information on your automatic message, **(8)** .... 'I am unable to deal with your email at the moment'. Don't help criminals by telling them too much!

Writing
Report (Part 2) ▶ CB page 128

1 Look at the task. Which three of the following do students **not** have to do in their report?

> The director of the college where you study is concerned about security, and is planning to either put security cameras in the college or install new devices for students to lock up their bicycles. As there is not much money to spend, the director has asked students to write a report assessing the value of both ideas and recommending which one most students would find useful.
>
> **Write your report.**

1 Describe both ideas.
2 Consider the advantages and disadvantages of each idea.
3 Describe security arrangements in the college.
4 Explain the opinions of other students.
5 Recommend one idea.
6 Give reasons for recommendations.
7 Think of a new idea to recommend.
8 Explain the purpose of the report.

2 **Rewrite the sentences with the correct form of the word in brackets.**

1 I suggest .... (spend) money on security cameras.
2 It is recommended that students .... (fill in) a questionnaire.
3 My suggestion would be .... (consult) as many people as possible.
4 I recommend the director .... (ask) students for their opinions.
5 It is my suggestion that students should be able .... (lock up) their bikes.
6 I recommend .... (talk) to students about this.

3 **Read the report below that was written in answer to the task in Activity 1 and do the following:**

1 Underline two pieces of unnecessary information the student has included.
2 Correct ten mistakes with spelling and grammar.
3 Choose a heading for each paragraph. There are two headings you do not need to use.

A Introduction
B Ideas from students
C Recommendations
D The cost of suggestions
E Locking devices for bicycles
F Security cameras

....

The purpose of this report is to asess the value of improving security by either puting security cameras into the college or providing devices to allow students to lock up their bicycles. I consulted many students, and this report is based in their responses.

....

Students felt there would be an overall benefit in instaling security cameras, but it could turn up to be expensive. The cameras in the new shopping centre cost a fortune! In addition, someone must watch the screens, which seems a waste of time and money.

....

It is a big problem for everyone when bicycles are stolen, as many students come to college by bikes. At the moment they leave them at the entrance, but several have been stolen. Last week a red one was taken. It would not being very expensive to install bicycle racks in the front of the college, and students were liking this idea.

....

Based on the views expressed by students, and on the fact that cameras would be expensive, I recommend install devices for students to lock up their bicycles. This would encourage even more students cycling, which is good for the environment and also for the health and fitness of students.

4 **Write your own answer to the task below. Remember to make recommendations, giving good reasons for your suggestions. Write 140–190 words.**

> You have recently been on a holiday where several things went wrong. You lost your wallet and some jewellery was stolen from your hotel room. The manager of the hotel has asked you to write a report for the hotel security team. You should explain what happened, and say how you think security at the hotel could be improved.

Multiple-choice cloze (Part 1)

For questions 1–8, read the text below and decide which answer (A, B, C or D) best fits each gap. There is an example at the beginning (0).

An escapist read!

This book **(0)** *A kept* me enthralled for a whole weekend. It describes an incident in which a scientist was standing on top of a Colombian volcano when it erupted, killing several of his colleagues **(1)** .... He tried to scramble down the incredibly steep side of the volcano, but was caught by a heavy shower of white-hot rocks. Several of these hit him, **(2)** .... him so badly that he feared he would not survive. However, **(3)** .... the dangers, two very brave women **(4)** .... an extraordinary rescue, and helped him to safety.

This book describes the work of scientists who place themselves in danger in the search to understand volcanoes, and shows why they choose to **(5)** .... such risks. They hope to develop the technique of **(6)** .... accurately when the next eruption might occur **(7)** .... to give people living in the area **(8)** .... warning which would save lives. It is a thought-provoking and fascinating book, which I recommend.

0	**A** kept	**B** held	**C** got	**D** made
1	**A** actually	**B** directly	**C** instantly	**D** momentarily
2	**A** damaging	**B** injuring	**C** spoiling	**D** smashing
3	**A** despite	**B** even	**C** providing	**D** consequently
4	**A** took up	**B** made up	**C** set out	**D** carried out
5	**A** get	**B** take	**C** have	**D** do
6	**A** planning	**B** forecasting	**C** projecting	**D** viewing
7	**A** so that	**B** in order	**C** in case	**D** though
8	**A** future	**B** ahead	**C** advance	**D** before

Open cloze (Part 2)

For questions 9–16, read the text below and think of the word which best fits each gap. Use only one word in each gap. There is an example at the beginning (0).

Cheerleading may be riskier than sport!

Cheerleading **(0)** *has* become a mainstream activity – many sports would be nothing today without groups of chanting young people dancing on the sidelines. But would you believe that showing support for a team **(9)** .... this way may be almost as risky as playing the game **(10)** ....? Each season, just as the players undergo trials for their sport, young people try out for their cheerleading team, hoping to join that elite group of people **(11)** .... spend the game urging their team on to greater efforts. What they do during the game is a key factor in creating an atmosphere within a stadium. In the past, cheerleading **(12)** .... to be fun, but now it may have a darker side. Cheerleading once simply involved performing a simple routine while at the same time making a lot of noise. But now it's turned into serious gymnastics and is competitive in its **(13)** .... right. Each season thousands of young people strive to come up with **(14)** .... most dramatic display of choreography they can, and as **(15)** .... result they end up needing emergency hospital treatment. Although sport itself is well-regulated, cheerleading is **(16)** ...., so maybe what it now needs are some serious rules!

Word formation (Part 3)

For questions 17–24. read the text below. Use the word given in capitals at the end of some of the lines to form a word that fits the gap in the same line. There is an example at the beginning (0).

Mountain storm nightmare

A young couple had a **(0)** _miraculous_ escape during a back-packing holiday in the mountains. Sally and Chris found themselves stranded in freezing conditions, surrounded by sheer rock faces in every **(17)** _____ . They tried to call the emergency services, but to their horror discovered they were **(18)** _____ to get a signal. They made the difficult **(19)** _____ to camp where they were and wait for morning, even though the weather was appalling. As daylight approached, Sally knew that she was **(20)** _____ of climbing down unaided and Chris set off to find help alone. Hours passed until she heard a helicopter in the distance, and waved **(21)** _____ to attract the pilot's attention. She was taken to hospital where she learned that Chris had fallen during his descent due to the **(22)** _____ conditions, and been forced to crawl for hours before reaching a small village. After an **(23)** _____ reunion, the couple decided to choose less **(24)** _____ holidays in future!

MIRACLE

DIRECT

ABLE

DECIDE

CAPABLE

FRANTIC

ICE

EMOTION
ADVENTURE

Key word transformations (Part 4)

For questions 25–30, complete the second sentence so that it has a similar meaning to the first sentence, using the word given. Do not change the word given. You must use between two and five words, including the word given. Here is an example (0).

Example:

0 A very friendly woman gave us directions when we got lost.

GIVEN

When we got lost we _were given directions by_ a very friendly woman.

25 I prefer playing football to tennis.

RATHER

I _____ tennis.

26 Do you think I have to get a visa to visit the country?

NECESSARY

Do you think _____ to get a visa to visit the country?

27 If no one turns up for the meeting, you can go home.

LONG

You can go home, _____ turns up for the meeting.

28 If it isn't too cold, we'll go skiing tomorrow.

UNLESS

We'll go skiing tomorrow _____ too cold.

29 The plane was so crowded that I couldn't sleep on the long flight.

TOO

The plane was _____ sleep on the long flight.

30 'Don't leave the building without locking up, John,' said the manager.

LEAVING

The manager reminded John _____ the building.

Who are you again?

Vocabulary

memory and understanding

1 Complete sentences 1–6 with the correct form of the verbs in the box. There are three verbs you do not need to use.

---
cross   follow   mislead   trigger   go
mistake   confuse   occur   stay
---

1 I once .... a complete stranger for someone I used to go out with. It was terribly embarrassing.

2 I really liked Elena but it never .... my mind that she might be falling in love with me.

3 I was trying to remember the speech from memory but halfway through my mind .... blank and I had to refer to my notes.

4 His films are great but sometimes I find it hard to .... the plot.

5 Smells often .... very vivid memories for me. The other day someone's perfume made me think about my grandmother.

6 I think my instructions might have .... you. The hotel is actually opposite the station, not behind it.

Reading

Multiple matching (Part 7) ▶ CB page 130

1 You are going to read an article about different kinds of amnesia. Read the article. Which thing is <u>not</u> mentioned?

A temporary memory loss   **B** people who fake amnesia

2 Read the article again. For questions 1–10, choose from the people A–D. The people may be chosen more than once.

Which person

may have reacted to stress at work?	1
had medical treatment that caused the memory problem?	2
seemed to be suffering from another medical condition?	3
had had an accident?	4
has only forgotten the events of one day?	5
enjoyed doing something which was also beneficial?	6
cannot remember relatives or past experiences?	7
is now thinking about many important issues?	8
had been exercising just before the problem started?	9
could not offer an explanation of what happened?	10

Amnesia

It's the subject of many books and films and fascinates us all but stories of real-life amnesiacs are also stories of suffering.

A Hannah Upp

One August morning, a twenty-three-year-old schoolteacher went jogging. That is the last thing that Hannah Upp says she remembers before she was rescued from New York Harbor almost three weeks later. She disappeared the day before the start of term, leaving behind her wallet and her mobile phone. Was she running away from an overly demanding job? Escaping from a city that can <u>overwhelm</u> many people? What did she eat? Where did she sleep? How on earth did she survive for so long without money or any identification in one of the world's biggest cities? Miss Upp is as much in the dark about all this as anyone else. While she was recovering after her rescue she was told that she was suffering from 'disassociative fugue', a <u>rare</u> form of amnesia that causes people to forget their identity. The condition can last from a few hours to years. It happens suddenly and, without warning, can end just as suddenly and has no physical cause. 'It has all been very weird,' Miss Upp said. 'It's definitely made me reconsider everything. Who was I before? Who was I then? Who am I now?'

B Scott Bolzan

The videos show scenes from a full and <u>prosperous</u> life: a couple getting married, bringing up their children and going on family holidays. They're precious memories. But the man who lived them cannot remember any of them. In fact, Scott Bolzan has no memory of any part of his life story. He has an extreme case of what is known as 'severe retrograde amnesia'. He <u>slipped</u> and hit his head on the hard flooring of a bathroom and can remember nothing that happened before that. Over the past sixteen months, he has had to re-meet family and friends, re-learn his life story and rebuild a sense of identity. Doctors could find no physical explanation for his rare condition at first. 'Then they worked out

that I have no blood flow going to the right temporal lobe of my brain,' said Bolzan. This is where all long-term memory is <u>stored</u>. Sadly, he'll never recover. But he continues one day at a time, to create memories that will, hopefully, last a lifetime.

C Ralph Gilbert

Susan Gilbert thought her husband Ralph had had a stroke. What else could cause a healthy person suddenly to become disorientated and confused? More than eight hours after the onset of his symptoms Ralph was diagnosed with 'transient global amnesia', a temporary condition that affects a small percentage of people every year. There was no <u>warning</u>. He had been lifting weights to fill in time before going out to lunch with Susan's parents. The amnesia came only moments after he finished his workout. He couldn't remember where he and Susan were going and had dressed himself in clothes he claimed he had never seen before. In hospital, although he remembered who Susan was and his own name, he didn't remember being taken there. Ralph was allowed to go home that same evening by which time his memory had, for the most part returned, except for the previous eight hours. That has forever been <u>erased</u>.

D Henry Gustav Molaison

Henry Gustav Molaison became the most studied patient in the history of brain science after an operation in 1953 left him unable to form new memories. Mr Molaison performed memory tests, filled in questionnaires and sat for brain scans each time as if for the first time. In between it all he did puzzles, hundreds and hundreds of them. In one experiment crosswords were used to test Mr Molaison's capacity to learn new facts. The researchers found that he was just as good at solving puzzles as healthy people his own age if he could draw on what he'd learned in the years before the operation. Mr Molaison stunned researchers over the years by learning some new facts. In particular, he seemed to be able to <u>update</u> pre-1953 memories. 'One thing I found out is that I fool around a lot with crossword puzzles,' he said. 'And it helps me, in a way.' 'It helps you remember?' his doctor asked. It did, he said. And, he added, 'You have fun while doing it too.'

---

3 **Complete sentences 1–8 with the underlined words and phrases from the article in Activity 2. Sometimes you will need to change the form of the word.**

1 I must remember to .... my profile on Facebook. I haven't told anyone about my new job yet.

2 We're always being told that .... is just around the corner but the economy seems to be in a real mess.

3 The teacher didn't .... us that we were going to have a test, so none of us had prepared.

4 There's not much .... space in this house. We've only got one large cupboard and some shelves.

5 He was thrilled to get a photograph of a very .... bird while he was on holiday.

6 The roads are often very .... after it's been raining, so do drive carefully.

7 She was completely .... by the response to her new record. She received thousands of letters from fans.

8 I accidentally .... some important files from my computer.

Vocabulary

phrasal verbs with *come* ▶ CB page 131

1 **Replace the underlined words and phrases in sentences 1–8 with a phrasal verb with *come*. You may need to add another preposition or phrase to complete the sentence.**

1 <u>By chance I found</u> a fascinating old diary when I was clearing out my grandmother's house.

2 After a lot of time <u>I thought of</u> a solution to the problem.

3 When my uncle in Australia died, <u>I inherited</u> enough money to buy a swimming pool.

4 I don't feel well – I think <u>I'm getting</u> some kind of virus.

5 I have to persuade my friend to come on holiday; I hope <u>she'll agree to</u> the idea.

6 It's been a difficult time for us all but <u>we've all survived</u> it.

7 <u>He's really made a great deal of progress</u> since he joined the class.

8 Some people say <u>I give the impression that I am</u> over-confident.

Grammar

ability: *can/could; be able to*
▶ CB page 132

1 **Complete the sentences with the correct form of *can/could/could have* or *be able to* and a verb in the box. There may be more than one possible answer.**

speak	hear	go	finish	buy	stay up
sleep	live	accept	get	play	contact

1 I'm really sorry but I .... to the cinema with you because I've got too much work.

2 When I was young I .... all night but now I get too tired!

3 He must .... Italian – he lived there for five years!

4 This phone line is awful; I .... you clearly.

5 If you'd told me it was your birthday, I .... you a present.

6 I expect I'll .... the report by the end of the week.

7 Eventually we .... the car to start but it took ages!

8 I'm so tired – I .... very well last night because it was noisy outside.

9 I used to .... tennis really well but I don't have time now.

10 I .... the promotion but I didn't want to work such long hours.

11 I just .... in such a big city – it's too polluted!

12 You won't .... him today as he's in a meeting.

Speaking

Long turn (Part 2) ▶ CB page 133

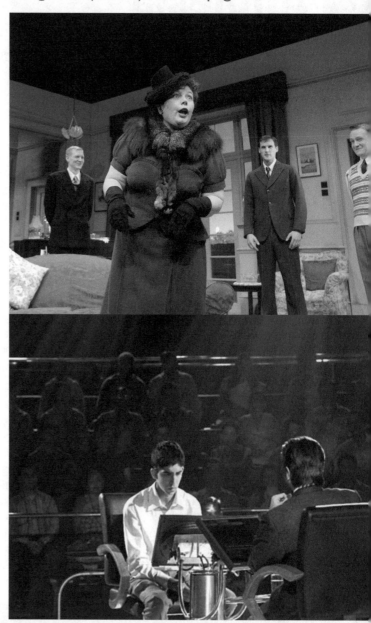

1 **▶ 25 Look at the two photographs and listen to the examiner's instructions to the candidate. Decide whether statements 1–4 below are true (T) or false (F).**

1 The examiner tells the candidate where each of the photographs was taken.

2 The examiner tells the candidate one thing that the two photographs have in common.

3 The candidate has to choose one of the photographs and justify this choice.

4 The candidate has to find similarities and differences between the two photographs.

2 Look at what the candidate said about the photographs. In each sentence there is an extra word. Cross out the extra words.

1 The two photographs are similar in many of ways.
2 One thing they have in the common is that the people are performing in front of live audiences.
3 The first one photograph was probably taken in a theatre.
4 It shows of actors performing on stage in a play of some kind.
5 In the second picture, we are see a contestant in a quiz show.
6 There is too a quiz master who is asking a question of some kind and the contestant is trying hard to remember the answer.
7 For the people in the both photographs, having a good memory is very important.
8 To win a quiz show like to this you have to remember a lot of facts and figures and answer the questions correctly under enormous pressure.
9 Despite of having to learn and remember their lines, they usually have someone standing at the side of the stage with a copy of the script to remind them if they forget.

3 Look at the sentences in Activity 2 again. Does the candidate perform the task well?

4 ▶ 26 Listen to what the other candidate said and decide which of these two questions the examiner asked him.

1 Which of these two activities would you rather take part in?
2 Which of these two activities would you find more nerve-racking?

Vocabulary

expressions with *mind*; verbs with similar meanings
▶ CB page 134

1 Complete the expressions with *mind* with the correct form of the words in the box. There are two words you do not need.

| lose | bear | cross | slip | in | change |
| off | take | on | make | put | blank |

1 I can't remember her address. My mind's gone _____!
2 You've given me some good advice. I'll _____ it in mind when I decide what to do.
3 I can't decide whether to go to the cinema or not; I'm _____ two minds about it.
4 I was so upset I couldn't think straight. I thought I was _____ my mind.
5 I'm sorry I forgot to post the letter; it just _____ my mind.
6 I've been very worried recently so I need something to _____ my mind off the problems.
7 That didn't _____ my mind. I just didn't think of it at all.
8 I'm going to phone Sue to tell her the good news; it'll _____ her mind at rest.
9 Please _____ up your mind what you want to do tonight because I need to know what to wear!
10 I just can't make decisions when I'm shopping. I keep _____ my mind.

2 Replace the underlined words and phrases in sentences 1–6 with expressions with *mind*.

1 She must be crazy if she's thinking of leaving him – he's a real catch!
2 The idea that he might buy me a present never occurred to me.
3 I was supposed to be going to the cinema tonight but I forgot about it.
4 I listen to music when I want to forget my problems.
5 I wish she'd decide which dress she's going to buy because I'm getting so bored waiting for her!
6 I thought the film would be terrible but after seeing it I don't think that any more.

3 Complete sentences 1–8 with the correct form of the verbs in the box.

| remember | record | preserve | remind |
| believe | consider | reflect | judge |

1 I don't keep important documents in a damp place because I want to _____ them in good condition.
2 I keep my old family photos to _____ me of my grandparents.
3 I _____ meeting Joe for the first time in London.
4 I _____ myself to be a fair person, though others may disagree!
5 I think that digital photos are the best way of _____ special events.
6 It's important to _____ on things that happen so you can learn from them.
7 Science fiction is totally unrealistic – I just don't _____ it!
8 Sometimes it's difficult for football referees to _____ whether a ball is in or out.

Use of English

Multiple-choice cloze (Part 1) ▶ CB page 135

1 **For questions 1–8, read the text below and decide which word (A, B, C or D) best fits each gap. There is an example at the beginning (0).**

Memories are made of sleep

Teenagers often choose not to spend time **(0)** _A catching_ up on their sleep. However, recent studies show they need more sleep than they realise – up to nine hours a night. There also seems to be a direct **(1)** _____ between sleep and academic success. Studies show that our ability to sleep is directly related to our ability to learn, suggesting that good sleep **(2)** _____ are essential to good study techniques. **(3)** _____, it may be useful for students to study for a test just before going to bed because sleep will help them store important information they need to remember the next day. **(4)** _____, information becomes 'cemented' in our brains as we sleep.

However, for older people it may be more appropriate to establish a regular **(5)** _____ of taking several short naps during the day. **(6)** _____ we all need to experience both light and **(7)** _____ sleep, regular napping can mean we are actually less **(8)** _____ to forget things.

0	**A** catching	**B** getting	**C** taking	**D** making
1	**A** bond	**B** union	**C** link	**D** attachment
2	**A** customs	**B** traditions	**C** habits	**D** manners
3	**A** Consequently	**B** However	**C** Eventually	**D** Finally
4	**A** Apparently	**B** Fortunately	**C** Obviously	**D** Clearly
5	**A** method	**B** tradition	**C** order	**D** routine
6	**A** But	**B** Although	**C** Unless	**D** Providing
7	**A** deep	**B** long	**C** big	**D** large
8	**A** possible	**B** probably	**C** likely	**D** usual

Listening

Multiple choice (Part 1) ▶ CB page 136

1 **● 27 You will hear people talking in eight different situations. For questions 1–8, choose the best answer (A, B or C).**

1 You hear two friends talking about a newspaper article about a dog. What do they agree about the article?
   A It's amusing.
   B It's fairly pointless.
   C It's an unusual topic.

2 You hear a voicemail message a woman has left on your phone. Why is she calling?
   A to describe a special offer
   B to explain a new phone contract
   C to clarify some confusing information

3 You overhear a couple talking at a bus station. How does the woman feel?
   A angry about a social situation
   B suspicious of a group of people
   C anxious about the time of the bus

4 You hear part of a radio programme. What is the focus of the programme?
   A vital environmental issues
   B using different types of energy
   C increasing people's awareness

5 You hear two friends talking about a football match. How does the girl feel about it?
   A angry about some things that happened on the pitch
   B upset that she couldn't play herself
   C disappointed that her team lost the match

6 You hear two students talking about a history lesson. What do they agree about?
   A It was good to find out about the past.
   B It was better than they'd expected.
   C It was too complicated to understand easily.

7 You hear two friends talking about shopping for clothes. What do they agree about?
   A There are good copies of fashionable clothes.
   B It's best to buy top quality clothes.
   C Trendy clothes cost too much money.

8 You overhear a man leaving a voicemail message. What is he doing?
   A changing an existing arrangement
   B warning about a potential problem
   C recommending a place to eat

Vocabulary

expressions with *time* ▶ CB page 136

1 **Complete the sentences 1–4 with an expression with *time* in the box.**

time is money	time flies
not before time	ahead of their time

1 Is it really ten o'clock already? It's amazing how _____!

2 I can't stop now; I'm supposed to be working, and _____.

3 The first science fiction films introduced such modern ideas that they were _____.

4 At last you've arrived, and _____ – I've been waiting for hours!

Grammar

reflexive pronouns ▶ CB page 137

1 Underline the correct alternatives to complete the sentences.

1 I leave notes on the fridge door to remind *me/myself/–* of things I have to do.

2 Please stop making jokes – you're upsetting *me/myself/–*.

3 You must remember *you/yourself/–* to lock up at night.

4 Tell him to be careful because that plate is very hot and he might burn *him/himself/–*.

5 When I'm on holiday I try to relax *me/myself/–* as much as possible.

6 I didn't like the hotel *it/itself/–* very much; it was rather dark and cold.

2 Put the missing pronouns in the correct place in sentences 1–6.

1 I knew that I couldn't rely on my friend to post the letter, so I did it.

2 We often forget to buy milk, so we have to remind by putting a note by the front door.

3 I had to remind to paint the front door, otherwise he would never have done it.

4 He really enjoyed at the party last night.

5 Stop pulling my arm – you're hurting.

6 The thieves caught sight of on the CCTV screen as they left the shop.

Writing

Informal email (Part 2) ▶ CB page 138

1 Look at the task and an email a student has written in response. The underlined expressions the student has used are too formal. Rewrite the email using the words and phrases below.

You have received this email from your English-speaking friend, Sara.

From: Sara
Subject: Catching up
Haven't heard from you for ages!
I've been having a great time as it was my birthday last week and we went to the beach for the weekend. I didn't hear from you though.
Hope all's well – let me know what you're doing,
Love
Sara

Write your email. Write 140–190 words.

Hi Sara,

I was distraught when I got your email! I cannot apologise enough! It's all my fault as I totally failed to recall when your birthday was. My only excuse is that I have recently been concerned about my exams and I've been doing nothing else but study. I suppose that was the reason the date passed me by. I sincerely trust that I can make amends for this in some way. I've got a really special present for you that I know you'll just love. I wonder if having dinner on Tuesday, 14th July at Chez Maurice might appeal to you. I could give you your present then, which would make me feel a whole lot better! I look forward to receiving your reply.

I owe you a big apology.

Yours sincerely,

Anya

1 I didn't realise it was your birthday until it was too late

2 Do you fancy meeting up for dinner at Chez Maurice next Tuesday?

3 I've been worrying about my exams lately

4 I can't begin to tell you how sorry I am.

5 I completely forgot

6 I really hope I can make it up to you somehow.

8 Love,

8 Please reply soon and let me know if you can come.

9 I felt terrible

10 I'm so sorry.

2 Write your answer to the task below. Remember to use informal language.

You have received this email from your English-speaking friend, Tom.

From: Tom
Subject: Next Saturday
We're planning a get-together next Saturday in town to celebrate Jo's birthday. What do you think we should do? What should we get her as a present? What's the best way to get everyone here? Let me know what you think!
Best wishes
Tom

Write your email.

Say what you mean

Vocabulary

communication

1 **Complete the article with the words in the box.**

actions	words	messages	communication
body	tell	accent	talking

Getting the message

Good **(1)** _____ happens in different ways – spoken **(2)** _____ , signals and **(3)** _____ language. However, there can be problems. A strong **(4)** _____ or dialect can prevent the listener understanding what is being said, and body language can give different **(5)** _____ in different cultures. However, it does help you to **(6)** _____ whether the person you are **(7)** _____ to is happy, sad or irritated. Their **(8)** _____ may also indicate whether they are lying or bored.

Listening

Multiple matching (Part 3)   ▶ CB page 140

1 **Underline the correct alternatives to complete the phrases.**

1 *raise/cross* your eyebrow

2 *shake/shrug* your shoulders

3 *shake/roll* your head

4 *cross/raise* your fingers

5 *nod/roll* your eyes

6 *shrug/nod* your head

2 ▶ 28 **You will hear five different people talking about being a good presenter. For questions 1–5, choose from the list (A–H) which skill each speaker thinks is most important. Use each letter only once. There are three extra letters that you do not need to use.**

A including specialist vocabulary

B having good material

C speaking clearly

D believing in what you're saying

E making good eye contact

F using body language

G being good with technology

H keeping presentations short

Speaker 1 [   ]

Speaker 2 [   ]

Speaker 3 [   ]

Speaker 4 [   ]

Speaker 5 [   ]

Vocabulary

say, speak, talk and *tell*; ways of speaking
▶ CB page 141

1 **Underline the correct alternatives to complete the sentences.**

1 There are times when it's better not to *tell/talk* the truth, though *telling/saying* lies is not usually a good idea.

2 I can't *speak/talk* Russian, but I'd love to learn; it'd be wonderful to be able to *talk/say* with Russians.

3 I'm not sure whether it's raining as I can't *tell/say* by looking out of the window.

4 I love it when my teacher *tells/says* us funny jokes.

5 Everyone *said/told* me they enjoyed the show, though the critics didn't have a good word to *say/tell* about it.

6 Please don't *tell/say* a word to Chris about the present because it's a surprise for her!

7 It can be difficult to *talk/tell* to people face-to-face and sometimes it's easier to *speak/tell* on the phone.

8 Please don't *say/tell* you've forgotten to buy any food because I *told/spoke* you this morning that the fridge was empty!

9 Generally *speaking/saying*, men make better chefs than women – though women may disagree!

10 I can't imagine what you're going to *say/speak* to the boss as it goes without *saying/telling* that you're going to be in trouble!

2 **Replace the underlined phrases in sentences 1–6 with a phrase using the words in brackets.**

1 <u>Everyone knows</u> that it's more difficult to learn a language when you're older. (*saying*)

2 <u>On the whole</u> men are stronger than women physically. (*generally*)

3 <u>He's very quiet</u> – maybe he's shy. (*hasn't*)

4 People <u>who say what they think</u> are often easier to work with. (*mind*)

5 I think that <u>what you do is more important than what you say</u>. (*actions*)

6 <u>Let me know</u> if I can do anything to help you. (*word*)

3 **Correct the mistakes in sentences 1–6 using the correct form of the verbs in the box.**

whisper	yell	mutter	mumble	scream	cry

1 You have to yell in a library so you don't disturb other people.

2 Don't scream – I can't hear you properly.

3 He always cries to himself angrily if he doesn't like what politicians say.

4 The girl mumbled as she fell off the cliff, but luckily her boyfriend heard and caught her!

5 The boy muttered at his friend as she was going to get on the wrong bus.

6 A baby whispers when it is hungry.

Grammar

it is, there is
▶ CB page 142

1 **Complete the sentences with the correct form of *it* or *there* + *to be*. Remember that some sentences are questions and negatives.**

1 The journey took hours because .... such a lot of traffic.

2 I couldn't go out yesterday because .... much too cold and wet.

3 I really wanted to visit the town centre, but unfortunately .... enough time before the bus left.

4 .... such a beautiful day yesterday that we went to the beach.

5 In some countries .... quite normal to eat dinner at 10p.m.

6 I think .... really important to tip waiters.

7 The ballet was so good that .... a standing ovation for the dancers at the end.

8 Last night .... an accident on the motorway but .... serious.

9 I see .... a new department store in town – .... any good?

10 She said .... a wonderful party.

2 **Find and correct the mistakes in sentences 1–8. Tick the sentences that are correct.**

1 Last week it was quite miserable and it was a lot of rain every day.

2 After the presentation it will be a chance for you to ask questions.

3 I enjoyed the trip and there was wonderful seeing old friends.

4 This is such a dangerous road I think it should be a lower speed limit.

5 I was told there would be a taxi for me at ten, but it didn't turn up.

6 Everyone says it's certain to be a close match between the two players.

7 There's a long way from my flat to the nearest Tube station.

8 It's too far for me to walk to the station every morning, but luckily there's a regular bus.

Speaking

Interview (Part 1); Long turn
(Part 2) ▶ CB page 143

1 ▶ 29 **Listen to an examiner asking students questions in Part 1. Match the candidates' answers, A–J, with the examiner's questions, 1–10.**

A Xàtiva. It's a town near here. I moved there about six months ago.

B Well, there are seven of us. Three girls and four boys. I'm the oldest but only by eighteen months. My youngest sister is only five.

C Living on an island, I don't have much choice really but if I lived on the mainland I'd get trains whenever I could.

D I used to do tai chi but that's more of a martial art than a sport, I suppose. I'm thinking of taking up paddle tennis now. It looks like really good fun.

E I actually like travel documentaries best, especially if they're about places I haven't ever visited.

F Yes, very much. We have a really good teacher and we have great fun in class.

G Well, I don't read many actually but sometimes when I'm in an airport I buy one on computers or cars.

H A little French. Just enough to get by on holiday really.

I Walking in the countryside and meeting up with friends for a drink or a meal. But most of all I like sleeping in on Saturday morning.

J I was born in Besançon.

2 **Look at the examiner's instructions. Then read the list of comments a candidate made about each photograph. Mark the comments R (relevant) or I (irrelevant).**

Examiner: Here are your two photographs. They show two kinds of non-verbal communication. I'd like you to compare the people and animals and say how easy or difficult it would be to communicate in this way.

Photograph 1

1 There is a woman checking in at the airport, with a dog sitting in front of her.

2 The woman has four bags with her.

3 There is something white tied to the big suitcase.

4 The lady at the check-in desk is looking at the dog.

5 Perhaps the woman can't hear and the dog is helping her communicate.

6 The dog is wearing some kind of special coat.

7 Maybe he is a special helper dog of some kind.

8 He is watching what the two women are doing carefully.

9 The dog does not look excited.

10 She is wearing black trousers and a white cardigan.

Photograph 2

1 The woman and the boy are in a park.

2 The woman is touching her hand to communicate something.

3 The woman is wearing a green top.

4 The boy is concentrating on what the woman is trying to say.

5 She is smiling.

6 The boy is wearing jeans and a red T-shirt.

7 The boy and the woman both have blonde hair.

8 The woman seems to be speaking at the same time as using gestures.

9 The boy looks calm and serious.

10 There are lots of trees behind them.

Reading

Gapped text (Part 6) ▶ CB page 144

The chimp that learned sign language

Back in the 1970s, a chimpanzee named Nim Chimpsky took part in a Columbia University research study called Project Nim. The project was led by Herbert Terrace, a psychologist at the university who was attempting to find out if a chimpanzee could learn to communicate using American
5 Sign Language. 'Everyone knows that words are learned one at a time, but something happens when children begin to combine words and create true language,' Terrace says. [1]

The name Nim Chimpsky was a <u>twist</u> on Noam Chomsky, the famous American linguist who theorised that language as we know it is unique to
10 humans. Terrace wanted to disprove this and show that a chimpanzee could develop real language. Nim was the chimp he chose.

To <u>immerse</u> Nim in a world where he would be taught sign language in the same way a human child would, Terrace brought him to live with a family in New York City in 1973, not long after the chimp was born. [2] Nim's
15 surrogate mother was Stephanie LaFarge, a psychology student studying with Terrace. She carried the chimp around on her body for almost two years.

But it wasn't easy to raise a chimp in a Manhattan <u>brownstone</u>. [3] Soon he was breaking things all over the house. LaFarge's husband was
20 never comfortable with Nim, and as the chimp entered his 'terrible twos', he became too much of a <u>handful</u>. So Terrace took Nim to live in a mansion that was part of Columbia University. By that time, Nim had learned about 125 signs. But the question remained: Was he really learning language?

[4] He says that while watching a video of Nim signing with a
25 teacher, he realised that the chimp was <u>tracking</u> most of his teacher's signs, imitating most of them, but he almost never made a sign spontaneously. In the end, Terrace came to believe that Chomsky was right, that Nim would never use language the way humans do to form sentences and express ideas.

He ended the project in 1977 and Nim went to the Institute for Primate
30 Studies in Norman, Oklahoma, to live a very different life. [5] Bob Ingersoll, who worked at the institute and got close to Nim, says that while in Oklahoma, Nim was learning how to be a chimp again. 'He was with his brothers. He got to have a chimp group and have a life that wasn't always controlled by humans.'

35 Research is not a secure proposition, and in 1981, all funding ended for the Oklahoma research programme. There was no plan for what would happen to the chimps afterwards. [6] Because he was a famous chimp, who had even appeared on the children's television programme *Sesame Street*, Nim's supporters were able to rescue him. He lived out the rest of his days
40 at an animal sanctuary in Texas. He died in 2000.

Elizabeth Hess, in a new book called *Nim Chimpsky: The Chimp Who Would Be Human* says that while the debate over whether chimps have language, and what kind of language, continues, most researchers are no longer trying to teach animals our language. Instead, they focus on the <u>myriad</u> ways
45 animals communicate.

---

1 You are going to read an article about a famous chimpanzee who took part in research into language learning. Read the article and decide if the following statement is true or false.

The chimpanzee in the story was well-known at the time.

2 Read the article again and decide where the sentences go in the text. There is one extra sentence which you do not need to use.

A There, Nim joined a large, chaotic family with many human siblings who could teach him sign language.

B Terrace doubts it.

C He was often in a cage with other chimps.

D The children loved having Nim around.

E The question was, could Nim do this?

F Nim was active, playful and strong.

G Within a year Nim was sold to a laboratory for tuberculosis research.

3 Choose the definition, A or B, that matches the meaning of words 1–6 in the context of the article in Activity 2.

1 *twist* (line 8)
  A a shape that you make by bending or twisting something
  B an unexpected change

2 *immerse* (line 12)
  A completely involve
  B put in liquid

3 *brownstone* (line 18)
  A a kind of house
  B a kind of stone

4 *handful* (line 21)
  A a small number or amount
  B a person or animal who is difficult to deal with

5 *tracking* (line 25)
  A tracing someone's steps
  B following and repeating

6 *myriad* (line 44)
  A countless
  B wonderful

Vocabulary

idioms: animals ▶ CB page 144

1 **Complete the idioms with an animal from the box.**

duck	cat	fish	kittens	birds	cat

1 She doesn't care what people say; it's water off a ....'s back.

2 If we work while we eat lunch we can kill two .... with one stone.

3 If the boss finds out we're late for the meeting, it will put the .... among the pigeons.

4 I was really worried about what to do; I was having ....

5 My company is not very big but I've got an important job there – I'm a big .... in a little pond.

6 I was furious when Peter let the .... out of the bag and told Mary about the party.

Grammar

subject/verb agreement
▶ CB page 146

1 **Complete sentences 1–8 with the correct form of *be* or *have*.**

1 Research into chimps' use of language .... still inconclusive.

2 Many researchers, not all of whom are animal lovers, ... tried to look into this question.

3 None of these early studies .... really established that chimps can learn languages.

4 Many chimps acquire quite an extensive vocabulary of signs, which .... sometimes led researchers to believe they are actually learning a language.

5 News of Nim's transfer to the laboratory .... what made people start a campaign to have him transferred to the sanctuary.

6 Learning hundreds of signs .... very difficult for a human and even more so for a chimpanzee.

7 Noam Chomsky believes that only people .... capable of learning a language.

8 Knowledge of how people learn languages .... advanced considerably since the 1960s.

2 **Find and correct the mistakes with subject/ verb agreement in sentences 1–8 below. There are mistakes in five of the sentences. Tick the sentences that are correct.**

1 The police is looking for a man with a tattoo of a tiger on his chest.

2 The advice they gave me on places to stay in London were really useful.

3 A hundred pounds do not sound like a big reward for someone who finds a much-loved pet you have lost.

4 Both my cats knows how to communicate with us, though they do it in quite different ways.

5 Everyone was very surprised when I told them I was going to learn Tibetan.

6 Neither of the researchers was very kind to Nim.

7 There is a few dog biscuits left in the packet.

8 The furniture in our flat is getting very old.

Use of English

Open cloze (Part 2) ▶ CB page 147

1 **For questions 1–8, read the text below and think of the word which best fits each gap. Use only one word in each gap. There is an example at the beginning (0).**

Can you speak 'Dog'?

We think we understand dogs, but are often wrong about **(0)** _what_ they are trying to 'say'. Imagine being in a foreign country trying to speak to someone who doesn't understand your language. Dogs find **(1)** .... in this exact situation, and **(2)** .... are many examples of misunderstandings.

If a dog is panting, we assume he's hot. Of course, that may be true, but it could also mean the dog is stressed. **(3)** .... yawning might indicate tiredness, it could also signify other emotions. Dogs yawn **(4)** .... a message of peace towards other dogs acting aggressively, in **(5)** .... to get them to change their behaviour.

Humans think a dog wags its tail because it's happy, but tail wags have different meanings, depending **(6)** .... the position of the tail and type of wag. For example, a tail held high and stiff **(7)** .... wagging in short movements indicates a warning. A dog does this if he thinks someone is trying to take his food, and may bite if the signal is ignored. So **(8)** .... can be important to understand 'Dog'!

Writing

writing round-up

1 Read the extracts from candidates' answers to Writing Parts 1 and 2. Match their answers, 1–8, with the writing tasks A–H below.

A	report	**E**	application
B	informal email	**F**	essay
C	formal letter	**G**	review
D	article	**H**	semi-formal letter

1 I have a number of criticisms of the service you provide. To begin with, the reception staff were most unhelpful. They took over five minutes to find my reservation.

2 It was great to get your message the other day. I know it's been ages since I've been in touch. I've had exams and then went on an end-of-term trip with some of my classmates.

3 There were some spectacular special effects, though the plot itself was rather disappointing.

4 Two-thirds of those students we interviewed were in favour of having optional activities on Friday afternoons instead of classes.

5 Finally, I would like to know if it would be possible to work longer hours on Mondays and have Tuesdays free.

6 There are also some great little beaches in the south of the island, some with excellent beach bars with music and food. I'd definitely try to fit in a visit to one or two of these if you can.

7 In my view, it is a gross exaggeration to say that young people are addicted to junk food. Among my own friends, I can only think of two or three people who do not eat what I would regard as a healthy diet.

8 Everyone has their favourite ways of studying but have you ever stopped to ask yourself how effective these methods are?

2 Look at the extracts in Activity 1 again and decide which part of the candidates' answers they come from: the beginning (B), the middle (M) or the end (E).

3 Look at some comments teachers wrote on earlier drafts of the writing tasks in Activity 1. Which of the extracts do they apply to?

A Don't forget, you're also supposed to recommend some places to visit, as well as describing them.

B Make sure you include the points from the notes (rude reception staff, dirty room) among your complaints but use different wording.

C Even though this is an article, you should mainly give advice and not just make a list of favourite study techniques.

D I like the informal tone of your email and the way you included the apology for not attending the party.

E It's always good to back up your opinion with an example, just as you have done here.

F You should explain what you like or don't like about the film or book, and whether you would recommend it to others.

4 Choose one of the tasks below and write your answer in 140–190 words, using your own ideas and language from Activities 1–3 where possible.

1

Film reviews wanted

Have you seen a film recently that had exceptionally good special effects?

Write us a review of the film, explaining what the special effects are and why you think they were exceptionally good. Tell us whether you would recommend the film to other people.

The best reviews will be published in the magazine.

2

You have received this email from an English-speaking colleague in another country.

From: Sam
Subject: Conference next week
I'm going to the conference in London next week, and I'd like to meet up with you one evening. Can you tell me about some things we could do together? What's the best way to get round the city?
Thanks,
Ben

Multiple-choice cloze (Part I)

For questions 1–8, read the text below and decide which answer (A, B, C or D) best fits each gap. There is an example at the beginning (0).

Dolphin talk

We have long suspected that there is some kind of **(0)** _empathy_ between dolphins and humans – but can we communicate with them? Captive dolphins can be **(1)** .... to understand hundreds of words, and can **(2)** .... understand some simple grammar. However, until now people could neither understand nor **(3)** .... to the underwater noises dolphins use to communicate with each other.

Now scientists are building a small device made up of a computer and two hydrophones which are **(4)** .... of detecting the full range of dolphin sounds. A diver **(5)** .... the computer in a waterproof case strapped to his chest, and lights show the origin of any sound it **(6)** .... up. The diver also has an instrument that enables him to choose the sound he should **(7)** .... in response.

But will we really be able to understand dolphins' words? Do they use words? And what if it **(8)** .... that they're terrible conversationalists? That would be a real disappointment!

0	**A** empathy	**B** sense	**C** comfort	**D** support
1	**A** trained	**B** exercised	**C** practised	**D** rehearsed
2	**A** yet	**B** still	**C** even	**D** however
3	**A** respond	**B** answer	**C** return	**D** acknowledge
4	**A** suited	**B** capable	**C** competent	**D** able
5	**A** fetches	**B** brings	**C** gets	**D** carries
6	**A** picks	**B** takes	**C** finds	**D** selects
7	**A** have	**B** do	**C** make	**D** be
8	**A** gives up	**B** comes across	**C** goes on	**D** turns out

Open cloze (Part 2)

For questions 9–16, read the text below and think of the word which best fits each gap. Use only one word in each gap. There is an example at the beginning (0).

Why people love postcards

In this age of instant digital communication, it seems to be **(0)** _an_ odd contradiction that the humble holiday postcard **(9)** .... never been so popular. There are more postcards being sent from exotic locations **(10)** .... ever before. Emailing and texting may be perfect for communicating short pieces of information, **(11)** .... for many holidaymakers the picture postcard is the best way of sharing **(12)** .... own travel experiences with friends and family back home. **(13)** .... is a more thoughtful means of communication, and for the sender, **(14)** .... is a certain pleasure in struggling to produce a perfect message that includes all the important information in just a **(15)** .... words. People choose a card with a picture that conveys a genuine sense of the place being visited. This could **(16)** .... simply so they can share the experience with others, but sometimes the message really being sent is – 'I'm here in this amazing place – and you aren't!'

Word formation (Part 3)

For questions 17–24, read the text below. Use the word given in capitals at the end of some of the lines to form a word that fits in the gap in the same line. There is an example at the beginning (0).

Improve your memory!

The human brain is perhaps the most complex information (0) _retrieval_ system in the world. **RETRIEVE**
No matter how much information you memorise, your brain will not run out of room. The only (17) .... is **LIMIT**
the time you spend committing facts to memory and how you do this. You can't learn anything unless you use your full (18) .... – too **CONCENTRATE**
many people waste time on mindless (19) .... of basic facts. **REPEAT**
However, you can improve your memory with a few simple techniques.

Your brain is a part of your body, so (20) .... habits and **HEALTH**
good nutrition all contribute to the (21) .... of your memory. **EFFECTIVE**
Exercise increases your overall blood (22) .... and especially **CIRCULATE**
blood flow to the brain. Deal with any physical problems before trying to study. Too little sleep can have a (23) .... impact on memory **DEVASTATE**
because the phase of sleep when dreams occur is essential for the (24) .... of memories. **CONSOLIDATE**

The good news is that like most skills, memory improves with practice!

Key word transformations (Part 4)

For questions 25–30, complete the second sentence so that it has a similar meaning to the first sentence, using the word given. Do not change the word given. You must use between two and five words, including the word given. Here is an example (0).

Example:

0 Those twins are identical; they look just the same!

DIFFERENCE

Those twins are identical; it's impossible _to tell the difference_ between them.

25 He said he was very happy that everyone had come to the party.

WONDERFUL

He said .... that everyone had come to the party.

26 It's said that the benefits of eating vegetables every day are enormous.

THERE

It's said that .... to eating vegetables every day.

27 People think he is living in London now.

THOUGHT

It .... he is living in London now.

28 I feel quite ill – maybe I'm getting a cold.

COMING

I feel quite ill – maybe .... a cold.

29 He inherited a lot of money when his father died.

INTO

He .... a lot of money when his father died.

30 I didn't try to get in the team, even though I was offered a trial.

COULD

I .... to get into the team when I was offered a trial, but I didn't.

Use of English

General advice

- Read the title and text first in Parts 1–3 to clarify the type and style of words required.
- Read the instructions – they tell you the text type and how many words to write.
- Check your spelling, as all words must be correct.

Part 1: Multiple-choice cloze

1 **Match pieces of advice 1–3 with reasons A–C.**

1 Read the words before and after the gap before choosing your answer.

2 Think what the answer might be before you read the options.

3 Read the whole sentence before choosing an answer.

A This part often tests collocations.

B If the missing word is a linking word, you must understand the meaning of the sentence.

C You may already know the answer, so you can confirm this when you read the options.

2 **Look at the extract from the full task below. The student chose options 1D and 2A, which are wrong. Which piece of advice have they forgotten? What are the correct answers?**

> Of those three routes that might lead to a happy, satisfied life, it is interesting that, **(1)** .... to what you might expect, pleasure seems to play the smallest part. **(2)** ...., it is ironic that many people build their lives around the pursuit of pleasure, feeling that enjoyment is the key to happiness.
>
> 1 **A** against **B** opposing
> **C** contrary **D** contrast
> 2 **A** On top of that **B** So that
> **C** In that case **D** As a result

Part 2: Open cloze

3 **Match pieces of advice 1–3 with reasons A–C.**

1 Don't write a word in a gap before you have read the whole sentence.

2 Don't write more than one word.

3 Never write contractions such as *didn't* in a gap.

A These count as two words and will be wrong.

B You may miss the need for a negative, or a linking word like 'however'.

C Even if you think more than one answer is possible, you must only write one.

Strategy:

In the exam you need to be aware of strategies that will help you with the exam tasks. Here are some tips for approaching each paper and examples of common mistakes students might make.

4 **Look at the short extract from a full task below. The student has written their answers, which are wrong. Which piece of advice have they forgotten? What are the correct answers?**

There are many stories of dolphins helping people, **(0)** _such_ as saving swimmers from shark attacks by gathering round them or shepherding them to safety. **(1)** _Supposing/If_ these stories are true, are dolphins really the good guys of the deep, always ready to extend a flipper towards humans **(2)** _and their_ distress?

Part 3: Word formation

5 **Match pieces of advice 1–3 with reasons A–C.**

1 Always change the word in capitals.

2 Think about the grammar of the sentence and the missing word.

3 Read the whole sentence, not just the line, before changing the word.

A This will help you decide whether you need a noun, adjective, adverb, etc.

B You will not be able to use the word in the same form as the word in capitals.

C This will help you spot suffixes, prefixes, negatives and plurals.

6 **Look at the extract from a full task below. The student has written their answer, which is wrong. Which piece of advice have they forgotten? What is the correct answer?**

But if you are the sort of person who worries about where the brakes are, this may not be the thing for you – **(8)** _adventurous_ types should probably give it a miss! **ADVENTURE**

Part 4: Key word transformations

7 **Match pieces of advice 1–3 with reasons A–C.**

1 Keep your sentence as close as possible to the meaning of the original.

2 Don't rewrite more than necessary or make up details.

3 Never change the given word, but remember to include it in your answer.

A You must think of a structure that contains the given word.

B You are being tested on your ability to paraphrase.

C If you write more than five words you have made a mistake, so go back and check.

8 **Look at the question below. The student has written their answer, which is wrong. Which piece of advice have they forgotten? What is the correct answer?**

I had never seen a glacier before I went to Norway.

I

When I was in Norway I _was thrilled to see a glacier for_ the first time.

Reading

General advice

- Read different things in English, as there are different types of text in Paper 1.
- Read all the rubrics (instructions) carefully to identify the type of text and the topic.
- Read the title of the text, which introduces the topic of the text.

Part 5: Multiple choice (long text)

1 **Match pieces of advice 1–3 with reasons A–C.**

1 Read all the options carefully, especially if you must complete a sentence.

2 Be careful if you see the same word in the option and the text.

3 Think about what the text is actually saying.

A This does not mean it is the correct answer.

B Incorrect options may not reflect the true meaning of the text accurately.

C Each option may be true, but only one completes the sentence correctly.

2 **Look at the extract from a task below. The student chose option D, which is wrong. Which piece of advice have they forgotten? What is the correct answer?**

But things weren't always that easy. Despite an IQ of 132, Louis dropped out of school when he was only eleven, frustrated and disheartened. 'It was terribly difficult for him,' his mother Mary explains. 'His handwriting was really bad and he struggled with spelling.' The problem was that Louis was, in his own words, 'dyslexic, dyspraxic and dyscalculic'. Nothing the school system had to offer made any sense to him.

Why did Louis Barnett leave school?

A He wasn't very bright.

B The teachers didn't understand him.

C He had special problems.

D He kept failing spelling tests.

Part 6: Gapped text

3 Match pieces of advice 1–3 with reasons A–C.

1 Read the sentences immediately before and after each gap carefully.

2 Read the main text before reading the missing sentences, and reread after doing the task.

3 Make sure linking words, tenses and time references in the main text match your answer.

A This helps you predict what kind of information is missing.

B This helps you understand text structure and topic, and check your answers make sense.

C Words like these: *firstly*, *secondly* and *last night*, help you make the correct choice.

4 **Look at the extract and limited options from a full task below. The student chose sentence A from the options, which is wrong. Which piece of advice have they forgotten? What is the correct answer?**

As Fred and George Weasley, respectively, Ron Weasley's mischievous older twin brothers in the Harry Potter films, James and Oliver Phelps must be one of the most famous sets of twins in the world. They were fourteen when they auditioned for the role and had no acting experience other than a bit of drama at school. [**1**] 'I felt like I wasn't a proper actor for about three or four years,' says James, who still occasionally takes acting lessons. 'I'm very aware that I'm lucky to call it my job.'

A Now they were known as the twins again, this time on a global scale.

B James shares this view.

C They seem to have fallen into acting by accident, rather than it being a burning passion.

Part 7: Multiple matching

5 Match pieces of advice 1–3 with reasons A–C.

1 First, read the texts very quickly, but don't spend time on them.

2 Second, read all the options carefully and scan the texts to find each answer.

3 Be careful if you see the same word in the text and in the question.

A You should look out for paraphrases, not the identical word.

B You only need to get a general idea of what they are about.

C Different texts have similar information, but only one text matches each option.

6 **Look at the extract and limited options from a full task below. The student chose option 1, which is wrong. Which piece of advice have they forgotten? What is the correct answer?**

Which person

was very unhappy before he started working from home?	1
had to control the amount of time he was spending on work?	2
likes to spend longer in bed in the mornings?	3

C Mervin: musical supplier

I am the UK's leading supplier of music rolls for mechanical organs. For me working from home has all the usual advantages like not having to get up at some ungodly hour to go out to work, especially when it's freezing outside; no office politics, no boss looking over my shoulder and I can sit in the garden with my wife when the sun comes out. I can't think of any disadvantages but there are some things to take into account. Firstly, a home-based business sometimes has less credibility than a 'proper' one.

Writing

General advice

- Read the question carefully and make sure that your answer is relevant.

- Use paragraphing and clear linking words to make your writing easy to follow.

- Check grammar and spelling – mistakes have a negative effect on the target reader.

- Use a style of language that is suitable for the person you are writing to.

Part 1: Compulsory question

1 Match pieces of advice 1–4 with reasons A–D.

1 Don't copy the same words from the question.

2 Make sure you include all the content points you are given.

3 Think of an idea for the last point.

4 Use an appropriate style of language.

A It is important to have one good idea of your own.

B They may be too informal for an essay.

C You must make a clear argument using the ideas you are given.

D An essay should be written in a semi-formal style.

2 Look at the essay task on page 17 and read the short extract from a student's answer. Which piece of advice has the student forgotten?

> It's great to grow up in a large family because there are always lots of people to talk to and do stuff with. It's another great advantage to have people to ask for advice, and that helps a lot.

Part 2

3 Match pieces of advice 1–4 with reasons A–D.

1 Choose the type of writing you are good at – if you are good at narrative, write the story.

2 Allow enough time for Part 2. Don't rush through it.

3 Make a short plan before you start writing.

4 Expand on your ideas using a variety of language.

A This helps you organise your answer and checks that you have enough relevant ideas.

B This gives you the chance to show how good you are.

C All questions carry equal marks.

D This makes your writing interesting for the reader.

4 Look at the task and the short extract from a student's answer below. Which piece of advice has the student forgotten?

You have had a class discussion on the nicest place to live. Your teacher has asked you to write an essay explaining whether you think it is nicer to live in the country or in a city.

> It is much nicer to live in the country. There are nice trees, flowers and animals. The city is not nice it is busy and noisy. In the country it is easy to be nice and quiet. The city traffic is hard and it is difficult to move around. In the country it is nice and easy to move around.

Listening

General advice

- Listen to and read the instructions, as they give you context and introduce the topic.

- Don't worry about understanding everything – concentrate on the task.

- Answer all the questions – there is no negative marking, so guess if you are not sure.

Part 1: Multiple choice (short extracts)

1 Match pieces of advice 1–3 with reasons A–C.

1 Remember the extracts are separate and not connected.

2 Don't spend too much time worrying about each answer.

3 Read the question carefully and identify key words such as *feel*, *think* and *why*.

A You may miss the next extract.

B This means if you are not sure of one answer, put something then wait for the next extract.

C Each extract has a different focus, e.g. feeling, opinion, purpose.

2 Look at the single extract below. The student chose option A, which is wrong. Which piece of advice have they forgotten? What is the correct answer?

> You hear part of a radio phone-in programme.
>
> Why has the person called the programme?
> **A** to complain about something
> **B** to clarify some facts
> **C** to make a suggestion
>
> *Thanks for finally having me on – I've been waiting absolutely ages! But at least I can have my say now. I've been listening for the last hour and I can't believe what your callers are saying. They must know that whatever anyone does on the recycling front – big or small – makes a difference. We're all responsible for the world we live in – how can they moan about being asked to put rubbish in different bins? But I accept that not everyone sees it like that, so what I think is that we should be given incentives to do it – that would get people on our side, and it would be pretty easy to put into operation I'd have thought.*

Part 2: Sentence completion

3 **Match pieces of advice 1–3 with reasons A–C.**

1 Read through the whole printed text first.

2 Read what is written before and after each gap.

3 Listen carefully to the exact words used on the recording.

A This shows you the structure of the recording and helps you follow it.

B You must write the exact word you hear in the gap, not a paraphrase.

C This helps you identify the kind of information that is missing.

4 **Look at the short extract from a full task below. The student has written their answer, which is wrong. Which piece of advice have they forgotten? What is the correct answer?**

> Steve likes going **(1)** _walking_ and rock-climbing in his spare time.
>
> _I also love adventure. My favourite leisure activities include going rock-climbing and hiking and once I started travelling round the world to remote places like rainforests and deserts I got completely hooked on the plight of endangered animals and ways of trying to save them._

Part 3: Multiple matching

5 **Match pieces of advice 1–3 with reasons A–C.**

1 Check each option carefully when you listen.

2 Don't be distracted if you hear the exact word you see in one of the options.

3 If you are unsure of an answer, note down your idea and confirm it with the second listening.

A You should be listening for gist and paraphrases of ideas.

B If you get one wrong, this may affect your other answers.

C Make sure that the one you have chosen is actually what the speaker means.

6 **Look at the single extract from a full task below and limited options. The student chose option A, which is wrong. Which piece of advice have they forgotten? What is the correct answer?**

> **A** following a parent's example
> **B** pursuing a dream
> **C** the salary
>
> **Speaker 1**
>
> _I got interested in the whole area of sport when I started school, though I'd loved playing with a ball from a very early age. My parents always encouraged me, though I think they regarded it as a hobby rather than an actual career – we didn't know what the opportunities were then. I went on adventure holidays where sporting activities were top of my list, but it wasn't until I talked to a careers advisor that I realised how many possibilities sport offered apart from playing, and more importantly, how much money I could earn! That's when I decided I wanted to become a personal trainer._

Part 4: Multiple choice (long text)

7 **Match pieces of advice 1–3 with reasons A–C.**

1 Check that the option really matches the unfinished sentence or question.

2 Check the question carefully for key words and phrases such as _feel, the first time._

3 Think about whether you are listening for gist, attitude, opinion or facts.

A These words will help you to listen for the right thing.

B The options may be correct, but not answer the question asked.

C Understanding what to listen for focuses you on only the information you need.

8 **Look at the single extract from a full task below. The student chose option A, which is wrong. Which piece of advice have they forgotten? What is the correct answer?**

> _There's a gap between imagining something and doing it! Those first days were the hardest, 'cos there were loads of technical problems which got me down – I even thought I might have to give up! That would've been disappointing, but I carried on, sleeping in periods of twenty to forty minutes, eating rehydrated meals. Some people said I'd be lonely, but my mates had put loads of music on my iPod which was great. I'd stuck photos everywhere and packed loads of clothes so I didn't need to worry about doing washing!_
>
> When he started the trip, Alan
> **A** found it too physically demanding.
> **B** was upset by difficulties with the boat.
> **C** worried about the prospect of the loneliness.

Speaking
General advice

- Listen carefully to instructions given by the interlocutor throughout the test.
- Ask the interlocutor to repeat instructions or questions if you are not sure.
- Speak clearly so that both the assessor and the interlocutor can hear you.

Part 1: Interview

1 **Match pieces of advice 1–3 with reasons A–C.**

1 Don't prepare long speeches in advance.
2 Practise talking about different topics in English.
3 Give details but not too many.

A This gives you confidence.
B You won't answer questions appropriately.
C Your answers should be suitable for a social situation, and not too long.

2 **Look at the question and answer given below. Which piece of advice has the student forgotten?**

> **Q:** *Do you ever listen to the radio?*
>
> **A:** *I think that people watch too much television these days and not many people listen to the radio, but the radio is good for concentrating on facts and getting information quickly and easily. The internet is also a good way of getting information.*

Part 2: Long turn

3 **Match pieces of advice 1–3 with reasons A–C.**

1 Remember the questions are at the top of your task.
2 Don't try to give your opinions during your partner's long turn.
3 Don't describe the pictures – you should compare them, then answer the question.

A This means you won't forget what you have to talk about.
B The language you use when you describe is simple and you won't show how good you are.
C In this part of the test you have to give an extended talk on your own.

4 **Look at the extract from a long turn given below. Which piece of advice has the student forgotten?**

> *In the first picture I can see a man. He is wearing a red shirt and a hat. He is walking in front of a building which is quite tall and he is with a friend who is wearing a scarf. In the bottom corner I can see a tree which is also quite tall.*

Part 3: Collaborative task

5 **Match pieces of advice 1–3 with reasons A–C.**

1 Respond to what your partner says and invite them to give their views.
2 Don't worry if you disagree with your partner, although you should be polite.
3 Say as much as you can about each option on the mind map before you move on to the next.

A This gives you more to say on the topic and you won't make your decision too early.
B This often makes the discussion more interesting and lively.
C This is part of interactive communication, which is a communication skill.

6 **Look at the extract from a Part 3 discussion given below. Which piece of advice have the students forgotten?**

> **A:** *OK, we'll start with this picture – it's people working in an office.*
>
> **B:** *Yes – and the next one is in a factory or something like that.*
>
> **A:** *I agree. What do you think the next one is?*
>
> **B:** *It's a school. So which one is the most difficult to work in?*

Part 4: Discussion

7 **Match pieces of advice 1–3 with reasons A–C.**

1 Listen to what your partner says and think about whether you agree.
2 Try to give interesting reasons for your opinions and extend your answers.
3 Remember there are no right or wrong answers!

A The examiner just wants to hear you give your opinions in English.
B This is a real-life skill and gives you and your partner more to discuss.
C You may be asked whether you agree or not.

8 **Look at the question and answer from Part 4 given below. Which piece of advice has the student forgotten?**

> **Q:** *Why do people often want to live in the country?*
>
> **A:** *Fresh air, quiet, animals. It's good to live there.*

Common language errors

Writing

Part 1 (essay)

1 **Read what a student wrote for the task below and find and correct the mistakes with**

1 articles (find five errors)
2 prepositions (find two errors)
3 spelling (find three errors)
4 verb forms (find three errors)

> In your English class you have been talking about travelling to other countries. Now, your English teacher has asked you to write an essay.
>
> Write an essay using all the notes and give reasons for your point of view.
>
> > It is a good thing for young people to travel to other countries. Do you agree?
> > **Notes**
> > Write about:
> > 1 culture
> > 2 independence
> > 3 .... (your own idea)

Some people think it's a good idea for young people to travel to other countries, but are there really advantages for them in doing this?

In a first place, it gives young people the opportunity to experience different cultures. This means that they can learning about different ways of life, which helps them to be more open-minded. As bonus, they can also learn to speaking other languages.

Secondly, it helps young people to become more independent, and this is good thing. When they are older and are working they have to think to themselves, and if they travel to other countreys when they are young, they might have a more independent spirit.

Lastly, going travelling gives young people the chance to making friends from other cultures, and in the today's world it is posible to keep in touch with people all over world through social networking sites. This will help to increas understanding in different nations in future.

To sum up, for the reasons given above, I agree that it is a good thing for young people to travel to other countries.

Part 2 (formal letter)

2 **Read the text below and find and correct the mistakes with**

1   articles. (find five errors)
2   prepositions. (find three errors)
3   question forms. (find four errors)

Dear Sir/Madam,

I am writing because I am very interested for the advertisement you put on Daily Mail last Monday for a course to become watersports instructor. I have been very keen in the waterskiing since I was a child and I also enjoy scuba diving.

Although you gave a very complete information in your ad, I would like to ask some other questions. First of all, how much your course cost? I would also like to know is it possible to study part-time and will I have to do an exam at end of the course. Finally, could you tell me is certificate you mention for one sport or for more than one?

I look forward to receiving your reply.

Yours faithfully,

Anya Braun

Part 2 (article)

3 **Read what a student wrote for the task below. Divide it into paragraphs. Then find and correct the errors with**

1   quantifiers. (find two errors)
2   linking words/phrases. (find two errors)
3   relative clauses. (find one error)

> You have been asked to write an article for a local English language newspaper on the topic:
> *Money or job satisfaction: which is more important?*
> Write your article.

Have you had a job you loved but for which you got very few money? I have, in my mother's bookshop, and I'm still working there. Choosing between money or job satisfaction has not been difficult for me but I'm unusual I think. Most people, of course, would rather have a job with a good salary that is interesting at the same time. Unfortunately, a few of us have such job prospects. Everybody looks for the best job which they can find. This usually means a well-paid job. Some people, such as scientists or young people, will be interested in getting as exciting and interesting a job as possible. On the contrary, there are other people who are content with a badly-paid, undemanding job if they have enough money to get by. They are not concerned about getting a better standard of living. Moreover, there are some people who do dangerous or dirty jobs with very high wages in order to do what they like in their spare time. In my opinion, enjoying your work is the priority. If you are unhappy at work you probably won't be happy in your spare time either. No amount of money can change that.

Part 2 (report)

4 Read what a student wrote for the task below and then find twenty mistakes and correct them.

> Your college is planning to build a new sports centre for students. The school director has asked you to write a report on students' sports preferences, recommending which sports should be catered for in the centre. Write your report.

Introduction
I have interviewed students in the canteen during the last week of term to find out their sports preferences. Here are results of my survey and my recommendations.

Results
There are basically two kinds of sports that students participate: indoor and outdoor sports.

Indoor sports: Many students say they enjoy often to play table tennis (fifty percent) and even more say that they at least once a week will swim if there was an indoor swimming pool available. Other indoor sports that frequently students mentioned were fencing, badminton, basketball and aerobics.

Outdoor sports: These were not so popular than indoor sports because of the cold winter. Nevertheless, the following sports several times were mentioned: ice-hockey, football and golf.

Conclusions
Obviously it would be too much expensive to have built a golf field or an ice hockey stadium. A swimming complex is in our city already, though students say it should renovate itself. Around the city also are many places to play football.

Therefore, I recommend to build an indoor sports centre that can use for table tennis, basketball, badminton and aerobics. In this way we would provide the needs of majority of students.

Speaking

There are one or two typical Cambridge English: First language mistakes in each of these extracts from speaking tasks. Find the mistakes and correct them.

E = Examiner, **C** = Candidate,
A = Candidate A, **B** = Candidate B

Part 1

1 **E:** What kind of music do you like?
   C: I like all kinds of music but I listen rock and pop most.

2 **E:** What plans do you have for the future?
   C: Well, when I will finish university, I want to work in advertising agency.

3 **E:** What free-time activities do you enjoy?
   C: I make lots of sports like tennis and football but I also like reading and go to the cinema.

Part 2

4 **C:** I'm not sure how say this in English but it's something you use for opening bottles. Anyway, the man on the first photo is giving one to his friend.

5 **C:** We all like joining our friends and family for meals as those we see here.

6 **C:** I'm not sure what they're doing – it looks they might be going on holiday.

Part 3

7 **A:** I think cooking is an important skill. Are you agree with me?
   B: I am agree. But being able to read a map is important too.

8 **A:** I think we should definitely take the tablet computers. They're light.
   B: Yes, that's good point.

9 **A:** I don't think it's such a good idea for a family with children to have …
   B: I think dogs make great pets. Sorry to interrupted you. What you saying?

Part 4

10 **E:** What are the advantages and disadvantages of tourism for a country?
   A: Well, is difficult to say. There are lots of advantages but are also disadvantages.

11 **A:** I don't think people should borrow money to pay for university education. What I mean is, the Government should pay.
   B: So what are you saying is university education should be free.

12 **E:** Do you think sportspeople should be role models?
   C: I sorry, did you say 'sportspeople'?

Practice test

Reading and Use of English

Part 1

For questions **1–8**, read the text below and decide which answer (**A, B, C** or **D**) best fits each gap. There is an example at the beginning (**0**).

Example

0 **A** in **B** at **C** under **D** with

Mark your answers **on the separate answer sheet**.

Making the most of your time

Nowadays we are all **(0)** _C under_____ pressure to increase the amount of work we can achieve in the shortest possible time. **(1)** _____ of this we may spend time looking **(2)** _____ short-cuts in our working lives. However, many of these time-saving measures may actually cause more problems than they **(3)** _____ .

Some organisations seem to expect their staff to work more than the usual eight or nine hours, without recognising the fact that tiredness causes people to **(4)** _____ silly mistakes. We all tend to **(5)** _____ those who can multi-task because we think they are working hard – but do all the electronic gadgets they use make them more efficient in the long **(6)** _____ ? It's possible they actually distract them from the task **(7)** _____ and lead to a loss of concentration. So maybe **(8)** _____ every email or answering every mobile phone call immediately is not the most efficient use of our time.

1	**A** As a result	**B** Therefore	**C** Owing	**D** Due
2	**A** through	**B** out	**C** for	**D** in
3	**A** answer	**B** solve	**C** explain	**D** settle
4	**A** do	**B** get	**C** make	**D** have
5	**A** look up to	**B** get through to	**C** catch up with	**D** go out with
6	**A** walk	**B** run	**C** race	**D** hike
7	**A** in hand	**B** on hand	**C** by hand	**D** with hand
8	**A** A keeping in	**B** setting out	**C** taking on	**D** dealing with

Part 2

For questions **9–16**, read the text below and think of the word which best fits each gap. Use only **one** word in each gap. There is an example at the beginning (**0**).

Write your answers **IN CAPITAL LETTERS on the separate answer sheet**.

Example

0		F	O	R	

Can you give a dog a yawn?

Everyone who has sat **(0)** ___*for*___ ages in a doctor's waiting room knows yawning is infectious – once one person yawns, everyone starts.

But did you know dogs can catch yawns too? When twenty-nine dogs were placed in a room with a man **(9)** _____ was yawning, twenty-one of them also yawned. To see **(10)** _____ this was a genuine response by the dogs, researchers then put **(11)** _____ in a room with a man pulling different facial expressions. Nothing other **(12)** _____ yawning provoked any reaction from the animals.

But why does anyone yawn? People who yawn with others may be more sensitive to others' moods, so **(13)** _____ is possible that yawning isn't always a sign of boredom. In **(14)** _____ words, yawning during a conversation doesn't mean the person isn't interested. And **(15)** _____ from indicating sleepiness, yawning actually creates a feeling of alertness **(16)** _____ of the rush of cold air we breathe in – maybe even in dogs!

Part 3

For questions **17–24**, read the text below. Use the word given in capitals at the end of some of the lines to form a word that fits in the gap **in the same line**. There is an example at the beginning (**0**).

Write your answers **IN CAPITAL LETTERS on the separate answer sheet**.

Example

0		D	I	F	F	E	R	E	N	C	E	

Tourist or traveller?

People assume there is a **(0)** ___*difference*___ between a tourist and a traveller – that a tourist is a negative term. In general, a tourist goes to a new place to have a fun, **(17)** _____ time, and replace the energy used up by working in a **(18)** _____ job. A traveller wanders from place to place driven by a deep **(19)** _____ about everything new and the desire to explore. A tourist goes somewhere, is amazed, returns, with his everyday life **(20)** _____ by what he has experienced, while the traveller roams around, seeking anything that improves his **(21)** _____ of the world. The tourist escapes from the **(22)** _____ routine of everyday life seeking relaxation, whereas all the traveller wants is to be on the road. The tourist goes home. The traveller moves on, perhaps because he doesn't want to stop anywhere permanently. But is it possible that the two are **(23)** _____ the same? They share a pleasure in the world and a **(24)** _____ with the wonders in it.

DIFFERENT

ENJOY
STRESS
CURIOUS
CHANGE

UNDERSTAND
BORE

ACTUAL
FASCINATE

Part 4

For questions **25–30**, complete the second sentence so that it has a similar meaning to the first sentence, using the word given. **Do not change the word given.** You must use between two and five words, including the word given.

Here is an example (**0**).

Example

0   In class you have to do precisely what your teacher tells you.

CARRY

In class you have to .... instructions precisely.

The gap can be filled by 'carry out your teacher's', so you write:

Example

0	CARRY OUT YOUR TEACHER'S

Write your answers **IN CAPITAL LETTERS on the separate answer sheet.**

---

25   The moment I arrived at the hotel I checked my email.

SOON

I checked my email .... to the hotel.

26   They cancelled the meeting because the boss was ill.

OFF

The meeting .... the boss's illness.

27   I had never seen such an amazing waterfall before.

FIRST

It .... I had seen such an amazing waterfall.

28   It's a shame the school holidays are quite short in the summer.

WISH

I .... school holidays in the summer.

29   I always use my dictionary to check any words I'm not sure of.

UP

If I'm not sure of a word, ... my dictionary.

30   'You'd better hurry if you want to catch the bus, Joe,' said Juan.

ADVISED

Juan .... he would miss the bus.

Part 5

You are going to read part of a magazine article about psychology. For questions **31–36**, choose the answer (**A**, **B**, **C** or **D**) which you think fits best according to the text.

Mark your answers **on the separate answer sheet**.

Focus! It's the key to happiness

Many religious and philosophical traditions have spoken of the benefits of living in the present moment but, until recently, there has not been much scientific evidence to support this advice. Now, a study by psychologists in the USA has shown that if we learn to live in the now we can be happier. Apparently, the problem is that we spend nearly half our time thinking about something other than what we are doing.

Of course, it is not possible to measure happiness by simply observing people. When researchers want to look into a question such as this they have to rely on their subjects' ability to look at their thoughts and emotions and then be able to say what they are feeling. That would be relatively easy if you planned to study only a small number of subjects but in a project like this one involving several thousand, things become rather more complicated.

To be able to reach as many people as possible, the psychologists designed a new mobile phone application that sent volunteers text messages at various times during the day. They were asked what they were doing and then told to rate their happiness on a scale from zero to 100. They also had to say whether they were concentrating on what they were doing or daydreaming about something positive, negative or neutral. 'We never anticipated getting so many responses,' says Matthew Killingsworth, one of the main researchers on the team. 'People are naturally concerned about this issue but I doubt that they would have been so keen to take part if we had tried to interview them on the street or sent out online questionnaires. The mobile phone application was the key.'

The study produced one surprising result. Although activities that demanded people's full attention, like exercise and conversation, made them happiest, even the most engaging tasks failed to hold their full attention. Volunteers admitted to thinking about something else at least thirty percent of the time even if they were doing something they enjoyed. People were least happy when working, resting or using a home computer because it was then that their minds wandered more. In fact they reported being distracted for as much as forty-six percent of the time.

The psychologists say that happiness was more affected by how often people drifted off than by the activity they were doing at the time. But couldn't it be that we daydream so much because we are unhappy? The Harvard team say that <u>this</u> is not the *line 48* case. Remembering, thinking ahead or imagining things tend to make people more miserable, even when they are thinking about something pleasant. This is what convinces the researchers that we become unhappy because we think too much and not the other way round.

So how can we overcome the problem? It seems that we might not want to. 'The unique human ability to focus on things that are not happening right now allows us to reflect on the past and learn from it. It also helps us anticipate and plan for the future,' said Killingsworth. If we could not do this, we probably wouldn't survive. So our wandering minds benefit us some of the time. The trouble is we also let them make us unhappy.

31 According to the writer, it is quite difficult to investigate happiness because

    A people do not really know how they feel.

    B people may look happy when they are not.

    C people do not like to talk about their feelings.

    D people are reluctant to take part in scientific studies.

32 How did the researchers feel about the way they conducted their survey?

    A confident that their results were correct

    B disappointed by the way people responded

    C amazed that so many people agreed to take part

    D uncertain about why their methods were successful

33 What surprised researchers when they examined the results of the study?

    A People often didn't concentrate even if they were enjoying themselves.

    B People spent more time daydreaming when they were working.

    C Working and resting made people equally unhappy.

    D People were not thinking about what they were doing most of the time.

34 What does <u>this</u> refer to in line 48?

    A That what you are doing makes you unhappy.

    B That feeling sad makes you drift off into fantasy.

    C That thinking about the past makes you unhappy.

    D That people's minds wander all the time.

35 Changing the way our minds work may not be a good idea because

    A we enjoy daydreaming.

    B we find thinking about the present is boring.

    C we need the ability to think about the past and the future.

    D we think of it as one of our special human characteristics.

36 The purpose of the article is to

    A describe how happy people think.

    B indicate the best way to conduct research.

    C persuade people to change their approach to life.

    D show the connection between daydreaming and unhappiness.

Part 6

You are going to read an article about a woman who got lost while she was on holiday. Six sentences have been removed from the article. Choose from the sentences **A–G** the one which fits each gap (**37–42**). There is one extra sentence which you do not need to use.

Mark your answers **on the separate answer sheet**.

Lost in paradise

On my second trip to Greece I had a very embarrassing experience. I had arrived in Athens very early in the morning after a delayed flight from London on which I had barely slept a wink. My plan was to go to an island called Skopelos that a friend had recommended. It turned out that this involved a five-hour bus trip, at the end of which I had to catch a ferry to the island. By the time I got there, I had been travelling for over twenty-four hours.

As soon as the ferry docked at the little port, the other tourists and I were surrounded by local people offering us accommodation in their homes. I attached myself to a lovely woman called Nina and she led me up a winding path to her house, where she showed me to a pretty room with a private bathroom. [37] After getting dressed, I went down to the kitchen.

There, Nina was sitting with a young woman called Anika, who spoke Greek and English. While we had coffee, Anika acted as an interpreter. It turned out that Nina's daughter Olga was studying abroad, so Anika was staying in her room. Nina had suggested she should show me around the town. [38] We finished our coffee, said goodbye to Nina and headed out the door.

As we headed in the direction of the port, Anika pointed out various landmarks for me to remember: a house with a blue door and a lemon tree in a pot, a little chapel with a small bench outside, a café on a corner where there was a friendly little dog. [39] I wondered if I should go back to the house and have an early night but

decided that I would be better off having something to eat before retracing my steps.

By the time Anika and I reached the port, it was time for her to go to work. [40] Although I was very hungry, I decided to make sure I could find my way back to Nina's while there was still some light.

From the port, I walked up a narrow path I could have sworn was the same one Nina and I had followed earlier that day. There was a café on a corner but no friendly dog, a little chapel but the bench was nowhere to be seen and there were several houses with blue doors and lemon trees. I had no idea where I was. [41] I began to wonder if Nina and her house were just a figment of my imagination.

Eventually, I realised that the simplest thing to do was to go back to the port and ask the tourist police to help me. [42] The police laughed when I told them that. It turned out that there were twenty women called Nina who rented out rooms and ten of them had daughters called Olga who were studying abroad.

The police were very kind, nevertheless, and telephoned every one of those women until on the tenth call they managed to find 'my Nina'. She came to get me and guided me back up to the house, chuckling to herself all the way. I collapsed into bed and slept for almost ten hours. The next day at breakfast I met an English couple who had had exactly the same experience.

A I hadn't asked Nina to write down her address but at least I knew her name.

B This meant that I was on my own, and the sun was beginning to set.

C The harder I tried to remember exactly what Anika had said, the more lost I became.

D Since it was late June, it would still be light for a couple of hours.

E I had a much needed shower and unpacked.

F Surely he would know where Nina lived.

G I tried to pay attention but my tiredness made it difficult to take it all in.

Part 7

You are going to read some information about five musicians and the instruments they play. For questions **43–52**, choose from the musicians (**A–E**). The musicians may be chosen more than once.

Mark your answers **on the separate answer sheet**.

Which musician

was inspired by seeing someone perform?	43	
feels the instrument suits their personality?	44	
stopped playing the instrument at one stage?	45	
says the instrument suits them physically?	46	
feels their instrument is sometimes a nuisance?	47	
had never seriously considered playing this instrument at first?	48	
did not make the decision to play an instrument?	49	
did not find it difficult to learn the basics?	50	
travels frequently?	51	
plays an instrument that was previously owned by someone else?	52	

Heart strings

A The guitarist

My father played the guitar and the banjo and had learnt both from my grandfather. All my uncles played too. By the time I came along, it was a well-established family tradition. There was just no question about whether I would learn to play an instrument or not and what instrument that would be. I got my first guitar when I was seven. My father bought me a second-hand instrument because they are easier to play and tune. Since that time, I have owned more than twenty guitars. I've sold some of them, lost one and had two stolen, but I've always managed to hang on to that original guitar. I've played it often and looked after it carefully over the years, so it is still in quite good condition.

B The mandolin player

My mother came home from work one evening with a mandolin. I already knew how to play the guitar so it didn't take me long to work out how to play a few chords. I strummed it from time to time, showed it to all my friends and then stuck it behind the sofa where it stayed for several years. In my second term at college, my parents phoned to say they were planning to come and visit me and asked me if there was anything in particular I would like them to bring from home. I don't know why but suddenly I realised I badly wanted the mandolin. So they brought it with them and I've never looked back.

C The double bass player

Children didn't normally learn the double bass in the past. The instruments were just too big for tiny fingers and little arms. As a result, most of my friends who play started with the violin but my teacher managed to get me an instrument specially designed for children. It was a tenth the normal size and very cute. Size is always a problem though. We play abroad quite a lot and getting my instrument through security is a real headache. Even getting round town is not easy. Despite all the inconvenience, I love my bass. It's a perfect instrument for someone like me who is rather shy and not really interested in being centre stage. I'd much rather make music with other people.

D The harp player

My parents took me to a concert but from where we were sitting, I couldn't see the strings of the harp. I just saw the hands move through the air and heard these beautiful sounds that took me into another world. Much later, when I started to play myself, I realised that because of the way you sit behind the harp and take its weight on your shoulders, you feel every sound as a vibration that passes through your body. It's wonderful. Unfortunately, not all concert music includes a part for the harp, so you don't have as many opportunities to play with others as some musicians do. I think that's a great pity.

E The viola player

A lot of people don't even know the difference between a viola and a cello. They just know that they're not violins. I was a bit the same when I was younger because my father was a concert violinist and he really didn't take the viola seriously, so I played violin. When I was studying violin at university I attended a chamber music class with a famous professor. He took a viola out of its case and said, 'You will play the viola.' I was very reluctant even to touch it but I have fairly long arms and the violin had always been a bit uncomfortable for me. The viola felt much less cramped. I played the first note and said to myself, 'My goodness, this is fun!'

Writing

Part 1

You **must** answer this question. Write your answer in **140–190** words in an appropriate style.

In your English class you have been talking about the advantages and disadvantages of buying things online instead of in person in a shop. Now, your English teacher has asked you to write an essay.

Write an essay using **all** the notes and give reasons for your point of view.

Is it better to buy things online, or in person in a shop?

Notes

Write about:

1 which gives greater choice

2 which is more convenient

3 _____ (your own idea)

Part 2

Write an answer to **one** of the questions **2–4** in this part. Write your answer in **140–190** words in an appropriate style.

---

2   This is part of a letter you have received from an English friend.

> In our school we are producing a series of reports for our school magazine on food and eating around the world and I want to include one on your country. Could you send me a report about the food people like to prepare and eat in your country, and where they like to eat?

Write your **report**.

3   You have seen this announcement in an international film magazine.

> **Film reviews wanted!**
> We're asking readers to send in a review of the best or worst film they have ever seen. We will publish the most interesting reviews!

Write your **review**.

4   You have received a letter from your American friend, Jack. Read this part of his letter and then write your letter to Jack.

> I'm planning to visit your country in July and I'd like to spend a short time seeing the most important sights and then find a part-time job for a few weeks to help me learn the language.
>
> Can you give me some advice on what to see and working in your country?
>
> Many thanks,
>
> Jack

Write your **letter**.

Listening

Part 1 ▶ 30

You will hear people talking in eight different situations. For questions **1–8**, choose the best answer (**A**, **B** or **C**).

1   You overhear a woman leaving a voicemail message on a theatre answerphone.
    What does she want to do?
    A get her money back
    B go to a different performance
    C change her seats for better ones

2   You hear two people talking about a film they have just seen.
    What do they agree about?
    A The film was not as good as they'd expected.
    B The acting was exceptionally good.
    C The special effects were outstanding.

3   You overhear two people talking at an airport.
    Why is the man annoyed?
    A He doesn't want to miss his meeting.
    B He doesn't like flying with a particular airline.
    C He doesn't understand why the flight is delayed.

4   You overhear a woman on the phone talking about her course at college.
    What does she think about the course?
    A It is more difficult than she'd expected.
    B It is less interesting than she'd hoped.
    C It is more time-consuming than she'd anticipated.

5   You hear two people talking about a type of television programme called a game show.
    What do they agree about game shows?
    A They are becoming ridiculous.
    B They are unreasonably expensive.
    C They are quite amusing.

6   You hear a young singer talking on a radio chat show.
    How does he feel about his career?
    A disappointed not to be doing better
    B upset by people's attitude towards him
    C sorry that he can't sing the kind of songs he likes

7   You hear a woman talking on the radio about chewing gum.
    What is she doing?
    A outlining the growth of the industry
    B highlighting a problem with the product
    C explaining the popularity of the product

8   You hear part of a phone-in programme on the radio.
    Why has the man called the programme?
    A to complain about the attitude of other listeners
    B to suggest a way of changing the programme
    C to criticise the way the programme is organised

Part 2 ▶ 31

You hear a woman called Anne Roberts talking to a group of students about doing a job called a runner in the film industry. For questions **9–18**, complete the sentences.

Working as a runner in the film industry

Anne says that her ambition is to be a (**9**) .... in films.

Anne uses the words (**10**) .... to describe the kind of work she does as a runner.

Anne found it odd that she did a lot of (**11**) .... on her first job as a runner.

Anne was amused when she had to collect some (**12**) .... that had been forgotten.

Anne found working with the (**13**) .... very useful in a practical way.

Anne says it's most important for a runner to be what she calls a good (**14**) .... person.

According to Anne, good (**15**) .... skills are important for a runner.

Anne says it is difficult finding work through (**16**) ....

Anne thinks that people become runners because they hope to make useful (**17**) .... in the industry.

What Anne likes most about working in films is the sense of (**18**) .... on the set.

Part 3 ▶ 32

You will hear five different people talking about a holiday they have had recently. For questions **19–23**, choose from the list (**A–H**) what each speaker says they enjoyed most about their holiday. Use each letter only once. There are three extra letters which you do not need to use.

A	spending time with friends	Speaker 1	19
B	eating interesting food	Speaker 2	20
C	being able to relax	Speaker 3	21
D	getting exercise	Speaker 4	22
E	finding out about the culture	Speaker 5	23
F	going shopping		
G	speaking a different language		
H	seeing famous places		

Part 4 ▶ 33

You will hear an interview with Kris Ashton, a successful young tennis player. For questions **24–30**, choose the best answer (**A**, **B** or **C**).

24 How did Kris feel about tennis when he was young?
 A upset because he preferred a different sport
 B frustrated because he couldn't practise often enough
 C annoyed because his parents forced him to play tennis

25 What is Kris's attitude now to his experiences at school?
 A He accepts that it was important to study.
 B He is glad that it showed him how to be successful.
 C He appreciates the opportunity he had to make lasting friendships.

26 What does Kris say about his early competitive years?
 A It was fortunate that older players accepted him.
 B He had to grow up more quickly than other people.
 C It would have been better to have spent more time at college.

27 What does Kris say about his exercise routine and diet?
 A He finds it difficult to eat healthy meals.
 B He understands that his training has to be varied.
 C He resents the need for strict discipline.

28 What does Kris enjoy most about being a tennis professional?
 A making a lot of money
 B travelling round the world
 C meeting new people

29 What advice would Kris give to young players?
 A Enjoy yourself as much as you can.
 B Listen to people who know more than you.
 C Try to achieve your ambitions as quickly as possible.

30 What ambitions does Kris have for the future?
 A to help younger players achieve their potential
 B to work in the media
 C to be successful in another sport

Speaking

Part 1

The Interlocutor will ask you and the other candidate some questions about yourselves.

▶ 34 Listen to the recording and answer the questions. Pause the recording after each bleep and give your answer.

Part 2

The Interlocutor will ask you and the other candidate to talk on your own about some photographs.

▶ 35 Listen to the recording and answer the questions. When you hear two bleeps, pause the recording for one minute and answer the question. Then start the recording again. When you hear one bleep, pause the recording for 20 seconds and answer the question.

Candidate A

What do you think the people are enjoying about learning these different things?

Candidate B

Why do you think this moment is important to the people?

Part 3

The Interlocutor will ask you and the other candidate to discuss something together.

▶ 36 Look at the task and listen to the Interlocutor's instructions. When you hear the bleep, pause the recording for two minutes and discuss the task.

Listen to the Interlocutor's instructions. When you hear the bleep, pause the recording for one minute and make your decision.

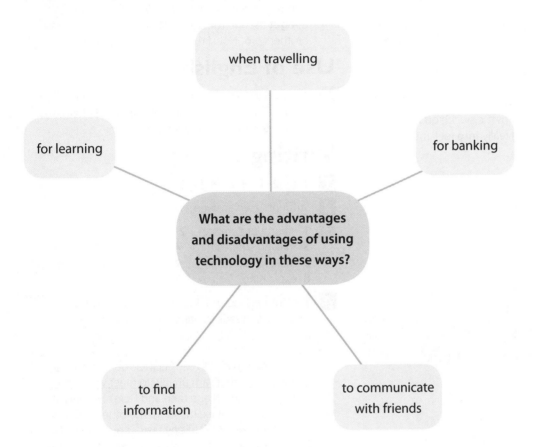

Part 4

The Interlocutor will ask you and the other candidate questions related to the topic of Part 3.

▶ 37 Listen to the recording and answer the Interlocutor's questions. Pause the recording when you hear each bleep and discuss the question with the other candidate.

Answer key

UNIT 1
Vocabulary

1 guitar   concert   audience   instrument   punk
performance   culture   drummer

2 **1** I really think listening **to** music is relaxing.   **2** Can
you play ~~at~~ a musical instrument?   **3** I try to go **to** as
many live concerts as possible – they're great!
4 I watch ~~at~~ television in the evenings after work.
5 It's much easier if I can ~~make~~ **do** the shopping at
the weekends.   **6** I tend **to** stay at home on Sundays.
7 ~~Making~~ **Doing** yoga helps me switch off from
problems at work.   **8** I'm really **into** rock music – I
love the strong beat.

Speaking

1 **1** C   **2** E   **3** G   **4** I   **5** B   **6** F   **7** A

Reading

1 2

2 **1** D   **2** F   **3** B   **4** E   **5** G   **6** A

3 **1** your mind   **2** a dish   **3** a jacket

4 **1** A   **2** A   **3** B   **4** B   **5** B

5 **1** famine   **2** lyrics   **3** recruited   **4** trend

6 **1** A   **2** B   **3** A

Grammar

1 **1** have, am getting   **2** come   **3** are performing,
tells   **4** are becoming, know, are downloading
5 understand, hear   **6** know, is working   **7** says, are
really looking forward   **8** love, play   **9** sound, like
10 criticise, disagree

Use of English

1 **1** B   **2** B   **3** D   **4** C   **5** A   **6** C   **7** A   **8** A

2 **1** looking for (2), came across (7),   **2** put us in touch
with (1), composing music (3), doing experiments (6)
3 common knowledge (4)

Listening

1 **1** F   **2** E   **3** A   **4** D   **5** G

Grammar

1 **1** did, had used to, would believe   **2** would, hadn't
used to

2 **1** When I was a child I used **to** hate classical music, but
I loved rock.   **2** Every time I went to a concert I **would**
buy a T-shirt to remind me of it.   **3** My brothers **used**
to go to football matches instead of coming to rock
concerts with me.   **4** After a while I **got** used to going
to music events on my own.   **5** My mother could
not **get** used to me doing different things from my
brothers.   **6** Now I think she's got used **to** it.

Use of English

1 **1** I used to live in   **2** I would go to   **3** got used to
singing live   **4** makes me feel relaxed   **5** hardly ever
go to   **6** came across your message by

Writing

1 **1** F   **2** T   **3** F   **4** F   **5** T

2 Students' own answers.

3 **1** stating preferences   **2** refusing an invitation
3 making suggestions   **4** explaining   **5** inviting
6 making suggestions   **7** making offers
8 explaining

4 The answer does not include information about
whether Jo needs to bring anything with her.

Hi Jo,

I'm looking forward to ~~see~~ SEEING you, too! I am sorry
to inform you that I am unable to meet you at the
station. I'll be in college then and I can't ~~missing~~ MISS
it because I've got exams soon. The other bad news
is that there ~~isn't~~ AREN'T any taxis at our station, but
there is a very good bus service – every 10 minutes,
and it's better because it's a lot cheaper! Get the
number 18 and get off at the post office – you know
how to ~~walking~~ WALK to my house from there. Good
news about the festival – I've got front row tickets!!
There are loads of great bands and we'll have a lot of
fun. It's in the local football stadium, so there'll be lots
of people there.

That's all for now – see you next week.

Yours sincerely

Inga

UNIT 2

Vocabulary

1 harmful, depressing, confusing, frustrating, irritated

2 **1** confusing   **2** independent   **3** relaxed   **4** harmful
5 frustrating/depressing   **6** irritated

3 1 pessimistic 2 emotional 3 creative 4 sociable
5 sympathetic 6 realistic 7 reliable 8 thoughtful

Use of English

1 1 inaccurate 2 relationships 3 unhappiness
4 depressing 5 unpleasant 6 unacceptable
7 actually 8 healthy

Listening

1 1 B 2 B 3 C 4 A 5 A 6 B 7 A

Grammar

1 1 We followed her directions as ~~close~~ **closely** as we
could, but we still got lost on the way to the farm.
2 In the afternoons we were free to do whatever
we liked. ✔ 3 She handed in her essay too ~~lately~~
late and the teacher refused to mark it. 4 As ~~hardly~~
hard as I try, I can never manage to remember all my
relatives' birthdays. 5 I'm not as close to my sister as I
am to my brother. ✔ 6 She spent her money so ~~free~~
freely that at the end of the month she had nothing
left. 7 I've been seeing a lot of Alicia lately. We've
become really good friends. ✔ 8 It's strange that we
get on so well because we have hardly anything in
common. ✔

2 1 difficult 2 brilliant 3 angry 4 impossible
5 exhausted 6 frightened 7 enormous 8 tired

Reading

1 1 F 2 F

2 1 B 2 A 3 B 4 C 5 D 6 B 7 D 8 C 9 A
10 C

3 1 looking into 2 grow up 3 came out
4 taken up 5 longed for 6 came through
7 taken up 8 found out

Grammar

1 1 it was raining too hard 2 I couldn't think what to
say 3 but I couldn't remember where I put it 4 you
have not got the job

2 1 dancing 2 telling 3 to be 4 to buy 5 going
6 watching

3 1 She made him help her do the cooking, but he
wasn't very good at it! ✔ 2 I stopped ~~to smoke~~
smoking over five years ago and now I feel great!
3 He tried ~~to phone~~ **phoning** her number, but she
didn't answer. 4 I'll never forget ~~to see~~ **seeing** the
Royal Wedding on television – it was beautiful.
5 I regret ~~informing~~ **to inform** you that your
application for the job has been unsuccessful.
6 I'm keen on doing as much sport as possible
to keep fit. ✔

Speaking

1 1 So do I. 2 I'm not sure about that. 3 I hadn't
thought of that. 4 Exactly! 5 What about you?
6 I'm not convinced. 7 I see what you mean but …
8 What's your view on that? 9 Well, actually …
10 Good point. 11 That's very true. 12 Neither
do I. 13 I suppose so. 14 What do you think?
15 I'm not sure about that.

Writing

2 1 as 2 as well as 3 in spite of 4 However
5 although 6 whereas

3 internet, parents pay for everything/can live in a flat

4 This is a difficult question to answer <u>as</u> we can't choose
our family, and every family is different. We can only
experience our own family! <u>However</u>, there are points I
can make.

In a big family with lots of siblings there is always
someone to talk to and listen to your problems,
<u>because</u> they know you well and can really help
you. <u>On the other hand</u>, siblings can also be very
competitive, and that can cause problems.

The problem with a small family is that life can be very
quiet, and possibly boring, <u>even though</u> it does teach
people to be independent, which is a good thing.
<u>Nevertheless,</u> they need to make lots of friends outside
their family.

It is a great advantage when grandparents live in
the family as well, <u>since</u> they can teach you about
life in the past. They also have more time to listen
to you <u>as</u> they don't go out to work like parents do,
<u>but</u> sometimes they have problems understanding
modern technology.

On balance, it seems that there is no right answer,
<u>but</u> there are more advantages than disadvantages to
living in a bigger family.

USE OF ENGLISH I

Part I

1 C 2 A 3 C 4 A 5 A 6 C 7 A 8 B

Part 2

9 though 10 the 11 how 12 and 13 themselves
14 who/that 15 to 16 their

Part 3

17 proof 18 pointless 19 impossible 20 performance
21 original 22 useful 23 personal 24 necessarily

Part 4

25 stopped watching television **26** came across an old diary **27** I used to listen **28** would (always) go **29** haven't finished **30** is very likely that

UNIT 3
Reading

1 False

2 **1** A **2** C **3** C **4** B **5** D **6** B

3 **1** brainchild **2** pulled off **3** give it a go **4** swelled **5** paid off **6** crucial **7** charisma **8** nationwide

Vocabulary

1 **1** I get really annoyed ~~of~~ by/with people talking loudly on their mobile phones during concerts. **2** I'm quite frightened ~~with~~ by/of snakes, though I know it's stupid! **3** I worry a lot ~~with~~ about the environment; we really have to do more to look after the planet. **4** My brother is really interested ~~on~~ in sport – he loves it. **5** I get quite embarrassed ~~of~~ by bad behaviour in sports events – I feel really bad about it. **6** We're going on holiday next week – I'm so excited ~~with~~ about it!

2 **1** embarrassed **2** annoying **3** excited **4** worried **5** interesting **6** frustrated

Grammar

1 **1** have been **2** 've owned **3** started **4** bought **5** used to get **6** haven't had to **7** has been **8** have gone

2 **1** have actually started **2** has become **3** have been having **4** have had **5** have learned **6** has got **7** have been reading **8** has given

Use of English

1 **1** up – phrasal verb **2** sure – collocation **3** through – phrasal verb **4** keep – collocation **5** like – grammatical word **6** as – grammatical word

2 **1** at **2** but/though **3** that/which **4** keep/put **5** however **6** has **7** course **8** up

Vocabulary

1 **1** to **2** away **3** of **4** within **5** to **6** on

2 **1** got money to burn **2** be in debt **3** made of money **4** a higher standard of living **5** worth a fortune **6** is (a bit) tight

Listening

1 **1** farm **2** eggs **3** hiking **4** tough **5** conservation **6** involvement **7** crocodile **8** climate **9** technology **10** rat

Grammar

1 **1** the biggest **2** the sunniest **3** more polluted **4** the rarest **5** the most intelligent **6** the best

2 **A 4** ~~Fewest~~ Fewer than two or three crystals of painite, which is said to be the rarest, are found each year. **B 6** Switzerland, but my country, Australia, is much ~~worser~~ worse than I thought. **C 2** Yuma in Arizona. The sun shines for more ~~that~~ than 90 percent of the time. **D 5** In Korea students get by far the ~~high~~ highest scores on maths tests but they're not as ~~better~~ good at some other subjects. **E 1** France has the ~~more~~ most tourist visitors, but China is getting more and more popular. **F 3** London, though they are trying to get ~~lesser~~ fewer people to drive their cars in the centre of the city.

3 **1** most **2** as important as **3** happier **4** just as happy **5** the best

Speaking

1 Yes

2 **1** very different **2** whereas **3** like **4** Although **5** more relaxed **6** look **7** look as if **8** while

Writing

1 **1** B **2** G **3** C **4** D **5** E **6** A **7** F

2 B

3 B

UNIT 4
Listening

1 **1** C **2** C **3** B **4** B **5** B **6** A **7** A

Vocabulary

1 **1** B/C **2** F **3** A/H **4** D **5** G **6** A/H **7** E **8** B/C

2 **1** cost an arm and a leg **2** keep a straight face **3** getting cold feet **4** can't face **5** to get my head around **6** keep an eye on **7** putting my foot in it **8** caught my eye

Grammar

1 **1** I ~~walked~~ **was walking** down the street when I saw my friend Brenda getting out of a sports car. **2** The man who was driving it ~~was looking~~ **looked** slightly familiar.   **3** I was sure I had seen him somewhere before. ✓   **4** As he drove off, I ~~was realising~~ I **realised** that I had met him at a party at Brenda's boyfriend's house.   **5** He had been talking to my boyfriend just before we left the party. ✓   **6** Later that night my boyfriend ~~had told~~ **told** me that the man had been telling him a story about a friend who had disappeared.   **7** Apparently this person was missing for several months before he was found living in France. ✓   **8** He had been working as a waiter in a restaurant and using a false name. ✓   **9** The man who told my boyfriend the story ~~had had~~ **was having** dinner in the restaurant and had recognised the missing man.   **10** I still wonder what Brenda ~~did~~ **was doing** getting out of his car that day.

2 **1** was jogging   **2** noticed   **3** was waving   **4** didn't stop   **5** ran   **6** had completed   **7** wanted   **8** had learned   **9** swam   **10** had seen   **11** got   **12** had disappeared   **13** looked   **14** was   **15** felt   **16** was/had been   **17** had failed   **18** was walking   **19** saw   **20** was talking   **21** were laughing   **22** turned out   **23** had known   **24** had lost   **25** had been waving   **26** was drowning

Speaking

1 **1** would be quite useful   **2** less hot   **3** more sensible than   **4** the least important skill   **5** less water than   **6** last skill

Reading

1 crime

2 **1** D   **2** C   **3** B   **4** C   **5** D   **6** C   **7** B   **8** A   **9** A   **10** B

3 **1** legendary   **2** affordable   **3** testify   **4** livelihood   **5** tease   **6** diverted   **7** adapt   **8** witnessed

Vocabulary

1 **1** absolutely   **2** soaking   **3** strong   **4** dense   **5** strong   **6** freezing   **7** pitch   **8** hard

Grammar

1 **1** That's a lovely house over there and it's got ~~the~~ **a** beautiful garden.   **2** We had dinner last night in ~~a~~ **the** most expensive restaurant in town.   **3** How often do you play ~~the~~ golf every month?   **4** I had to go to **the** dentist last week as my tooth was very painful!   **5** Where did you have ~~the~~ lunch yesterday?   **6** The most important thing we can all do for **the** planet is to recycle more.   **7** I'm staying at ~~the~~ home today.   **8** I love ~~a~~ snow – it's great for skiing!   **9** I could hear ~~a~~ **the** rain beating on the roof of the tent all night.   **10** I could see it was raining, so I just grabbed ~~the~~ **an** umbrella from the collection in the cupboard.

2 **1** the   **2** –   **3** a   **4** the   **5** the   **6** –   **7** the   **8** the   **9** the   **10** the   **11** –   **12** the   **13** –   **14** –   **15** –   **16** the   **17** –   **18** the   **19** a   **20** the

Use of English

1 **1** discouraged   **2** unhealthy   **3** unfortunate   **4** immature   **5** irresponsible   **6** misunderstand   **7** disadvantage   **8** impatient

2 **1** unsuccessful   **2** discouraged   **3** unfortunate   **4** impatient

3 **1** successful   **2** competitive   **3** survival   **4** inexperienced   **5** unprepared   **6** unsatisfying   **7** pleasant   **8** irresponsible

Writing

2 **1** In my view   **2** in order to   **3** would lead to   **4** as a result/because of this   **5** In addition to, apart from   **6** as well as   **7** I believe   **8** because of this/as a result

3 c

4 **1** However   **2** if   **3** also   **4** in order to   **5** Instead of   **6** as a result   **7** and   **8** While

USE OF ENGLISH 2

Part 1

1 B **2** C **3** A **4** B **5** C **6** A **7** D **8** C

Part 2

9 If **10** what **11** who **12** there **13** most **14** a **15** each **16** It

Part 3

17 frightening **18** connection **19** amazing **20** pointless **21** useful **22** commercial **23** locations **24** unadventurous

Part 4

25 more irritating than   **26** were so excited by   **27** is very interesting for   **28** get very worried about/by   **29** find it boring   **30** I saw a glacier for

UNIT 5

Vocabulary

1 **1** vegetarian   **2** high-fat   **3** well-balanced   **4** vitamins   **5** salt-free

Grammar

1 **1** some **2** much **3** much **4** hardly any, too much **5** few **6** hardly any **7** a lot of **8** lots of **9** some **10** a little **11** no **12** a bit of

2 **1** few **2** A few **3** a little **4** a little **5** a few **6** little **7** a few **8** a little

Use of English

1 **1** not **2** have **3** than **4** they **5** used **6** to **7** like **8** of

2 **1** a comparative – rather than (3) **2** a verb + preposition – agree on (0) **3** a quantifier – a bit of (8) **4** a pronoun – they (4) **5** an auxiliary – have (2) **6** an uncountable noun – pepper (8)

Listening

1 **1** D **2** C **3** B **4** A **5** C

2 **1** biology **2** research **3** 125 **4** big **5** paperwork **6** rewarding **7** money **8** big business **9** moderation **10** toast

Reading

1 2

2 **1** C **2** B **3** C **4** D **5** A **6** A

3 **1** reluctant **2** upmarket **3** intriguing **4** daunting **5** heartened **6** pushy **7** sponsor

Vocabulary

1 **1** off **2** down **3** on **4** up **5** out **6** away

2 **1** turned up **2** turned down **3** turned on **4** turned away

Grammar

1 **1** Rice is always ~~serve~~ **served** with your meal so there's no need to order it separately. **2** Are you ~~been~~ **being** picked up at the station or shall I meet you there? **3** Turkey ~~are~~ **is** eaten every year at Christmas in the UK. **4** The cookery book was ~~wrote~~ **written** by a famous television chef. **5** In the past, women ~~was~~ **were** expected to do all the cooking. **6** Too much fast food ~~are~~ **is** eaten nowadays – people should be educated about healthy eating. **7** It is ~~believe~~ **believed** that people should be educated about the health benefits of regular exercise. **8** People are expected **to** throw their litter in the bins, not on the pavement. **9** Orders for our special banquet menu must **be** placed at least two days in advance. **10** She was always being ~~ask~~ **asked** to prepare the food for parties since everyone knew she was such a good cook.

2 **1** has happened **2** has been stolen **3** hid **4** didn't notice **5** had been touched **6** had been taken **7** are known **8** was being watched **9** were hidden **10** will be found

3 **1** was given the recipe by **2** were brought up in/by **3** was baked by Mary **4** is not permitted **5** washing-up has been done **6** had been opened by

Speaking

1 2

2 **1** shows **2** seems **3** looks **4** see **5** obviously **6** of **7** similar **8** if **9** both **10** clear

3 **1** like those we see **2** like breakfast **3** when there's a bit more time

Writing

1 B

2 very busy so there can be queues – but worth it

rather loud music

some meals expensive, but there are cheap sandwiches and interesting salads

UNIT 6

Speaking

1 **1** T **2** T **3** F **4** F **5** T **6** F **7** T **8** F

2 **1** ✓ **4** ✓ **6** ✓ **8** ✓ **9** ✓

3 **1** I think **2** In my opinion **3** As far as I'm concerned **4** Would you agree? **5** Is that what you think too? **6** Well, I suppose you're right up to a point **7** I see what you mean but … **8** I'm not sure about that. **9** What you're saying is … **10** The point you're trying to make is …

Vocabulary

1

Film	Art	Drama	Musical show
costumes	exhibition	costumes	costumes
production	painting	production	production
premiere	gallery	premiere	premiere
set	director	actors	conductor
actors	critics	performances	scenery
screenplay	review	scenery	stage
performances		stage	director
director		play	critics
location		director	review
critics		critics	
review		review	

2 **1** review, critics **2** screenplay, actors **3** location **4** exhibition **5** stage **6** premiere, director **7** conductor **8** play, costumes

Listening

1 **1** C **2** A **3** B **4** C **5** A **6** A **7** C **8** B

Grammar

1 **1** am meeting (fixed arrangement) **2** leaves (schedule) am going to get (intention) **3** will check (offer) **4** could be (future possibility) **5** going to be finished (prediction based on fact) **6** will raise (prediction based on opinion) **7** ends (after time expression *as soon as*) **8** arrives (after time expression *when*)

2 **Dialogue 1** **1** are you doing **2** 'm studying **3** are going to live **4** I am **5** I'll probably share **6** does **7** is going to be **8** will really enjoy

Dialogue 2 **1** will change **2** will disappear **3** We'll download **4** are probably not going to be **5** will still be **6** there'll be **7** will even remember **8** will read

Reading

1 **1** T **2** F

2 **1** F **2** A **3** E **4** D **5** G **6** B

3 **1** script **2** role **3** auditioned **4** set **5** casting director **6** typecast

4 **1** mischievous **2** lucky **3** insulting **4** gratitude **5** safety **6** argument **7** perception **8** success **9** ignore **10** temptation

5 **1** successful **2** luck **3** grateful **4** mischief **5** argument

Grammar

1 **1** Directors will **have** started to make most of their films in places other than Hollywood. **2** All video clubs **will** have closed down. Everyone will be able to watch whatever they want via the internet. **3** People won't have stopped going to big music festivals like Glastonbury and Benicassim every summer. They'll still be very popular. ✓ **4** Many people will have stopped using mobile phones as a result of all the health warnings. ✓ **5** People will have **been** using smartphone applications for so long that they'll have got bored with them. **6** Webcams will have become 3D so that it will really feel as if the person you are talking to is in the room with you. ✓ **7** A lot of record companies will have gone out of business because most people **will** have started to make their own music and upload it to the internet. **8** People will **have** got used to paying for music and will accept this as only right and fair since the money will go directly to the performer.

Use of English

1 **1** B **2** A **3** F **4** E **5** D **6** C

2 **1** over **2** through **3** down **4** round to **5** away with **6** into **7** down **8** away

3 **1** A **2** B **3** B **4** C **5** A **6** D **7** A **8** B

Writing

1 **1** ✗ **2** ✓ **3** ✗ **4** ✗ **5** ✓ **6** ✓ **7** ✓ **8** ✓ **9** ✗ **10** ✓

3 **Report on performing arts proposal**
This report is to **suggest** ways in **which** we could establish a performing arts club in our school. I **interviewed** a number of students about this issue and the following were **their opinions**.

Different options
Most students were in favour of forming a choir. It was felt that almost everyone would enjoy this. Although it was acknowledged that singing ability varies, it was generally **agreed** that in a large group individual talent was not a problem.

Another opinion that was shared among the students was that the music chosen should be mostly rock or pop music rather than **classical.** Beatles songs were often mentioned in the survey as were Abba and Take That.

Improving facilities
Finally, a number of students raised the issue of **rehearsal space** and equipment. Although the common room is the obvious place to rehearse, it was pointed out that the piano needs to be **repaired**.

Recommendation
In my opinion a choir offers students an excellent way of taking part in performing arts, and the piano should be **repaired**.

USE OF ENGLISH 3

Part 1
1 A **2** A **3** C **4** D **5** C **6** C **7** C **8** A

Part 2
9 up **10** find **11** how **12** with **13** give **14** more **15** out **16** is

Part 3
17 ridiculous **18** allegedly **19** ecological **20** actually **21** customer **22** Surely **23** immoral **24** drinking/drinkable

Part 4

25 was looking forward to seeing **26** has not seen Joe since **27** reminded Tom to do/reminded Tom about doing **28** get round to reading **29** more irritating than **30** are very frightened by

UNIT 7

Vocabulary

1 **1** home town **2** feel at home **3** holiday home **4** stay at home **5** at home **6** home from home

Reading

1 True

2 **1** D **2** A **3** B **4** C **5** B **6** D

Vocabulary

1 **1** A **2** A **3** B **4** B **5** A **6** B **7** B **8** A **9** B **10** A

Grammar

1 **1** could have been **2** could/might be **3** can't have/might not have **4** must be **5** must have been **6** may/might have

2 **1** I don't know why I can't contact her – her mobile phone could be switched off. **2** He must have his own webpage. **3** They can't be eating outside because it's raining! **4** John might be arriving tonight. **5** We can't leave because it's too early. **6** The new student could be from Germany.

Speaking

1 1

2 **1** P **2** P **3** C **4** P **5** D **6** P **7** C **8** P **9** P **10** C

3 **1** I imagine **2** must have **3** They seem to be **4** look as if **5** They can't **6** I'm absolutely certain **7** are definitely **8** They must **9** could have **10** I suppose **11** might **12** As far as I can see **13** I'm fairly certain **14** It might even have

Listening

1 grandeur remarkable

2 **1** A **2** B **3** C **4** A **5** C **6** C **7** B

Vocabulary

1 **1** sightseeing tour **2** return ticket **3** camping trip **4** season ticket **5** Domestic flights **6** business trip **7** guided tour **8** package holiday

Grammar

1 and

2 **1** that (D) **2** which (ND) **3** whose (ND) **4** who (D) **5** when (D) **6** where (D) **7** which (ND) **8** who (ND) **9** that (D) **10** who's (D)

3 The island of Saint Brendon, which is situated in the northwest, is the largest in the area. To the east is La Esperanza, which is slightly smaller and from which there are breathtaking views of all the surrounding islands. Saint Brendon has a population which exceeds six million people, who all speak English. The island, whose climate is mild but changeable, has lush green vegetation which may be a result of the frequent showers of rain! However, this is what makes it so beautiful, and a place where tourists love to spend some time.

Use of English

1 **1** I am patient enough **2** so much (that) **3** too technical for me **4** never (before) seen such an **5** could have met him **6** cannot/can't be lying

Writing

2 **Para** 2 personal experience

Para 3 languages

Para 4 own idea (information and cost)

3 **Para** 2 having a real experience, not being able to see everything

Para 3 being able to learn, having fun

Para 4 finding facts, cost

4 **Para** 2: a d

Para 3: c e

Para 4: b f

5 **a** to introduce the general topic

b to give the writer's own opinion

6 **1** a **2** c **3** b **4** b **5** a **6** c **7** c **8** c

UNIT 8

Listening

1 **1** E **2** A **3** D **4** C **5** B

2 **1** D **2** C **3** F **4** B **5** E

Vocabulary

1 **Across** **2** occupation **4** exercise **6** agency
7 practise **9** career

Down **1** emotional **3** calculate **5** security
8 problem

Speaking

1 **1** colleagues **2** distraction **3** concentrate
4 desktop **5** self-disciplined **6** deadlines **7** desk
8 landline

3 **Agreeing** **1** I suppose so. **2** That's just what I was
going to say. **3** Yes, that's true. **4** I agree up to a point.

Asking for an opinion **5** So would you agree
that …? **6** What about communication?

Expressing opinions **7** I think… **8** you certainly
need an internet connection **9** actually I'm not
sure that it's necessary **10** that's why it would be
important

Grammar

1 **1** Carlos told **us** that he would meet us at the cinema.
2 Harry offered ~~giving~~ **to give** me a lift to the station.
3 Joe reminded me to call the hotel to cancel the
reservation.✓ **4** The boss accused me **of** using the
internet at work. **5** We warned him to avoid the
traffic jam in the Port Street. ✓ **6** Sue suggested ~~us to take~~ **taking** the bus because the trains were running
late. **7** Juan explained that the computer system had
crashed so emails weren't getting through. ✓ **8** Peter
refused ~~apologising~~ **to apologise** to Mary.

2 **1** advised me not to **2** denied writing/having
written **3** reminded me to send Bob **4** warned us
to lock up **5** recommended taking/that I take/
should take **6** offered to help me

Reading

1 A

2 **1** A **2** B **3** A **4** B **5** B **6** A **7** B

3 **1** C **2** A **3** A **4** D **5** B **6** C **7** A **8** B **9** D
10 B

4 **1** though **2** Another thing is that **3** as well **4** so
5 but **6** Despite

Grammar

1 **1** had studied **2** had taken **3** was working
4 worked/had worked **5** has worked/has been
working **6** was **7** would commute **8** preferred
9 is/was **10** are/were **11** was not being
12 needed **13** didn't have/hadn't got **14** would
15 was

Use of English

1 **1** tourism **2** applicant **3** representative
4 improvement **5** employer **6** behaviour

2 **1** impression **2** employer **3** applicants
4 appropriately **5** communication **6** naturally
7 inconvenient **8** personally

Writing

1 6, 5, 4, 1, 3, 2.

2 1 ✓ 2 ✓ 3 ✓ 4 X 5 ✓

3 **Suggested answer**

Dear Mr Ellington,

I am writing in reply to your advertisement in last
Tuesday's *Global News*. I would like to apply for the
position of trainee journalist on *Actualise it!* magazine.

I have a good knowledge of student life having just
completed a university degree and am in an excellent
position to write about young people's interests.

I would like to ask some questions about the position.
Firstly, I would like to know whether it would be
possible to work from home. In addition, I am very
interested in the on-the-job training opportunities you
mention in the advertisement, especially the language
courses. Also, would it be possible to do both the
languages you mention in your advertisement? I
have a good knowledge of English but can certainly
improve and I have always wanted to study Chinese.

I can be contacted by telephone on 01094893214 or
by email at SamRuffolo@ymail.com.

Yours sincerely,

Samuel Ruffolo

USE OF ENGLISH 4

Part 1

1 C **2** C **3** D **4** D **5** B **6** A **7** A **8** C

Part 2

9 a **10** despite **11** In **12** up **13** although **14** so
15 and **16** However

Part 3

17 successful **18** Professional **19** believable **20** scary
21 emotional **22** resolution **23** different **24** amazing

Part 4

25 not to open her present **26** apologised for being
27 get very worked up **28** are you getting on **29** should
not have told **30** rains such a lot

UNIT 9

Vocabulary

1   **1** gymnast   **2** championships   **3** athlete   **4** track   **5** medallist   **6** coach   **7** competitive   **8** rivals   **9** training   **10** laid-back   **11** scuba diving   **12** mascot

Reading

1   2

2   **1** G   **2** B   **3** D   **4** A   **5** E   **6** C

3   **1** threatened   **2** exhaustion   **3** decision   **4** losses   **5** harmless   **6** prevention

Vocabulary

1   **1** an enormous effort   **2** a good deed   **3** a strong demand   **4** a good try   **5** a difficult past

2   **1** with   **2** up   **3** on   **4** on   **5** for   **6** in

Speaking

1   a) give you time to think

2   **1** OK. Let me see.   **2** Do you mean   **3** Well, it's difficult to say   **4** I mean   **5** What I meant was   **6** Well, as far as I know,   **7** What I'm trying to say is   **8** I'm sorry, did you say   **9** Right.   **10** So what you're saying is

3   **1** those things that you use to climb up to paint the house   **2** how well you can do things   **3** not exactly afraid but kind of a bit worried and uncomfortable   **4** harm or damage to you physically   **5** a little thing that is supposed to be lucky   **6** the long thing that divides the court into two halves

Grammar

1   **1** I   **2** C   **3** F   **4** A   **5** G   **6** B

2   **1** smoke in restaurants you will   **2** would do my homework if   **3** it rains you will   **4** I were (any) good   **5** they are in noisy places   **6** would not go

Listening

1   **1** B   **2** C   **3** C   **4** A   **5** B   **6** B   **7** A

2   **1** C   **2** A   **3** F   **4** E   **5** B   **6** D

Use of English

1   **1** competitor   **2** competition   **3** competitive   **4** competitively

2   **1** intelligence   **2** improvement   **3** unfortunate   **4** solutions   **5** differently   **6** unhappiness   **7** behaviour   **8** annoying

Grammar

1   **1** would have won   **2** had known   **3** would have given   **4** wouldn't have gone out   **5** wouldn't have met   **6** had made   **7** might/could have seen   **8** might have bought

2   **1** had been given/had had more time   **2** had not invited him   **3** if his alarm had gone   **4** would not have lost   **5** had not got   **6** would not have had to

Writing

1   Plan A

2   **1** Many people claim that   **2** as an illustration of this point   **3** We can easily see   **4** nevertheless   **5** This can be said of   **6** In conclusion   **7** it is my view that

3   D, E, B, C, A

UNIT 10

Vocabulary

1   **1** friendship   **2** affection   **3** loyalty   **4** connection   **5** sensitive   **6** supportive   **7** emotional   **8** companionship

Listening

1   **1** C   **2** G   **3** E   **4** A   **5** F

Grammar

1   **1** as long as   **2** unless   **3** even if   **4** otherwise   **5** even if   **6** otherwise   **7** even if   **8** provided that   **9** as long as   **10** unless   **11** whether   **12** unless

2   **1** learn to   **2** had bought   **3** cook   **4** stand/are standing   **5** would argue

3   **1** unless I use   **2** help you as long as   **3** otherwise they will   **4** provided that they give me/I am given   **5** even if the job   **6** whether (or not) to invite

Use of English

1   **1** unique   **2** usual   **3** individual   **4** affect   **5** special   **6** actual

2   **1** B   **2** A   **3** D   **4** B   **5** C   **6** A   **7** B   **8** C

Reading

1   2 and 3

2   **1** D   **2** C   **3** D   **4** B   **5** C   **6** A

3   **1** dilute   **2** dumped   **3** tread   **4** cools   **5** reverse   **6** drift

4   **1** drifted   **2** diluted   **3** dumping   **4** reverse   **5** treading   **6** cools

Vocabulary

1　**1** cross　**2** heavy　**3** demanding　**4** hot

2　**1** even-tempered　**2** level-headed　**3** self-absorbed
4 cold-hearted

3　**1** self-conscious　**2** quick-tempered　**3** self-centred
4 empty-headed　**5** kind-hearted

Grammar

1　**1** There was a steel box in the cupboard which
contained lots of old photographs.　**2** That new
shop which is opening/which will be opening in the
High Street on Saturday looks like it'll be really good.
3 There is a path which leads down to the sea from
our hotel.　**4** She found the camera which belongs to
my sister.　**5** All those who wish to buy a ticket should
queue up near the Box Office.　**6** My best friend is a
lively person who is bursting with energy.　**7** I'd love
to get a job in film which involves set design.　**8** My
friend gave me a beautiful photograph which was
taken/which had been taken by her brother.

2　**1** I remember ~~meet~~ **meeting** my friend for the first
time – I didn't like him at first!　**2** He introduced
himself by ~~say~~ **saying** 'Howdie'!　**3** Once we became
friends we didn't stop ~~to talk~~ **talking**.　**4** We were
both ~~interesting~~ **interested** in playing football.
5 People said we would end up ~~play~~ **playing**
professionally together, though sadly that didn't
happen.　**6** When he moved to another town I
missed ~~to speak~~ **speaking** to him every day.　**7** After
~~have~~ **having** been so close, it was hard at first.
8 Now we share our experiences on Facebook and
that's ~~fascinated~~ **fascinating**.　**9** He's good at ~~take~~
taking photographs, so I like looking at them on the
computer.　**10** I hope that we'll carry on ~~be~~ **being**
friends for the rest of our lives.

Speaking

1　F

3　**1** D　**2** B　**3** E　**4** C　**5** F　**6** A

4　**1** matters　**2** influence　**3** matters　**4** vital　**5** vital
6 factors

Writing

1　2, 7 and 8 aren't relevant.

2　B

3　**1** exciting　**2** live　**3** challenging　**4** interesting
5 quiet　**6** convenient

4　B

USE OF ENGLISH 5

Part 1

1 B　**2** D　**3** C　**4** D　**5** B　**6** C　**7** A　**8** A

Part 2

9 of　**10** how　**11** from　**12** which　**13** what　**14** other
15 not　**16** so

Part 3

17 listeners　**18** sympathetic　**19** assistance
20 supportive　**21** impression　**22** unpleasant
23 unhappy　**24** instantly

Part 4

25 it snows heavily　**26** unless you do some　**27** as/so long
as there is　**28** you would have caught　**29** had enough
money, I would　**20** who lives next door

UNIT 11

Vocabulary

1　**1** B　**2** H　**3** E　**4** C　**5** F　**6** D　**7** A　**8** G

Reading

1　**1** T　**2** F　**3** F

2　**1** F　**2** A　**3** B　**4** G　**5** E　**6** C

3　**1** barefoot　**2** support vehicle　**3** agility
4 Endurance　**5** overcome　**6** challenged

Vocabulary

1　**1** H　**2** J　**3** D　**4** C　**5** B　**6** G　**7** A　**8** E　**9** F
10 I

2　**1** **over**weight　**2** **inter**national　**3** **re**read
4 **pre**-set　**5** **dis**organised　**6** **tri**-athlete
7 **hyper**active　**8** **mis**understood

Grammar

1　**1** A, B　**2** C　**3** A, C　**4** A, C

2　**1** won't be　**2** wouldn't be　**3** spoke/could speak
4 had met　**5** would be　**6** hadn't come, wouldn't
be helping　**7** plan/are planning, need/will need
8 want, is always/will always be

3　**1** If I ~~didn't spend~~ **hadn't spent** so much money
last Saturday, I would have more in my bank account
now.　**2** If I had been able to find a job in London, I

wouldn't ~~have lived~~ **live/be living** in Paris now.   **3** If I hadn't studied German for six years at school ~~I'm not~~ **I wouldn't be** so good at it now.   **4** If I had worked harder I ~~was~~ **would be** in a higher position in the company now.   **5** If I ~~could choose~~ **could have chosen** my name when I was born I would be called Chloe now.   **6** If I ~~would win~~ **won** the lottery, I would give all the money away.

Vocabulary

1 **1** intend intentional   **2** separate separate   **3** threaten threatening   **4** experience experienced   **5** support supportive   **6** weigh weighty   **7** strengthen strong   **8** terrify terrified/terrifying

2 **1** decisive   **2** terrifying   **3** threatening   **4** supportive   **5** strength   **6** weigh

Use of English

1 **1** unspoiled/unspoilt   **2** argument   **3** Critics   **4** rescuers   **5** safety   **6** choice   **7** entertainment   **8** preferable

Listening

1 **1** finance   **2** patience   **3** date   **4** dreams   **5** special   **6** invitations   **7** boredom   **8** scenery   **9** blog   **10** journalist

Vocabulary

1 **1** called   **2** cut   **3** told   **4** see   **5** putting   **6** wears

2 **1** about   **2** about   **3** to   **4** for   **5** on   **6** of   **7** on   **8** to   **9** to   **10** on   **11** with   **12** in   **13** by   **14** in

Grammar

1 **1** could run   **2** hadn't bet   **3** would take up   **4** were   **5** had never started   **6** could improve   **7** didn't live   **8** could have

2 **1** The film was so well made I felt as if I ~~have~~ **had** actually climbed Mount Everest myself.   **2** I'd rather you ~~don't~~ **didn't** invite Jamie to the party. He doesn't get on very well with Max.   **3** It's high time we ~~had~~ **left** for the station. We'll be lucky to catch the 9.30 train.   **4** It was very silly of you to go out on your bike without a helmet. Suppose you ~~fell off~~ **had fallen off** and hit your head?

Speaking

1 Yes

2 **1** B   **2** D   **3** A   **4** C

Writing

2 **1** give an opinion   **2** explain   **3** describe   **4** give an opinion   **5** describe   **6** give an opinion   **7** recommend   **8** recommend

3 **1** give an opinion, describe   **2** given an opinion, describe, explain   **3** give an opinion, recommend

4 **1** awesome   **2** progress   **3** thrilling   **4** irritated   **5** designed   **6** element

UNIT 12
Listening

1 **1** solving   **2** do   **3** passed on   **4** going through   **5** strike   **6** grab

2 **1** skill   **2** nightmare   **3** motivation   **4** departments   **5** special   **6** mystery   **7** rules   **8** editor   **9** short   **10** marketing

Vocabulary

1 **1** police   **2** facts   **3** evidence   **4** court   **5** trial   **6** defendants   **7** innocent   **8** sentences

2 **1** sentenced   **2** fined   **3** punishment   **4** had   **5** decide   **6** got

Grammar

1 **1** shouldn't   **2** needn't   **3** must   **4** supposed to   **5** need   **6** don't have to

2 **1** She had **to** leave home early to make sure she didn't miss the meeting.   **2** The teacher told me I needn't do the test again because my marks were good enough. ✓   **3** You are not allowed ~~driving~~ **to drive** at over 100mph on the motorway.   **4** You must ~~to~~ try not to get depressed – we know you're innocent.   **5** Witnesses may think they don't have to ~~telling~~ **tell** the truth to the judge, but they do.   **6** You are not allowed to drink and drive – it's illegal.   ✓   **7** You ~~mustn't~~ **don't have to/needn't** do the washing-up – it's not necessary because I can do it later.   **8** You ~~shouldn't~~ **mustn't** smoke anywhere in public buildings.

3 **1** are allowed to bring   **2** had to pay   **3** didn't need to   **4** I really have to   **5** I am supposed to   **6** I mustn't smoke

Speaking

1 **1** For example, if they're shopping online … particularly after what happened to my mother. I get a lot of unwanted messages on mine. Something really horrible happened to a friend of mine, for instance.   **2** Would you agree? Has anything like that ever happened to you? … don't you think?   **3** I certainly would … No, they're not. Yes and no.

Reading

1 True

2 **1** C **2** C **3** A **4** B **5** A **6** D

3 **1** pristine **2** wobbly **3** be long gone **4** gutted
5 shameful **6** be straight over **7** scary-looking
8 buckled **9** in one piece **10** catch up with

Vocabulary

1 **1** turned up **2** get away **3** looking for **4** go along with **5** catch up with **6** go ahead

Grammar

1 **1** had her bicycle stolen **2** has had it returned
3 had got/had it repainted **4** going to have/get it painted **5** have/get it repaired **6** had/got it fixed

Use of English

1 **1** ✓ **2** broken **3** being **4** ✓ **5** got **6** out
7 ✓ **8** ✓ **9** got/was **10** in

2 **1** how **2** if **3** an **4** what **5** at **6** where
7 into **8** like

Writing

1 1, 3 and 7

2 **1** spending **2** fill in **3** to consult **4** asks
5 to lock up **6** talking

3 **Introduction**
The purpose of this report is to **assess** the value of improving security by either **putting** security cameras into the college or providing devices to allow students to lock up their bicycles. I consulted many students, and this report is based **on** their responses.

Security cameras
Students felt there would be an overall benefit in **installing** security cameras, but it could **turn out** to be expensive. The cameras in the new shopping centre cost a fortune! In addition, someone must watch the screens, which seems a waste of time and money.

Locking devices for bicycles
It is a big problem for everyone when bicycles are stolen, as many students come to college **on their bike.** At the moment they leave them at the entrance, but several have been stolen. Last week a red one was taken. It would not **be** very expensive to install bicycle racks in the front of the college, and students **liked** this idea.

Recommendations
Based on the views expressed by students, and on the fact that cameras would be expensive, I recommend **installing** devices for students to lock up their bicycles. This would encourage even more students **to cycle**, which is good for the environment and also for the health and fitness of students.

Headings B and D are not needed.

USE OF ENGLISH 6

Part 1

1 C **2** B **3** A **4** D **5** B **6** B **7** B **8** C

Part 2

9 in **10** itself **11** who **12** used **13** own **14** the
15 a **16** not

Part 3

17 direction **18** unable **19** decision **20** incapable
21 frantically **22** icy **23** emotional **24** adventurous

Part 4

25 would rather play football than **26** it is necessary for me **27** as/so long as no one **28** unless it is **29** too crowded for me to **30** to lock up before leaving

UNIT 13

Vocabulary

1 **1** mistook **2** crossed **3** went **4** follow
5 trigger **6** misled

Reading

1 B

2 **1** A **2** D **3** C **4** B **5** C **6** D **7** B **8** A **9** C
10 A

3 **1** update **2** prosperity **3** warn **4** storage
5 rare **6** slippery **7** overwhelmed **8** erased

Vocabulary

1 **1** I came across **2** I came up with **3** I came into
4 I'm coming down with **5** she'll come round to
6 we've all come through **7** He's really come on
8 I come across as

Grammar

1 **1** can't/am not able to go **2** could stay up/was able to stay up **3** be able to speak **4** can't/am not able to hear **5** could have bought **6** be able to finish **7** were able to get **8** couldn't sleep **9** be able to play **10** could have accepted **11** couldn't live **12** be able to contact

Speaking

1 **1** F **2** T **3** F **4** T

2 **1** The two photographs are similar in many ~~of~~ ways. **2** One thing they have in ~~the~~ common is that the people are performing in front of live audiences. **3** The first ~~one~~ photograph was probably taken in a theatre. **4** It shows ~~of~~ actors performing on stage in a play of some kind. **5** In the second picture, we ~~are~~ see a contestant in a quiz show. **6** There is ~~too~~ a quiz master who is asking a question of some kind and the contestant is trying hard to remember the answer. **7** For the people in ~~the~~ both photographs, having a good memory is very important. **8** To win a quiz show like ~~to~~ this you have to remember a lot of facts and figures and answer the questions correctly under enormous pressure. **9** Despite ~~of~~ having to learn and remember their lines, they usually have someone standing at the side of the stage with a copy of the script to remind them if they forget.

3 Yes.

4 1

Vocabulary

1 **1** blank **2** bear **3** in **4** losing **5** slipped **6** take **7** cross **8** put **9** make **10** changing

2 **1** losing her mind **2** crossed my mind **3** it slipped my mind **4** take my mind off **5** make up her mind **6** have changed my mind

3 **1** preserve **2** remind **3** remember **4** consider **5** recording **6** reflect **7** believe **8** judge

Use of English

1 **1** C **2** C **3** A **4** A **5** D **6** B **7** A **8** C

Listening

1 **1** B **2** A **3** A **4** C **5** C **6** B **7** C **8** B

Vocabulary

1 **1** time flies **2** time is money **3** ahead of their time **4** not before time

Grammar

1 **1** myself **2** me **3** – **4** himself **5** – **6** –

2 **1** I knew that I couldn't rely on my friend to post the letter, so I did it **myself**. **2** We often forget to buy milk, so we have to remind **ourselves** by putting a note by the front door. **3** I had to remind **him** to paint the front door, otherwise he would never have done it. **4** He really enjoyed **himself** at the party last night. **5** Stop pulling my arm – you're hurting **me**. **6** The thieves caught sight of **themselves** on the CCTV screen as they left the shop.

Writing

1 Hi Sara

I felt terrible when I got your email! **I can't begin to tell you how sorry I am.** It's all my fault as **I completely forgot** when your birthday was. My only excuse is that **I've been worrying about my exams lately** and I've been doing nothing else but study. I suppose that was the reason **I didn't realise it was your birthday until it was too late.**

I really hope I can make it up to you somehow. I've got a very special present for you that I know you'll just love. **Do you fancy meeting up for dinner at Chez Maurice next Tuesday?** I could give you your present then, which would make me feel a whole lot better! **Please reply soon and let me know if you can come.**

I'm so sorry.

Love Anya

UNIT 14
Vocabulary

1 **1** communication **2** words **3** body **4** accent **5** messages **6** tell **7** talking **8** actions

Listening

1 **1** raise **2** shrug **3** shake **4** cross **5** roll **6** nod

2 **1** B **2** D **3** C **4** G **5** E

Vocabulary

1 **1** tell, telling **2** speak, talk **3** tell **4** tells **5** told, say **6** say **7** talk, speak **8** say, told **9** speaking **10** say, saying

2 **1** it goes without saying **2** Generally speaking **3** He hasn't got much to say for himself **4** who speak their mind **5** actions speak louder than words **6** Just say the word

3 **1** You have to ~~yell~~ **whisper** in a library so you don't disturb other people. **2** Don't ~~scream~~ **mumble** – I can't hear you properly. **3** He always ~~cries~~ **mutters** to himself angrily if he doesn't like what politicians say. **4** The girl ~~mumbled~~ **screamed** as she fell off the cliff, but luckily her boyfriend heard and caught her! **5** The boy ~~muttered~~ **yelled** at his friend as she was going to get on the wrong bus. **6** A baby ~~whispers~~ **cries** when it is hungry.

Grammar

1 **1** there was **2** it was **3** there wasn't **4** It was **5** it is **6** it is **7** there was **8** there was, it wasn't **9** there is, is it **10** it was

2 **1** Last week it was quite miserable and ~~it~~ **there** was a lot of rain every day. **2** After the presentation ~~it~~ **there** will be a chance for you to ask questions. **3** I enjoyed the trip and ~~there~~ **it** was wonderful seeing old friends. **4** This is such a dangerous road I think ~~it~~ **there** should be a lower speed limit. **5** I was told there would be a taxi for me at ten, but it didn't turn up. ✓ **6** Everyone says it's certain to be a close match between the two players. ✓ **7** ~~There's~~ **It's** a long way from my flat to the nearest tube station. **8** It's too far for me to walk to the station every morning, but luckily there's a regular bus. ✓

Speaking

1 **1** J **2** A **3** B **4** I **5** H **6** F **7** E **8** D **9** G **10** C

2 **Photograph 1**

1 R **2** I **3** I **4** R **5** R **6** R **7** R **8** R **9** I **10** I

Photograph 2

1 R **2** R **3** I **4** R **5** R **6** I **7** I **8** R **9** I **10** I

Reading

1 True

2 **1** E **2** A **3** F **4** B **5** C **6** G

3 **1** B **2** A **3** A **4** B **5** B **6** A

Vocabulary

1 **1** duck **2** birds **3** cat **4** kittens **5** fish **6** cat

Grammar

1 **1** is **2** have **3** has **4** has **5** was **6** is **7** are **8** has

2 **1** The police ~~is~~ **are** looking for a man with a tattoo of a tiger on his chest. **2** The advice they gave me on places to stay in London ~~were~~ **was** really useful. **3** A hundred pounds ~~do~~ **does** not sound like a big reward for someone who finds a much-loved pet

you have lost. **4** Both my cats ~~knows~~ **know** how to communicate with us, though they do it in quite different ways. **5** Everyone was very surprised when I told them I was going to learn Tibetan. ✓ **6** Neither of the researchers was very kind to Nim. ✓ **7** There ~~is~~ **are** a few dog biscuits left in the packet. **8** The furniture in our flat is getting very old. ✓

Use of English

1 **1** themselves **2** there **3** Although **4** as **5** order **6** on **7** while **8** it

Writing

1 **1** C **2** B **3** G **4** A **5** E **6** H **7** F **8** D

2 **1** M **2** B **3** M **4** M **5** E **6** M **7** E **8** B

3 **A** 6 **B** 1 **C** 8 **D** 2 **E** 7 **F** 3

USE OF ENGLISH 7

Part 1

1 A **2** C **3** A **4** B **5** D **6** A **7** C **8** D

Part 2

9 has **10** than **11** but **12** their **13** It **14** there **15** few **16** be

Part 3

17 limitation **18** concentration **19** repetition **20** healthy **21** effectiveness **22** circulation **23** devastating **24** consolidation

Part 4

25 it was wonderful **26** there are enormous benefits **27** is thought (that) **28** I'm coming down with **29** came into **30** could have tried

COMMON ERRORS AT CAMBRIDGE ENGLISH: FIRST

Use of English

1 **1** A **2** C **3** B

2 Forgot advice **3** B. The correct answers are **1** C **2** C.

3 **1** B **2** C **3** A

4 Forgot advice **2** C. The correct answers are: (**1**) either is possible but student should not write both. (**2**) *in* – student should not write two words.

5 **1** B **2** A **3** C

6 Forgot advice **3** C. The correct answer is *unadventurous*.

7 1 B **2** C **3** A

8 **1** Forgot advice **2** C. The correct answer is *saw a glacier for*.

Reading

1 1 C **2** A **3** B

2 Forgot advice **2** A. The correct answer is C.

3 1 A **2** B **3** C

4 Forgot advice **3** C. The correct answer C.

5 1 B **2** C **3** A

6 Forgot advice **3** A. The correct answer is **3** (paraphrase of 'not having to get up at some ungodly hour to go out to work').

Writing

1 1 B **2** C **3** A **4** D

2 4 A

3 1 B **2** C **3** A **4** D

4 Forgot advice **4** D.

Listening

1 1 B **2** A **3** C

2 Forgot advice **3** C. The correct answer is C. The speaker complains about waiting and explains her point of view, but the reason she has called ('why') – is to put forward a suggestion.

3 1 A **2** C **3** B

4 Forgot advice **3** B. The correct answer is *hiking*.

5 1 B **2** A **3** C

6 Forgot advice **2** A. The correct answer is C.

7 1 B **2** A **3** C

8 Forgot advice **2** A. The correct answer is B.

Speaking

1 1 B **2** A **3** C

2 Forgot advice **1** B.

3 1 A **2** C **3** B

4 3 B

5 1 C **2** B **3** A

6 Forgot advice **3** A.

7 1 C **2** B **3** A

8 Forgot advice **2** B.

Common language errors

Writing

1 **Part 1**

Some people think it's a good idea for young people to travel to other countries, but are there really advantages for them in doing this?

In **the** first place, it gives young people the opportunity to experience different cultures. This means that they can **learn** about different ways of life, which helps them to be more open-minded. As **a** bonus, they can also learn to **speak** other languages.

Secondly, it helps young people to become more independent, and this is **a** good thing. When they are older and are working they have to think **for/by** themselves, and if they travel to other **countries** when they are young, they might have a more independent spirit.

Lastly, going travelling gives young people the chance to **make** friends from other cultures, and in ~~the~~ today's world it is **possible** to keep in touch with people all over **the** world through social networking sites. This will help to **increase** understanding between **different** nations in future.

To sum up, for the reasons given above I agree that it is a good thing for young people to travel to other countries.

2 **Part 2 (formal letter)**

Dear Sir/Madam,

I am writing because I am very interested ~~for~~ **in** the advertisement you put ~~on~~ **in the** *Daily Mail* last Monday for a course to become **a** watersports instructor. I have been very keen ~~in~~ **on** ~~the~~ waterskiing since I was a child and I also enjoy scuba diving.

Although you gave ~~a~~ very complete information in your ad, I would like to ask some other questions. First of all, how much **does** your course cost? I would also like to know **if it is** possible to study part-time and **if I will** have to do an exam at **the** end of the course. Finally, could you tell me ~~is~~ **if the** certificate you mention **is** for one sport or for more than one?

I look forward to receiving your reply.

Yours faithfully,

Anya Braun

3 **Part 2 (article)**

Have you had a job you loved but for which you got very ~~few~~ **little** money? I have, in my mother's bookshop, and I'm still working there. Choosing between money or job satisfaction has not been difficult for me but I'm unusual I think.

Most people, of course, would rather have a job with a good salary that is interesting at the same time. Unfortunately, ~~a~~ few of us have such job prospects. Everybody looks for the best job ~~which~~ they can find. This usually means a well-paid job. Some people, such as scientists or young people, will be interested in getting as exciting and interesting a job as possible. ~~On the contrary~~ **At the same time/However/On the other hand**, there are other people who are content with a badly-paid, undemanding job if they have enough money to get by. They are not concerned about getting a better standard of living. ~~Moreover~~ **On the other hand/However**, there are some people who do dangerous or dirty jobs with very high wages in order to do what they like in their spare time.

In my opinion, enjoying your work is the priority. If you are unhappy at work you probably won't be happy in your spare time either. No amount of money can change that.

4 **Part 2 (report)**

Introduction
I ~~have~~ interviewed students in the canteen during the last week of term to find out their sports preferences. Here are **the** results of my survey and my recommendations.

Results
There are basically two kinds of sports that students participate **in**: indoor and outdoor sports.
Indoor sports: Many students say they **often enjoy** ~~to play~~ **playing** table tennis (fifty percent) and even more say that they **would** swim **at least once a week** if there was an indoor swimming pool available. Other indoor sports that students mentioned **frequently** were fencing, badminton, basketball and aerobics.

Outdoor sports: These were not so popular **as** ~~than~~ indoor sports because of the cold winter. Nevertheless, the following sports were mentioned **several times**: ice-hockey, football and golf.

Conclusions
Obviously it would be too ~~much~~ expensive to have a golf ~~field~~ **course** or an ice hockey stadium **built**. **There is** a swimming complex in our city already, though students say it should **be** renovate**d**. Around the city **there are** also many places to play football.

Therefore, I recommend ~~to build~~ **building** an indoor sports centre that can **be** use**d** for table tennis, basketball, badminton and aerobics. In this way we would provide **for** the needs of **the** majority of students.

Speaking

Part 1

1 I like all kinds of music but I **mainly** listen **to** rock and pop ~~most~~. **2** Well, when I ~~will~~ finish university, I want to work in **an** advertising agency. **3** I ~~make~~ **play** a lot of sports like tennis and football but I also like reading and **going** to the cinema.

Part 2

4 I'm not sure how **to** say this in English but it's something you use for opening bottles. Anyway, the man ~~on~~ **in** the first photo is giving one to his friend. **5** We all like joining our friends and family for meals **such as/like** those we see here. **6** I'm not sure what they're doing – it looks **like/as if** they might be going on holiday.

Part 3

7 ~~Are~~ **Do** you agree with me? I ~~am~~ agree. **8** Yes, that's **a** good point. **9** I think dogs make great pets. Sorry **I/to have** interrupted you. What **were** you saying?

Part 4

10 Well, ~~is~~ **it's** difficult to say. There are lots of advantages but **there** are also disadvantages. **11** So what **you are** saying is **that** university education should be free. **12** I'm sorry, did you say 'sportspeople'?

PRACTICE TEST
(Reading and Use of English)

Part 1

1 A **2** C **3** B **4** C **5** A **6** B **7** A **8** D

Part 2

9 who **10** whether/if **11** them **12** than **13** it
14 other **15** far **16** because

Part 3

17 enjoyable **18** stressful **19** curiosity **20** unchanged
21 understanding **22** boring **23** actually
24 fascination

Part 4

25 as soon as I got **26** was called off due to/owing to/
because of **27** was the first time **28** wish (that) we had
longer **29** I look it up in **30** advised Joe to hurry or/
otherwise

Part 5

31 B **32** C **33** A **34** B **35** C **36** D

Part 6

37 E **38** D **39** G **40** B **41** C **42** A

Part 7

43 D **44** C **45** B **46** E **47** C **48** E **49** E **50** B
51 C **52** A

Listening
Part 1

1 B **2** B **3** C **4** C **5** A **6** C **7** B **8** B

Part 2

9 producer **10** general tasks **11** photocopying
12 equipment **13** technical crew **14** ideas
15 communication **16** newspapers **17** contacts
18 teamwork

Part 3

19 E **20** A **21** C **22** G **23** B

Part 4

24 A **25** B **26** B **27** B **28** C **29** A **30** C

Audio scripts

Unit 1, Speaking Activity 1

Track 01

1 What kind of music do you enjoy listening to?
2 Do you have any brothers or sisters?
3 What do you like about the place where you were brought up?
4 What subject did you like most at school?
5 What do you think you'll be doing in five years' time?
6 Where do you think you'll go on holiday this year?
7 Who is your closest friend?

Unit 1, Listening Activity 1

Track 02

Speaker 1: I hadn't really got any particular expectations before I went, even though it was my first time – obviously my friends had told me about the last gig they went to, but nothing really prepared me for the sheer size of the venue. The stage was well lit but we were so far away from it that it might as well have been somewhere else. I did quite like the music, though I could have been listening on an MP3 player. And the cost of getting in seemed rather unfair – it wasn't very good value for money, given how little I could see.

Speaker 2: It was the band that attracted me to go in the first place – I love their music, and I've bought all their albums – and the cost of the gig seemed pretty reasonable. I went with three mates, and we had a good time watching the rest of the people and eating the food and drink that you could buy from loads of stalls around the site. The stage wasn't that great, and the view was pretty rubbish – but what really got me was what I'd actually gone for – the music was distorted and I couldn't hear it properly. My mates said the same thing.

Speaker 3: I've always liked the band, and have been to some of their concerts before so I thought I knew what to expect. I knew that the cost would be ridiculously high, the food would be expensive and poor and that the only way to see them properly would be to watch the big screens on either side of the stage – though one of my mates was really put out about that! It was what they chose to perform that I was less keen on – instead of doing their hits they tried this new experimental stuff. Not my thing at all, and I nearly left early.

Speaker 4: I really love listening to any live music, whatever it is – for me the whole experience is really improved by actually being there and sharing it with all the others. That's why I found this concert such a let-down – there was no atmosphere and instead of getting up and dancing everyone just sat watching the band on stage. Maybe they didn't like the music – I agree that it wasn't up to their normal standards – but if you make the effort to go to these things then at least join in! The place itself was impressive, though.

Speaker 5: I know that most people think that the only important thing is the music – and of course that's pretty important! But when I go out for the evening, I expect to have a good all-round experience, especially when the tickets are pretty pricey! This concert was let down not by the music, which I thought was cool, but the venue. OK, I could see the stage and there was a good atmosphere generally, but trying to get anything to eat was ridiculous – the queues were so long that you missed loads of music. And don't even get me started on the wait for the toilets.

Unit 2, Listening Activity 1

Track 03

Interviewer: Danny – you're only 18 and you've spent half your life making films. What was your family like?

Danny: I'm the youngest of four brothers, and we all got on very well – though it might have been easier if we hadn't all had ambitious plans for our futures! We were very competitive. My folks didn't really know much about the entertainment world, but they were incredibly supportive – it was probably the last thing they wanted me to do! But they were always there for me, and I'm very aware of how important they were in keeping a young person stable and on track.

Interviewer: How was life at school?

Danny: I had to go to school the whole time I was making films, and the other kids were pretty jealous of me. I'd miss a bit of school and then return with bright blond hair, or something that had been necessary for the film – needless to say, there was bullying. It wasn't physical, but there was name-calling and jealousy. But in some ways I'm grateful because I'd rather have had that than be sheltered my whole life and not realise people like that were out there. I feel like it made me stronger. I do still have a few close friends from school, but not many.

Interviewer: How do you feel now about being rich and famous?

Danny: Fame isn't a positive thing. The idea of it is a lot better than the reality. It's fantastic when you go to premieres and people cheer you, but it's not real. OK – I earned a lot but I bought a lot of rubbish things – skateboards and clothes and typical teenage stuff, and, as soon as I could, I wasted a lot of money on cars for myself and my family. Then I got into trouble because I couldn't manage it well. I actually envied my schoolfriends who didn't have to think about money!

Interviewer: What effect have relationships with people you work with had on you?

Danny: The film crew especially are the first people to whip us into shape and tell us we're no one special – they've kept my feet firmly on the ground. There are loads of jokes on set and that has been crucial in keeping us down-to-earth. I've been so lucky to work with the best – and what I've learned is not just acting, but how to act with the crew.

Interviewer: Who is your best friend and why are they important to you?

Danny: I'm incredibly close to another actor who's my age. Professionally, she's a phenomenal actor and she doesn't take anything as a given. In between films she takes acting classes trying to improve herself. She's very polite, terrifically good with names and hates people who are rude. But more than anything else she's exceptionally passionate about acting – she loves it. That's what I try to copy.

Interviewer: Do you regret anything about your life?

Danny: Well, it's been good and bad. I've been to places and done things that others my age can only dream of – but I've come in for a lot of negative reviews and I would say that I lost my childhood – and people think that money makes up for it. That's ridiculous – you can't put a price on childhood – you never get those years back. They're priceless, and they make you what you are. I sometimes wonder how I would've been different if my life had taken a different course.

Interviewer: But you've won awards, so it can't have been that bad.

Danny: I feel very embarrassed about anything like that. I won an award last year for the best screen baddie and I found it hard to accept it – making a speech was terrifying – I didn't enjoy one minute of it. I don't buy into all the razzmatazz. There was a big party afterwards and I stayed for about fifteen minutes before going back to my hotel for a cup of tea and a chocolate biscuit.

Interviewer: Danny – thank you for sharing your life with us …

Unit 2, Speaking Activity 1

Track 04

1

Woman: I think it's so important to get on well with your parents.

Man: So do I. I have a great relationship with my folks. I think it's more important than getting on with your brothers and sisters.

Woman: Hmm. I'm not sure about that. I mean, I think it's important to have a good relationship with them too.

Man: It's much more difficult if you come from a very large family.

Woman: I hadn't thought of that. I guess it's almost inevitable that there will be someone you don't get along so well with if there are a lot of you.

Man: Exactly! There are five of us and though I get on fine with my older brother and with my two sisters, my younger brother and I just don't have anything in common. What about you?

Woman: Well, I've only got one sister and I really enjoy doing things with her.

2

Woman 1: I saw a programme about relationships last night that said that friends were more important than family.

Woman 2: I saw it too – but I'm not convinced. Certainly friends are pretty crucial – it'd be a poor social life without them! But family must always come first.

Woman 1: I see what you mean but some things the programme said are certainly true for me. They said your friends have a lot more influence on you when you're young than your parents do. What's your view on that?

Woman 2: Well, actually in my case it was the other way round. I learnt my values from my parents. I think it's their responsibility to teach you how to behave.

Woman 1: Good point. Parents do need to teach their children how to behave but I think you can also learn from your friends.

3

Man: They say that people are having fewer and fewer children.

Woman: That's very true. I don't plan to have a large family myself.

Man: Neither do I. But in some ways, it's a pity. It must be fun to grow up with lots of brothers and sisters. I mean you always have someone to play with.

Woman: I suppose so. I'm an only child so I don't really know what it would be like. My friends who come from large families seem much more sociable than me. Being part of a big family might help you to get on better with other people. What do you think?

Man: I'm not sure about that. It depends a lot on the family.

Unit 3, Listening Activity 1

Track 05

Hi, everyone – it's great to be here and have the chance to share with you what I do and why I feel it's so important. I've been passionate about animals and the environment all my life – to me it's what matters most. Although it was quite near a town, I actually grew up on a small farm, so I was always surrounded by animals – all sorts of different things – ducks, chickens, horses – I used to milk the goats before I went to school every morning and collect the eggs when I got home – I loved that. But as I got older, I realised how other people aren't lucky enough to have this closeness to nature – particularly children brought up in cities who don't really see animals in their natural state.

I also love adventure – my favourite leisure activities include going rock-climbing and hiking – and once I started travelling round the world to remote places like rainforests and deserts I got completely hooked on the plight of endangered animals and ways of trying to save them. When I got the chance to audition as the presenter on a new children's television programme about dangerous animals, I jumped at it. Although I think the best word for me to describe it is tough, I love to be out there in the natural world, so it was the perfect job for me.

What makes it so perfect? What's crucial for me is that although we show lots of dangerous animals which engages the children's interest, the strong message that runs through every programme is conservation.

A large proportion of the animals we film are on the endangered list and we've done 'endangered animal special' programmes as well. It's my responsibility to present the wider picture that goes beyond just showing off a dangerous animal for the thrill of it.

The most important thing for me is that the programme speaks to young people – they're the future, and if we can save species under threat, then it's the children who'll do it. What I want is to give them a sense of involvement with my programme in ways they'll remember and that will affect their future thinking. Children want to know what it's really like to be with me in the Arctic or in the jungle.

When we're filming, we never know what's around the corner. It isn't scripted, so if I suddenly come across a giant snake, the film crew can capture my shock. Over the years I've been charged by an elephant, followed by a tiger – and the cameras were there last year when I tripped over a crocodile in swampland and needed hospital treatment! The children loved that!

How important is my work? I can't emphasise enough that TV does a remarkable job of bringing the major issues to light. It's made children more aware of things like climate change and how that affects wildlife. It's great watching them when they come across an animal they've never seen before. They're inspired and totally in awe.

I do know not everyone agrees with me – sociologists have argued that children's lives are becoming even more disconnected from the natural world because they're increasingly immersed in media and technology. I've even heard some say nature films lead children to believe that wildlife is exotic and inaccessible and that they actually dislocate children from the everyday nature in their own gardens.

If the success of my own programme is anything to go by, sociologists have got it wrong. Expeditions to the world's most remote places are still the most exciting thing for me – I've been inside a volcano, and found new species in jungles, such as the world's largest rat! But, I don't just show what's there – what's so important to me is to search for a way to save the places I explore. I can't bear the thought of being in this world without trying to do something to look after it – that's what matters to me. So does anyone have any questions …?

Unit 3, Speaking Activity 1

Track 06

Examiner: I'm going to give each of you two photographs to talk about. Carla, here are your two photographs. I'd like you to compare and contrast the photographs and say what the people are doing in the photographs and how they are feeling. You have about a minute to do this.

Carla: These photographs are similar because they both show groups of people but they are very different in other ways. The first photograph shows people on a beach, whereas the people in the second photograph are probably in a city or town. In the first photograph, the people look like environmental activists protesting

about some kind of problem. Although the people have signs, they look more relaxed than the people in the other picture. In the second photograph, the people seem to be watching something happening in front of them. Most of them look excited so I think they might be watching a football match. Most of the people look as if they are really upset about whatever has just happened, while one man is clapping. Perhaps the other team has just scored a goal.

Unit 4, Listening Activity 1

Track 07

Interviewer: Today in our series of incredible exploits we're talking to Alan Preston, a young man who sailed round the world alone at the age of sixteen. Alan, what were you like as a child?

Alan: My parents say I was born adventurous, and I love outdoor life. We spent our family holidays going camping, hiking, things like that – I was always ready to have a go at anything I hadn't done before. Once we went out in a small boat exploring. I loved it, and although my sister wasn't keen, that experience was the defining moment for me. I started reading about sailors and, although I was still fascinated by all kinds of adventure sports, it was sailing that had the edge. Dad encouraged me – he'd been in the navy and I think he hoped I'd follow him in that.

Interviewer: How did you start taking sailing seriously?

Alan: Dad had always wanted to sail across the Atlantic single-handed, but Mum discouraged him because she was worried. But he and I talked about it, and as I got better at sailing it kind of took on its own momentum. I was fourteen when I did it – but Dad followed me in a back-up boat to make sure I was all right. After that the sailing bug really took hold – I felt like I had a purpose in life. Although I still did teenage things, I had a kind of inner strength. I knew what I wanted to do.

Interviewer: What made you decide to sail round the world?

Alan: I was sixteen when I started planning and I had to get money somehow – Dad and I had to raise sponsorship. Some people criticised my parents for being pushy but they were just supportive. I'd never have left port unless I was committed to the challenge and knew I was capable. But I was lucky to be allowed to do it, given the dangers! I actually left the final decision to Mum who said making it was almost impossible, but in the end she went along with Dad and me.

Interviewer: How did it feel when you started out on such a long trip?

Alan: There's a gap between imagining something and doing it! Those first days were the hardest, 'cos there were loads of technical problems which got me down – I even thought I might have to give up! That would've been disappointing, but I carried on, sleeping in periods of 20–40 minutes, eating rehydrated meals – some people said I'd be lonely, but my mates had put loads of music on my iPod which was great. I'd stuck photos everywhere and packed loads of clothes so I didn't need to worry about doing any washing!

Interviewer: What was the worst moment?

Alan: I love the roller-coaster ride of huge seas – I was in tune with the boat, surfing down fifty-foot waves. I felt confident I could cope. But there was this one storm that I knew was forecast – it had massive waves and the boat turned over on its side. The damage meant I had to climb to the top of the seventy-foot mast to repair it in terrible winds – the only time I wore body armour and a helmet for protection! That was pretty scary – I was glad to get back to the cabin!

Interviewer: Why do you keep sailing?

Alan: It's the feeling of being completely in control and in tune with natural forces. I've had dolphins swimming alongside, seen stunning, vivid sunsets. It's those kinds of moments when it feels like the world stops and you believe anything is possible. It's not the racing against other people, though I'm proud to be doing it so young – I don't bother much about records and stuff.

Interviewer: What advice would you give young people about taking on this kind of challenge?

Alan: One thing is to be ready mentally for anything – sometimes during the voyage, I'd think, why am I here, this is awful. Then I'd remember Mum and Dad and what it would be like at the finish. That got me through. Listen to any advice you're given but decide for yourself, though probably the most crucial thing is, don't lose sight of what's real – I still have sailing ambitions but for now, it's back to ordinary life – I've got to go back to college to finish my exams.

Unit 4, Speaking Activity 1

Track 08

A: OK. Let's talk about what'd be useful on our trip. We have to eat so I reckon cooking would be quite useful.

B: I agree. The problem is, how would we do it? It'll be so hot we won't want a fire.

A: True, but we can cook at night when it's less hot – that'd be more sensible than in the daytime.

B: OK. I accept that. But what about fishing? That's the least important skill for anyone in the desert!

A: You mean because there's less water than anywhere else! I agree, that'd be pointless.

B: It's the last skill we'd need! Let's keep talking about other skills – there must be something more useful.

Unit 5, Listening Activity 2

Track 09

Hi, everyone – I'm Terri and I'm here to talk about my job, which is one that many of you may never have heard of!

I'm sure you've had experiences of diets of different kinds – well, I'm a nutritionist – but not for people, for horses. How did that come about? My childhood loves were animals and science, and my parents always imagined I'd be a vet – I did think about it, and also about studying medicine, but in the end I did a biology degree at university which was when I got interested in food and health in general. I then discovered that there was a module in animal nutrition – and everything took off from there. I now work in a department involved in research into the physical state of horses and what makes them fat, so I can advise horse breeders and owners on the best diet for the animals to follow. I've recently been involved in a study on how much grass horses eat compared with other food. During this trial, it was found that some horses ate up to five to seven percent of their own bodyweight in grass daily – which amounts to an extra weight gain of approximately three kilograms a day on average.

We used to think that horses ate around sixty-two kilos of the stuff in a day – however we now know that it's double this and is actually around a hundred and twenty-five kilograms every single day – incredible!

My work is pretty varied on a day-to-day basis – yesterday I spent the day out with a vet weighing and measuring a selection of horses. They were all pretty big so I spent most of my day standing on my toes and I ache all over now!

I'm not always out with the animals – I also spend a lot of time in the office having meetings and also doing paperwork – not my favourite occupation! We have a telephone helpline where people can call with questions or problems, and although some might find it challenging as you get put on the spot by callers, for me it's very rewarding.

As with any job there are highs and lows. I'm trying to get a message across – what makes horses fat – and work out how to educate people – it's a bit like dealing with human diets really. Once people understand, they are desperate to change things, but I have to work out ways of raising that awareness. I also get irritated that I have to rely on others for the money that enables me to do my work – we're not funded.

I'm actually still very interested in human nutrition – and now there is a massive demand for it – it's big business. I have to stay up to date with all the latest developments. My approach to any kind of diet though is the same – people often try to cut down on everything, but for me moderation is the key. I don't think anyone has to avoid eating bad things, but if you eat them you have to make compromises elsewhere – for example, if you have a chocolate bar, cut down on the toast! The main reason why both humans and horses put on weight is lack of exercise but you can't treat them the same. You have to treat horses like horses not people – and they need proper exercise.

The industry as a whole needs a bit of a shake-up. We seem to be at two ends of extremes – on the one hand we have ground-breaking science in the form of veterinary research such as stem cell treatments, but on the other people are still not open-minded to new approaches and tend to stick to what they know. But the great thing is that everyone who works with horses is passionate about them.

Unit 5, Speaking Activity 1

Track 10

Your pictures show people eating in different places. I'd like you to compare the pictures and say what the people are enjoying about eating in these different places.

Unit 5, Speaking Activity 3

Track 11

I think we all like joining our friends and family for meals like those we see in the photos. It's particularly enjoyable to eat in the open air but even an ordinary meal like breakfast in the kitchen is a good time for the family to get together and talk before the beginning of a busy working day or at the weekends when there's a bit more time.

Unit 6, Speaking Activity 1

Track 12

1

Examiner: Ana, what do you think would be hardest about being a famous actor or musician – the lack of privacy or the need to constantly compete with others?

Ana: Definitely the lack of privacy. I think it must be very difficult to be constantly surrounded by paparazzi and journalists watching everything you do. And often it's not just the actor or musician; it's their whole family. Competition is healthy in some ways because it makes us perform at our best, but never having a moment to yourself must be almost unbearable. Would you agree with that, Mario?

Mario: No. I think it would be good to be famous.

Ana: Well, I suppose you're right up to a point. The money would obviously be very useful and it would be great to feel that you had achieved something important but I still think that often the media are just waiting for the star to make some kind of mistake and then it's all over the front page of the newspapers.

2

Examiner: Celina, what do you think of international competitions like the *Eurovision Song Contest*?

Celina: I think they're great. It's like a huge party with young people from literally all over Europe taking part. We get to hear great pop music in all the European languages and see Europe's best young artists performing live.

Examiner: What do you think, Gabriel?

Gabriel: Like you, Celina, I'm a big fan of the *Eurovision Song Contest*. I never miss it. What you're saying is that it offers us the very best of European pop music. I'm not sure about that. I mean not all the acts are of equally high quality and sometimes the artists themselves are not really representative of the best their countries have to offer.

Unit 6, Listening Activity 1

Track 13

Extract 1

M: I just loved it – the music was brilliant!

F: I'm gutted that it was their last performance together. Did you read in the programme that they've filmed it and are going to put it out on DVD – ah, it'll be great to see it again, though it probably won't be the same as it was tonight. No atmosphere.

M: It'll be interesting when the lead singer goes into musicals on stage – he's talented enough on the singing front, but what about the acting?

F: Well, we'll have to give him a chance. I'll certainly go and see him, especially after tonight!

Extract 2

How did I start? Well, I'd never imagined that I'd actually be a teacher – that's what both my parents did and my grandparents as well, though they never pressured me into doing it. I was around sixteen when I really became interested in science and mechanical engineering, and so the idea of working in a college rather than a school seemed on the cards. It wasn't a particularly cool thing to do according to my mates, of course! I suppose I could say that I kind of stumbled into it, but I've been doing it for three years now and I can't say I've ever regretted the decision.

Extract 3

F: I'd really like to go home and see if it's OK.

M: But you always turn it off – it's just an automatic reaction. Don't be silly!

F: It's just that I can't remember doing it – I know you always laugh if I say that but you don't understand how it feels!

M: Well, I haven't got time to go back with you now – I've got a meeting in half an hour – and the bus is coming. If you want to then I'll have to go ahead and catch up with you at lunchtime.

F: Maybe that's the best thing to do.

Extract 4

Thanks for finally having me on – I've been waiting ages! At least I can have my say now. I've been listening for the last hour and I can't believe what your callers are saying. They must know whatever anyone does on the recycling front – big or small – makes a difference. We're all responsible for the world we live in – how can they moan about being asked to put rubbish in different bins? But I accept that not everyone sees it like that, so I think we should be given incentives to do it – that would get people on side, and be pretty easy to put into operation I'd have thought.

Extract 5

OK – let me just check that I've understood you. It's OK for me to come along next Tuesday afternoon and give it a go – if I'm interested in taking it further I pay a registration fee and fifty pounds for the orientation course which I can start immediately. After that I just pay a small fee every time I want to use the facilities, and I can also use your centres in other cities on the same basis when I'm travelling. Could you just repeat what you said about the rooms for classes, please? I didn't quite get that.

Extract 6

F: Well – that was pretty much a waste of time – after those fantastic reviews I'd had high hopes!

M: I'd been told that it was disappointing, so I was kind of prepared. But I hadn't thought that the actors would be so off – she's usually brilliant.

F: And he doesn't often put in a bad performance – pity it was this film! At least the technology didn't let anyone down – the flying scenes were spectacular.

M: But they didn't do anything really cutting edge, did they? I mean I've seen it all before.

F: They had me on the edge of my seat!

Extract 7

M: Did the meeting go OK?

F: I guess. When I presented the policy plan it seemed to go down well. Even the technology worked, which I had nightmares about because I knew the big bosses would be there! The question and answer session afterwards went well – the time I spent preparing paid off.

M: You said the kids got fed up with you working in the evenings so at least now you can spend some time with them.

F: Well, I've still got to write up the report – it'll be circulated next week. I haven't told my husband yet but next weekend will be busy!

M: I'll see it soon then.

Extract 8

We've been friends for a long time and it'd be a pity if we can't disagree on some things and still stay friends. You know that I don't think that what you're saying is right and it's difficult to go along with you when you say things like that – but we need to move on from the whole incident. OK, I may be wrong and you may be proved right in the end – but just now I think we must change the subject before we actually come to blows over it. That would be a big mistake!

Unit 7, Speaking Activity 1

Track 14

Here are your two photographs. They show people celebrating unusual weddings. Now talk to each other about why people choose to celebrate their weddings in situations like these.

Unit 7, Speaking Activity 3

Track 15

Well, the first couple have chosen to have a cycling wedding. I imagine they are on their way to the reception in the photograph and that the wedding ceremony itself must have already taken place. They seem to be very happy about it, and the other members of the wedding party look as if they are enjoying it too. The other couple have decided to have one of their wedding photos taken under water. They can't have had the actual wedding there. I'm absolutely certain of that.

The first couple are definitely cycling fanatics. They must really love the sport if they have chosen to cycle to the reception. The other couple could have just wanted an unusual wedding photograph for their wedding album. I suppose an underwater photograph would be rather difficult to organise but it might be fun. As far as I can see there's nobody else in the photo, so I'm fairly certain it was also taken after the wedding itself. It might even have been taken the day after. It wouldn't be much fun sitting through the reception in a wet wedding dress!

Unit 7, Listening Activity 2

Track 16

Interviewer: Today we're talking to Karen Wilson, a talented musician and photographer who produces unusual, thought-provoking travel books. Karen, how did you start?

Karen: My home town was very traditional and I wasn't outstanding at school. I was persuaded to take up the classical guitar and learn music theory, but then I studied piano and drums – it was those classes that I found most engaging, and I thought it would be my only career. But I was always good at drawing – visual stuff appealed to me, though teachers didn't push me. Photography wasn't on the syllabus, and it was never suggested as a realistic career option.

Interviewer: How did you get started as a photographer?

Karen: I'd been taking photographs for years as a hobby, though I didn't really show them to many other people at the time. I loved photographing unusual things – empty places like airport buildings, theatres – stuff like that. I was travelling a lot for my music, and putting photographs I took during tours on a website. By chance a publisher saw them and asked me to write a book combining photographs with a travel diary. I couldn't turn down that opportunity to express myself and it all took off after that.

Interviewer: How do you approach your books?

Karen: I heard something in an interview that was a great influence on me – a photo-journalist said that photographers were privileged people who should record things other people don't get the chance to see – that it's our responsibility to open people's eyes to things they wouldn't otherwise be aware of. Most people think travel is always exciting and positive. I want to show the strangeness of it – make people realise it's not always glamorous, especially when you're doing it for work as I do.

Interviewer: What do you find fascinating about different places?

Karen: You think every big city is beautiful – and of course they are. But when I'm touring I have to go to parts of cities that aren't – like backstage in large venues outside the main tourist areas. It's weird – I read travel guides or look down at a city from a plane as it's coming in to land and it looks wonderful – but then I go to a characterless hotel room or desolate rehearsal space and it's not the same at all. I've talked to people about this contradiction, but they don't feel it like I do.

Interviewer: Tell us about a trip that you really enjoyed.

Karen: That would be when I went to the south of Argentina. Its beauty comes from a kind of stillness, a grandeur that's based on its landscape and wildlife. I did a few gigs at the start of the trip, which all went really well, then took time off and rented a car to drive along parts of the coastline. I hardly saw anyone – just birds and miles of remote countryside. It was so different from New York – you can't get away from people there.

Interviewer: What have you learned from your travel experiences?

Karen: Ah, before I became a touring musician I did loads of travelling with the family, but we only scratched the surface of places we visited. It was ticking boxes – been there, done that. Of course I still enjoy that part of it – some places are so remarkable you can't not enjoy them. But now I try to get beneath the surface, listen to the sounds and soak in the atmosphere. That's where photography comes in for me – it makes me concentrate on a single image which helps me comprehend much more about a place.

Interviewer: What do you think has made you so successful?

Karen: Well, I've been so fortunate to combine music and photography – clearly if you love what you do it helps! I've also had lots of support both personally and professionally, though that's just a bonus really. For me it's about not accepting the obvious but searching for things that lie deeper. If you push boundaries you enrich yourself personally – and that's really what I think has been the key!

Interviewer: Thank you, Karen – and good luck with the next tour!

Unit 8, Listening Activity 2

Track 17

Speaker 1: I got interested in the whole area of sport when I started school, though I'd loved playing with a ball from a very early age. My parents always encouraged me, though I think they regarded it as a hobby rather than an actual career – we didn't know what the opportunities were then. I went on adventure holidays where sporting activities were top of my list, but it wasn't until I talked to a careers adviser that I realised how many possibilities sport offered apart from playing and, more importantly, how much money I could earn! That's when I decided I wanted to become a personal trainer.

Speaker 2: I come from a family of teachers – in that kind of environment there's always an expectation you'll automatically do the same thing. I've always known it wasn't for me, but I also knew they'd be disappointed – that was hard. But since I was young I've had this ambition to become a dancer, though I know it's a very difficult life. I've taken the first steps towards achieving my ambition in that I'm at a vocational school, but whether I'll ever be good enough to earn big money like the stars, travelling all over the world, I don't know. But if I don't try I'll never know.

Speaker 3: I'd always intended to do something related to my main interest, which is music – my parents have always encouraged me to play various instruments since I was very young – we used to play music together as a family – and I can't imagine my life without it. Once I started looking into it, though, I found that unless you are really good there's just no money in it. So I've decided to leave music as a hobby and go into something with more of a future – so I'm going to study medicine, which gives me loads of opportunities for getting to the top.

Speaker 4: I was pretty rebellious when I was young – I hated school and never wanted to conform to anything. I had these grand ideas of travelling round the world. I was positive I'd never settle down to an office job – I was going to make my fortune, though I wasn't sure how – I just knew it'd be something I'd enjoy. Then I began to see sense, and started taking an interest in lessons – my parents ran their own business and they talked to me about what they did. It seemed pretty interesting so it wasn't long before I realised I wanted to do the same.

Speaker 5: Funnily enough, I've always been a home person – I love hanging out with the family and chilling with friends. I've got loads of hobbies, and we never went on exotic holidays as a family. Then I got interested in languages at school and found I was pretty good at them – but it's not much good understanding different languages if you don't use them, is it? So what I'm thinking of doing is going into the travel business – and I'm realising just how much of the world I want to see! It's very exciting.

Unit 9, Speaking Activity 2

Track 18

Examiner: Do you think luck is important in life?

David: OK. Let me see. Well, I always wish my friends good luck before an exam or job interview so I suppose that does mean I believe in it to some extent. What about you?

Sara: Me too – and I really believe it makes a difference. I always carry a – I'm not sure how to say this in English – it's a little thing that is supposed to be lucky. It's a silver bead that my grandmother gave me. If I did an exam without it, I know I would fail.

David: Do you mean that you actually think it affects your success in the exam?

Sara: Well, yes. I do.

David: Well, I suppose I do too now I come to think of it. I have things I always do like wearing the same socks and walking on the same side of the street on the way to the exam.

Examiner: How much does luck contribute to success in sporting events?

David: Well, it's difficult to say but not so much, in my opinion. I mean other things are more important like – I can't remember the word – how well you can do things like hit the ball or passing in football.

Sara: But in tennis for example you often see that for one player the ball hits the top of the – what's it called? – you know, the long thing that divides the court into two halves – and the ball doesn't go over. That's to do with luck if you ask me.

David: So you think luck is more important?

Sara: No, not always. What I meant was that in some sports it can play quite an important role. I'm very superstitious. There are a lot of things that I avoid doing, like stepping on the lines on the pavement or walking under those things that you use to climb up to paint the house – and if I do my English friends tell me to say 'bread and butter'!

David: Why?

Sara: Well, as far as I know, it's supposed to stop anything terrible happening to you.

David: But perhaps some superstitions are logical.

Sara: What do you mean?

David: What I'm trying to say is that sometimes there really is a danger. For example, the painter could drop something and it could fall on you and cause some kind of harm or damage to you physically.

Examiner: Do superstitions ever stop people doing things they might enjoy or benefit from?

David: I'm sorry, did you say enjoy?

Examiner: Yes.

David: Right. I suppose they do but I would never decide not to go on a trip or something because it was on the thirteenth of the month.

Sara: So what you're saying is that if you go to the airport and the airline gave you seat 13D on the plane you would still go?

David: Well, I might feel a bit … not exactly afraid but kind of a bit worried and uncomfortable but it wouldn't stop me flying.

Unit 9, Listening Activity 1

Track 19

Interviewer: We're talking to Carol Johnson, a successful young cyclist with big ambitions. Carol, tell us how it all started.

Carol: Mum's a nurse, Dad's a solicitor, my sister's into music – no sport at all at home! I remember going round to a friend's house when I was six. I couldn't ride a bike but she could – and her four-year-old brother! I hated that! My friend's dad helped me and eventually I managed to ride it. I pestered my parents to buy me a second-hand bike for five pounds and from that moment I was completely hooked – I rode it everywhere. It wasn't until I went to university to study sports science that I took up cycling competitively.

Interviewer: What kind of person are you?

Carol: I'm very competitive – my sister got irritated when I turned everything into a contest. But I don't understand athletes who boast about what they're going to achieve. You're better off keeping your mouth shut, training as hard as possible and when it comes to the day, doing all your talking on the track. I try to unleash my drive in training and my competitive spirit in races. When I'm racing I'm a different person.

Interviewer: How do you feel about training?

Carol: It hurts a lot but I wouldn't dream of missing a session. It may be the worst pain imaginable but you either do it a hundred percent or you don't do it at all – that's what makes the difference between you and others. You can give ninety-nine percent and the coach wouldn't know – only you would. It's being able to give everything, day in, day out, so if you get beaten you accept it because you've done your best. You get out what you put in. If you really work hard at something, you can achieve anything.

Interviewer: Are sportspeople arrogant or just confident?

Carol: It's a misconception that athletes are supremely confident – they're full of self doubt. That's what drives them because if you believed you were going to win all the time, that it was easy, why bother? Every day you have doubts about your fitness, your injury status. It's how you deal with those doubts, particularly on race day – that's the key. You have to be quite selfish as an athlete and I suppose that comes across as arrogance sometimes. But I don't race for second place.

Interviewer: What part does luck play?

Carol: People think athletes are superhuman but they're not – they can be lucky with their bodies and injuries but it's about drive, ambition and determination, not luck. My success is in my head as much as my body. If I think about the consequences of failure, I perform badly – it's not exactly fear of failure but fear of having sacrificed everything for nothing. When negative thoughts pop into my head I keep them out by visualising the race, what I want to happen. Lots of athletes go over a race in their heads before the start. The more you rehearse, the more it seems natural it will happen that way – is that luck?

Interviewer: What about the publicity?

Carol: I try to deal with journalists and photographers as I want to be treated myself. They're doing their job just like me. It's hard when you've just lost and you want to go and hide but you still have to do interviews and show up for sponsor events. I know that without financial backup I couldn't do it, so I try to focus on what's important and not let other things bother me. And it's nice when I win and everyone wants to interview me!

Interviewer: What advice would you give other young cyclists?

Carol: Being too goal-centred can be destructive. When I won my first big medal, I realised nothing changes. It's just a part of your life. It's not everything. It's about balance, and I'm aware of the dangers of being successful – sometimes achieving your goals can bring elation, then depression and a loss of focus. But it's exciting – and you have to feel that, to love it. That's probably the key piece of advice – all the money and success in the world won't be worth it if you hate what you're doing.

Interviewer: Thanks for talking to us, Carol …

Unit 10, Listening Activity 1

Track 20

Speaker 1: I think I have lots of friends, though in a way they're more acquaintances I suppose – I don't feel I can share my real innermost thoughts with them. It's not that I don't trust them, because on the whole I do – and I see them every day at school – it's more that I love sport and they don't, which makes it difficult for us to do things together. I regret that a lot and I feel quite jealous when I see groups of friends out together doing stuff. Maybe things will change as we get older.

Speaker 2: My closest friend doesn't live near me any more, so we have to keep in touch by phone and email. That's fine – we've known each other since school and our friendship is very deep. I don't think we're really alike – and that's what makes our friendship so interesting – we can tell each other about our doings which stops us getting bored! We love pulling one another's legs – she's the only one who really gets my jokes.

Speaker 3: We don't see each other very often now even though we both still live in the same town and grew up together. I think we've just grown apart and developed different interests – what's missing for me now is the feeling that I can go to him if I need help – I'm not sure that he'd be there for me. I think that's such a key thing in a friendship. Of course, I miss the fun we used to have, but I've got other friends now, and after all – life moves on.

Speaker 4: I often read those quizzes in magazines – you know, 'Are You a Good Friend' – that type of thing – I usually come out of them quite well. But what I know about myself is I need to have my friends around me – I'm a people person – and even though there's always Twitter and Facebook they're no real substitute for being together in person. It's not that important to be the same kind of person, nor to like the same kind of things – but you do need to be there all the time!

Speaker 5: Most of my friends like loads of different things – and it's great that we can give ourselves space and not worry about being together all the time. We have a good laugh together – though not all my mates get my idea of a joke! But we all have the same values, we're the same kind of people really. That's what supports a good friendship, not the other stuff – and if we don't meet up for a few days that's not a problem. We just pick up exactly where we left off!

Unit 10, Speaking Activity 1
Track 21

Here are some things that friends often think are important and a question for you to discuss. Talk to each other about how important they are in a good friendship.

Unit 11, Listening Activity 1
Track 22

Hi everyone – I'm Pete, and I'm here because you're all planning to go on your very first cycling expedition across Europe. I've been there, and I'd like to share some of my experiences with you and give you some tips for making the most of such a trip. It's incredibly exciting, but it can all go horribly wrong if you don't follow some simple guidelines. I'll answer any questions at the end, so don't worry if anything occurs to you while I'm speaking.

So, what will guarantee you a successful expedition? It may seem obvious, but in my opinion it's preparation! Read as much as you can about everywhere you're going, so you can anticipate any problems that might come up. On a practical level, the first thing you need to do is arrange all the finance for the trip, which may mean looking for people to back you. I hope you've already got some sponsors in place but you can never have too many – I emailed potential sponsors, then called, then sent letters. You'll need a great deal of patience but finding the right person to talk to is crucial, and don't get downhearted if it takes time. One thing I was told that really helped me was not to get bogged down in detail – to set the leaving date and stick to it. And that moment of departure is a great feeling!

Once you're out there on the road, there are loads of things to think about. I had this big idea of covering a pre-determined distance every day but people kept stopping me to talk about interesting things and opening up to me about their own dreams and ambitions. I got a glimpse into the day-to-day lives of people living in the different countries and cultures on the way. I felt it was important not to let the concept of cycling round Europe get in the way of the 'experience' which I describe as special and not something that many people get the chance to have. One family I stayed with cooked me a very traditional meal and invited the whole village to eat with us – I found that quite emotional!

So don't turn down any invitations you may get, but if you have the chance to stay with families on the way, be a good guest – which is a lot to do with trying to make conversation, even if you don't speak the language, and being tidy. I describe it as not acting like I was staying in a hotel and it taught me a lot.

A bike tour is full of ups and downs: you have to deal with tiredness, boredom – that was the worst for me! – and not having any personal space. On top of that you're exposed to the elements but remember – the lower the lows the better the highs! There are new challenges every day and there's also the constantly-changing scenery which I found kept things interesting.

But you have to think about why you're doing the trip at all – is it enough to do it for personal reasons? Having a goal in any challenge is important because it keeps you motivated and gives you a reason to keep going when things get tough. My motivation was raising awareness about a small, relatively unknown charity, which protects wilderness areas. What I had to do during the trip was observe climate change and write about my findings on a blog that I updated every evening – I loved doing that. I also sent back photos and videos, which had an extra benefit for me personally because it meant I developed certain skills in media and communication – not to mention photography! That should stand me in good stead in the future – I'm hoping to develop my career as a journalist once I've stopped going on expeditions!

So, now – is there anything you'd like to ask me?

Unit 11, Speaking Activity 1
Track 23

Examiner: In this part of the test I'm going to give each of you two photographs. I'd like you to talk about your photographs on your own for about a minute and also to answer a short question about your partner's photographs.

It's your turn first. Here are your two photographs. They show people travelling in remote regions. I'd like you to compare the photographs and say what people learn from going on trips like these.

Candidate: Both these photographs show people on expeditions. In the first photograph there is a group of people. I'm not sure exactly where they are but it could be the North Pole or somewhere like that because they are all wearing very warm outdoor clothing and there is a lot of snow on the ground. There is a light plane to their right, so they must be somewhere quite difficult to get to by road. I think the plane might have come to pick them up at the end of their journey. The people are all carrying heavy backpacks and are dragging big bags that might have tents or some other kind of equipment in them. It's hard to see their faces but I imagine they are looking forward to going home. They must have achieved what they set out to do.

In some ways the second photograph is similar because again we see someone in a very remote part of the world. Like the people in the first photograph, this person seems to be very warmly dressed and we can see some snow on the mountains in the background, so presumably it's very cold. The main difference is that this person is alone, or at least we don't see anyone else in the photograph. Also he is travelling by bicycle, whereas the people in the other photograph were probably using dog sleds or travelling on foot. It could be somewhere like the Himalayas or the Andes but I'm not really sure.

I think the people in both photographs must have learnt a lot about the environments they have travelled through but also about themselves. The people in the first photograph will have learnt about how to get on with each other and how to work in a team, while the person on the bicycle will have learnt to cope with loneliness and fear.

Unit 12, Listening Activity 2
Track 24

Hello, I'm Carrie, and it's great to be here and share my experiences of writing crime novels with you. I've been writing novels for ten years now. What do you imagine a writer's life is like? Do I sit for hours in my own world waiting for inspiration to strike and then dash off words at a furious rate? Definitely not! Writing isn't a random activity but a skill, which in theory anyone can master, but the reality is it's hard work, especially those times when your mind is completely empty – just like your computer screen! That's what's generally known as writer's block but I like to call it a nightmare!

So, now I'd like to pass on a few tips that helped me along the way. Before deciding to write a book, think about why you want to do it. Some people expect huge financial rewards but there are no guarantees of success and there are safer ways to make your fortune. Others want to be famous so you must identify your own motivation first. I believed that people wanted to read what I had to say and I could tell a good story. That sounds like the best reason, but it may not be enough to keep everyone going in difficult times.

Simply wanting to do it is not enough. You have to know how to write for the market. Crime is the number one best-selling genre in the world and you must do your research. I spent ages finding out about the way various police departments work, their systems and so on.

Identify what readers want. What I did was get hold of books by best-selling authors and analyse them chapter by chapter, line by line. That told me the main reason for their high sales figures and what makes them special.

If you're planning to write crime fiction you really need to understand what people enjoy about it. That helped me, but it's pretty complex. We're all competitive – we want to

be better than everyone else, and one of the ways we can do this is being the first to solve a mystery. Take a crossword for instance – finishing one gives a feeling of satisfaction and pride. People love quizzes and problems and that's why crime fiction is popular. Readers want to go through the clues and guess the identity of the murderer before the last page.

What about the practicalities of writing? The best piece of advice I was given was to remember that crime writing has rules and conventions, and to follow them. On a personal level I also learned very early that I shouldn't try to improve things while I'm writing – that slows me down. I have to finish the whole story before I go back and concentrate on details, though I know everyone's different. But you do have to work closely with your editor and listen to their advice rather than just your friends or family.

I find it hard to know when to stop but if you keep adding too many details they can interfere with the narrative, and make the plot difficult to follow.

Don't imagine you can relax when you've written the book – you still have to make sure it sells. There's the back cover of your book with the synopsis of your novel to do. It needs to be short but it must grab the reader's attention. So show your summary to friends – would it make them want to read the book? You also have to be quite good at marketing as you may need to do a lot of promotional work, making personal appearances, signing copies and so on.

I think I've been so lucky – I can't imagine wanting to do anything else, even though it is more difficult than you might think!

So now – have I covered everything?

Unit 13, Speaking Activity 1
Track 25

In this part of the test I'm going to give each of you two photographs. I'd like you to talk about your photographs on your own for about a minute and also to answer a short question about your partner's photographs.

It's your turn first. Here are your two photographs. They show people performing. I'd like you to compare the photographs and say what part memory plays in doing things like this.

Unit 13, Speaking Activity 4
Track 26

I think I would enjoy being in the play more. I've been in a couple of plays at school and although I was quite nervous it was really good fun.

Unit 13, Listening Activity 1
Track 27
Extract 1

M: That article was pretty funny – the one about the dog that skateboards!

F: I know it seems like that – but when you actually think about it, a dog whizzing round the street on a skateboard – ridiculous! It could get in people's way. I'm sure it makes children laugh, though! And it's certainly not something you see every day.

M: Some people reckon it's not worth writing about – it's irrelevant. I suppose they could be right.

F: There are more useful stories to put in the paper – though it's not exactly bad to have it, just out of touch with what's important.

M: Well, it made me smile anyway.

Extract 2

Oh, hi – I'm calling from Q3 Telephone Services. Do you know about some of our new special rates for international calls? Whatever you're currently paying on your existing deal, we guarantee you'll find our rates competitive and that you'll make substantial savings on your monthly bills. This opportunity will only run for a short time, so why not take us up on the trial period? Either call us on 0294 68500 or go on to our website, which sets out all the details. As you have been a customer of ours in the past you can take full advantage of this opportunity. Thanks for your time.

Extract 3

F: Did you see that group of young people hanging round when we came in?

M: Yes – they seemed a bit threatening to me – even though they weren't doing anything and I'm sure they're perfectly harmless really.

F: It's not that – it's just that there must be so many other things they could be doing – much more interesting for them.

M: I agree, and bus stations can be quite depressing enough without having to keep an eye on other people just in case! I hope the bus comes soon – it's late.

F: It infuriates me that there's not enough done for young people nowadays – and it's the same everywhere.

Extract 4

During my research for this programme – which was originally going to be concentrating on finding new and different forms of heating and so on – it became clear that we're just not doing enough to look after the planet in general terms – recycling, that sort of thing. I realise it's not easy, but I was taken aback by how little the average man in the street seemed to know or think about – so that caused a shift of emphasis. I now see it as a wake-up call, bringing the kinds of things we can all do out into the open.

Extract 5

F: Well, everyone thought it'd be a good game, but it turned out to be better than that.

M: It was certainly closer than anyone anticipated! And at least it was played in good spirit – none of those stupid arguments or refereeing decisions that spoil a game – they're so annoying!

F: But in the end it wasn't a good result, was it?

M: We've been playing so badly recently the coach wasn't too displeased with us! And personally I've missed so many matches with my knee I was relieved to finally be involved in a game. But a bad result like that is hard to deal with, especially after such a good game.

Extract 6

M: That lesson was more interesting than usual – I normally hate history!

F: I could actually see what the teacher was on about this time – what she meant and how it kind of fitted in with other things we've been studying. That was a first!

M: It was hard to get some of it – though there was stuff I hadn't realised before, like how past things still affect us – political decisions, I mean.

F: It put things into perspective for me – that's very positive, though what's gone is gone.

M: It still didn't really grab me, though – far too much detail. History's not really my scene.

Extract 7

F: Loads of shops sell copies of designer-branded clothes now. But if they're reasonable quality, does it matter if they're not real?

M: Personally I wouldn't go for them 'cos you can tell fake gear a mile off. I'd rather buy fewer clothes even though I know they're over-priced.

F: Ridiculously so – it's not for me. And I wouldn't get the fakes anyway. I don't want to stand out in something that's out of date. My friends would laugh at me!

M: If you can get hold of clothes with a slight fault – like a small hole – then they're much cheaper.

F: Not sure about that – and I hate mending, anyway!

M: Then what can you do?

Extract 8

Hi, I don't think I'm going to get away before five after all, so there's no chance of being able to eat with you before the film – a good thing we hadn't booked in anywhere! I'll probably stop off and get a sandwich on the way and just catch up with you at the box office, but you go ahead and get yourself something – there's that café opposite the cinema, though I don't know what it's like. According to the radio there's a lot of traffic building up on the motorway so I might get held up – if that happens I'll call you on the mobile and you'll just have to go on your own.

Unit 14, Listening Activity 2

Track 28

Speaker 1: I often have problems getting my message across. Some people seem to be natural communicators while others struggle. I find it hard to get to the point and not beat around the bush – which can be pretty confusing for the listeners, though my slides are good. People have very short attention spans, so you can't include too much redundant stuff and it's crucial to be direct about what you're trying to say. Of course things like good eye contact are useful, and some people say body language is the thing to concentrate on but I know it's all in the writing of the presentation.

Speaker 2: This may seem obvious to you but it's amazing how many people wear a kind of mask to impress others. I was guilty of this myself when I started out because I felt huge pressure to make a good impression on everyone else. But in the long run it didn't work – people see through you. It doesn't matter how good your speaking voice is, or how much of an actor you are, you have to speak from your heart. But nowadays, without being able to use slides effectively you may not be as good as you could be, though you have to retain your integrity.

Speaker 3: Some people are very animated when they're talking to others – they use lots of hand movements and different facial expressions. If this is your style, that's great! If not, don't worry about it. You have to find a way of expressing yourself that you're comfortable with and stick with it. As long as you're getting your views across, which means articulating your words well and not mumbling, that's the key – and if you can make sure everyone in the audience thinks that you are looking at them and talking directly to them then that's a bonus.

Speaker 4: When I'm passionate about something I tend to speak really fast, wave my arms around and try and get all of the words out at once. When you speak fast and have a lot to say, it's hard for all the information to be processed by the listeners at the end of it. But you need to support what you're saying, so mastering the computer is something I think should come first. The slides can actually slow your speaking down, which is no bad thing – and you can always use your body if you want to!

Speaker 5: People used to say I smiled too much – though I don't really get that! But seriously smiling did and still does have a very positive effect on others. When you smile your eyes light up and you can hear it in your voice. Good communication is always made better if people enjoy listening to you. But there's something I learned very early that for me is the number one tip – if you look away from your audience and have a miserable face, you may find that people don't warm to you, or worse still don't trust you. Slick computer skills can't make up for that!

Unit 14, Speaking Activity 1

Track 29

1 Where are you from?
2 Which town do you live in now?
3 Can you tell us something about your family?
4 What do you enjoy doing at the weekend?
5 Can you speak any other languages apart from English?
6 Do you enjoy learning English?
7 What kinds of films or television programmes do you enjoy watching?
8 Do you play any sports?
9 What kinds of magazines do you enjoy reading?
10 What kind of transport do you prefer to use when you travel?

Practice test, Listening Part 1

Track 30

Extract 1

Oh, hello, it's Sara Jones here. I've got two tickets for this evening's show, but unfortunately I'm not very well and won't be able to make it. I know you don't give a refund unless you can re-sell them, but would it be possible for me to come next Saturday instead? I'm quite prepared to pay

any admin fee and I don't mind which part of the theatre the seats are in – even the restricted view would be OK. The problem is I can't get the tickets back to you today. Could you call me on 786533 when you get this message, so I can give you the details? Many thanks.

Extract 2

M: Well, that was a load of hype! I really thought it'd be brilliant after all the trailers.

F: Bits of it were! The technical side for instance – I've never seen anything like it – it all looked so realistic to me.

M: Hm, I found it all a bit of a bore really. The only thing for me was the performance of the stars – they made it something to remember.

F: Hm, I was particularly moved by the young girl's scenes – it was her first film, wasn't it? She's so talented – we'll be seeing a lot of her in the future.

M: Hopefully not in films like this one!

Extract 3

M: I can't believe I'm still hanging round – I checked in ages ago! I don't normally have problems with this carrier – that's why I fly with them on business.

F: I've been waiting since ten! A friend's meeting me at the other end – she'll be really fed up!

M: It could be a problem with the incoming flight – bad weather conditions or something – but they're not exactly keeping us informed, are they? It'd make it easier if we knew what was happening.

F: I tried asking at the information desk but that didn't get me very far.

M: Well, if it takes much longer I'm going to see if I can change my ticket for another flight.

Extract 4

Hi, Jo – well, I got through the first semester but I'm not sure how! I knew it would be demanding – after all, I've never done anything like it before. I'm enjoying the challenge of the coursework and keeping up with the lectures, though some of it isn't exactly fascinating – I think it's the way the tutors deliver it rather than the subject itself, though. It's not the way I thought it would be, and it takes ages to get everything right – I don't mind putting in the hours but I know you're all a bit annoyed I can't go out as much as before! Next term should be better.

Extract 5

M: Do you like those game shows where people have to do extreme sports to win prizes? They're getting a bit silly, I think.

F: Some of the things they do are totally stupid – whoever dreams up the ideas must have a great sense of humour.

M: There was that one in the swimming pool with enormous red balls they had to run across – it wasn't people falling into the water that made me laugh but the fact that they bounced!

F: What must it cost to put on a game show? I can't imagine how television companies afford it.

M: I guess it's the adverts that pay for it – it probably doesn't cost the TV company much.

Extract 6

It was always my first love – my mother talks about how

I'd sing endlessly even when I was very young. At school I hated music lessons, not 'cos of the subject but 'cos it was done in such a boring way! My teachers were pretty annoyed with me, because they realised I was wasting my talent. I went in for a music competition when I was sixteen, which I didn't win, but it got me in touch with like-minded musicians. Now I've joined the band I have to go along with their choice of music, though, which has to be what works commercially, not what I'd choose myself. Once I've really made it things will be very different!

Extract 7

People have enjoyed chewing natural products like bark and tree resin for thousands of years, and such products were often believed to have medicinal properties. Now it is produced commercially in a vast industry with worldwide sales measured in billions of pounds. Although it is so widely used and there are a huge range of different forms of the product, including sugar-free and medicated gum, we're increasingly concerned about the environmental impact of the way people dispose of their gum. The cost of removing it from the streets is enormous, and some wildlife can be seriously harmed by eating it.

Extract 8

I'm pretty fed up with everything I've been hearing over the last few minutes. The people you are talking to seem to be just ringing in to moan and OK, they're taking the chance to say what they think – but they're all so critical. I know giving the opportunity to hear different opinions is the focus of a phone-in programme so if you changed the format it would become pretty pointless, but there seems to be little balance in what you're doing at the moment. I want to make the point that this kind of show should present a range of opinions, not just the negative views as it does now.

Practice test, Listening Part 2

Track 31

Hello, everybody – I'm Anne. I'm here to tell you about the work I do in the film industry, and give you some tips on how to get into it yourselves. I followed a popular route into working behind the scenes by becoming a runner – it's a very junior job but it can lead into any area of film making, from camera work to research to directing. My ultimate aim is to be a producer.

It's a rather strange name for a job, and in fact it's a difficult job to define, but you may have noticed it on the credits that come up on the cinema screen at the end of a film. Being a runner involves helping out on the production of a film with what's often referred to as 'odd jobs' but I prefer to call general tasks. I suppose it comes from the idea of running from one job to another! What I actually do varies depending on the film and the location, but I often help members of the production team with things like unpacking the gear, setting up for the shoot and getting food and drinks for the crew – though strangely what I seemed to spend most of my time doing on my very first

assignment was photocopying! A runner is really useful when things go wrong, because they can spend time away from the shoot sorting out problems while the film crew and the actors get on with their work. That's the part of the job I like best and no two days are the same. One day I was amused to be asked to go to another town to pick up some equipment that had actually been left behind! No matter how much planning has been done by the production team things can always change at the last minute.

What I've found most useful apart from following the director was working closely with the technical crew. From the practical point of view that was brilliant. I learned loads of really useful stuff, and lots of runners I know have gone on to become camera assistants.

There are certain qualities that make a good runner. Determination is quite important because it is so hard to break into the industry, and it's good if you are energetic, enthusiastic and patient – but it's most important to be what I call a good 'ideas' person. I also learned never to be late on the first day of a film shoot – it's the worst thing you can do, so you soon learn to be organised. You also meet people from many different backgrounds, so it's vital to have good communication skills.

When you're looking for work, one strategy is to send your details to loads of companies, in the hope of getting a job interview. The biggest problem is that most vacancies aren't advertised in the newspapers – you find out about them through word of mouth, and most of them are only short contracts with small salaries. I've put my CV on several media websites so companies can contact me when they are looking for runners.

People ask me if working as a runner is better than doing a course at college if you want to work in films. At the end of the day, the experience is fantastic but you do also need to have done the groundwork. I think many people who work as runners are attracted by the idea of making contacts that might lead to further opportunities but of course that's not guaranteed.

I have to say that working on any production is exciting because everyone is focused and dedicated to making it work. There is a really strong sense of teamwork which for me is something that is the best part of working in the industry. I love it!

So now – are there any questions?

Practice test, Listening Part 3

Track 32

Speaker 1: When we first arrived I thought we'd made a mistake and it was too quiet – not enough for us all to do – but when we found the wonderful strip of beach just along the coast I was thrilled. The number of places to eat and shop there was incredible, and prices were reasonable. It was important that we could all find things we liked – sport for some of us, walking for others. I always want to find out about the history of places I visit, so for me it's the museum that I'll actually remember. I think my understanding of the language improved too – a bonus!

Speaker 2: The resort was fantastic – though I'd expected that from the reviews – but it was the food that just blew everyone else away! There was so much choice and it was all good. What made it for me, though, was the chance to just hang out with my mates – chat, catch up on things – you're usually too busy for that. The shops were good too – lots of bargains! There were loads of beaches to walk along and other resorts to explore – really quiet areas for when I wanted to get away from things and relax – which wasn't often! I would definitely go there again.

Speaker 3: We stayed in a small resort but it was pretty easy to rent a car or take a bus to nearby larger places, though they were too far to walk to, which was a shame. My main aim in going there was to get away from the stresses of student life, and that was certainly what happened. In fact, it couldn't have been better. There was a lovely old town which had a great sense of history, and we all enjoyed wandering round in the evenings. I was even able to try out my primitive language skills which I'd hoped to do and I definitely got more confident!

Speaker 4: I love travelling, and I think it's important to be able to communicate with people in other countries. I often choose a place to go just so that I can practise the language, and this holiday was perfect for that as I was on my own. That had the double bonus of meaning I could do whatever I wanted without asking anyone else – go to galleries, relax, go swimming, cycling – I certainly got fitter! – but most importantly I had to talk to people in restaurants, shops and so on. Of course I learned a lot about their way of life as well and I didn't miss my friends at all!

Speaker 5: My last holiday was a cruise. I'd expected to hate being stuck with other people – I only went because my friend wanted to try it. We visited lots of different ports, and when we got off the boat we sampled loads of exotic dishes in all the different restaurants. I think that's what I look back on now with the greatest pleasure. The pace of life on the boat was slow and leisurely, which I found frustrating, but at least there was a gym on board so I was able to go running and swimming every day. Everyone on the boat spoke English, so my language skills didn't improve much!

Practice test, Listening Part 4

Track 33

Interviewer: Kris, you started tennis very young – how did that happen?

Kris: My parents worked at a leisure complex – Dad was a tennis coach. I began playing with him when I was four. At my first school I tried rugby which I actually liked better because I could play with my friends, so keeping on going with tennis was really tough. After one rugby match I went home with a cut on my forehead and my parents told me to give it up. Up until then I played tennis twice a week, but after that I played more often and improved rapidly.

That got me hooked and by the time I was twelve I was pretty good.

Interviewer: Were you a good student at school?

Kris: I enjoyed school on the whole and I wasn't bad academically, though I couldn't really see the point of it – I already knew what I was going to do. I still keep in touch occasionally with a few old classmates, though my life is very different from most of theirs – but I am grateful for the teachers who taught me that if you dedicate yourself to something, there's nothing that can't be achieved. I started competing seriously when I was fifteen.

Interviewer: You were successful in national tournaments very quickly. How were those early years?

Kris: I fell in love with the buzz of competition. Now the trend is for junior players to go to college first, take a few more years to grow up before trying to make it as a professional but I'm glad I didn't take that route. I just wanted to play, and I was lucky I was tall and strong enough to compete with older players quite easily, though some of them resented me. It taught me a lot about people, and I needed to mature faster – that's given me an edge.

Interviewer: Tell us about your exercise routine and diet on a normal day.

Kris: I try to follow a healthy lifestyle. It's important to avoid stuff like fast food, though I admit I really missed it at first! I train hard – my coach pushes me to build up my strength and stamina. I run first thing every day, then spend four hours working with him on my technique on the court. That's the bit I enjoy, though I know the rest of it is probably even more important. He's introduced me to yoga which is good for my flexibility – it's hard, though, and I try to avoid it. I don't enjoy the fact that it isn't competitive – I need that to spur me on, though I don't really mind being told what to do.

Interviewer: What do you like most about being a professional?

Kris: Of course it's great seeing places I wouldn't otherwise have the chance to visit – some tournaments take place in fascinating cities, and I always try to look round if I can. Spending so much time away from my family and friends isn't great, though, and hotel rooms are very lonely even when you're earning enough to do what you like. I find it a privilege to talk to loads of interesting people – it's something I never imagined I'd enjoy, but in fact that's what makes it really special.

Interviewer: Do you have any advice for young players who'd like to follow in your footsteps?

Kris: I believe setting goals and working as hard as you can for them is a big thing, though that's not something you can rush. Don't totally ignore those who want to help you – I was rather stubborn at times, and that didn't always make my life easy – though you know yourself best and sometimes you do have to stand up for yourself. Top of the list is how you feel – never underestimate how having a good time builds the real foundation for success.

Interviewer: Finally, is there anything you'd like to achieve?

Kris: Apart from winning that really big tournament?!

Many players want to coach, though I don't have the patience or selflessness for that. I'm attracted to the idea of taking up something completely different – say cycling – and getting to the top in that. The idea of becoming a television commentator has crossed my mind – it's glamorous, though probably harder than it looks!

Interviewer: Thanks for your time, Kris …

Practice test, Speaking Part 1

Track 34

Where are you from?

Do you use a computer much in your free time?

Tell us about a television programme you've enjoyed recently.

What's your favourite month of the year?

What do you enjoy most about learning English?

What sort of job would you like to do in the future?

Practice test, Speaking Part 2

Track 35

In this part of the test, I'm going to give each of you two photographs. I'd like you to talk about your photographs on your own for about a minute, and also to answer a question about your partner's photographs.

Candidate A, it's your turn first. Here are your photographs. They show people learning different things.

I'd like you to compare the photographs, and say what you think the people are enjoying about learning these different things.

All right?

Thank you.

Candidate B, who do you think is finding learning the easiest?

Thank you.

Now, Candidate B, here are your photographs. They show people sharing an important moment together.

I'd like you to compare the photographs and say why you think this moment is important to the people.

All right?

Thank you.

Candidate A, who do you think is enjoying the moment the most?

Thank you.

Practice test, Speaking Part 3

Track 36

Now, I'd like you to talk about something together for about two minutes.

I'd like you to imagine that a school is doing a project on how people use technology in their everyday lives. Here are some of the things they are going to include in the project and a question for you to discuss. First you have some time

to look at the task.

Now talk to each other about the advantages and disadvantages of using technology in these ways.

All right?

Thank you.

Now you have about a minute to decide which use of technology has had the greatest effect on people's everyday lives.

Thank you.

Practice test, Speaking Part 4

Track 37

Which aspect of technology do you think has been the least useful?

Some people dislike using technology. Why do you think this is?

What do you think is the future for newspapers and magazines?

Why do you think some people always want to have the newest gadgets?

Do you think using a computer saves time, or wastes time?

Some people say we were better off without technology. What do you think?

Pearson Education Limited
Edinburgh Gate
Harlow
Essex CM20 2JE
England
and Associated Companies throughout the world.

www.pearsonELT.com/examsplace

© Pearson Education Limited 2014

First published 2014
Third impression 2014
ISBN: 978-1-4479-0715-2 (Gold First New Edition Exam Maximiser with Key)
ISBN: 978-1-4479-0717-6 (Gold First New Edition Exam Maximiser without Key)

Set in Myriad Pro
Printed in Slovakia by Neografia

Acknowledgements

The publishers and authors would like to thank the following people and institutions for their feedback and comments during the development of the material:
Nora Brussolo, Adriana Lado (Argentina); Henrick Oprea, Atlantic Idiomas (Brazil); Anna Kraśko, Katarzyna Machala (Poland); Eleonora Olaru (Romania); Idiomas O'Clock team, Kamal K Sirra (Spain); Tina Casura-Risch, Riana Paola (Switzerland); Pauline Bokhari, Fiona Johnston, Jacky Newbrook, Judith Wilson (UK)

We are grateful to the following for permission to reproduce copyright material:

Text

Unit 1 Read.: adapted from The Word Issue 101, July 2011, p.61 Abridged version from Hope and Glory by Stuart Maconie; U. of E. 1 Part 3: adapted from http://seasideman.blog.co.uk/2009/07/12/talking-about-music-is-like-dancing-about-architecture-6496611/, tom@oldwood.demon.co.uk; U. of E. 2 Part 2: adapted from On a Role, The Guardian:, 06/05/2002 (Kate Figes); Unit 2 Read.: adapted from http://www.guardian.co.uk/lifeandstyle/2011/may/10/sisters-best-friends-20-years, Steven Morris 10/05/05; Unit 2 Read.: adapted fromhttp://www.telegraph.co.uk/news/worldnews/1567542/Identical-twins-reunited-after-35-years.html, Alex Spillins 27 October 2007, copyright (c) Telegraph Media Group Limited; Unit 2 U. of E.: adapted from Gossip is good for you, The Lady, 2-3 Dec 2003 Diana Hutchinson; Unit 2 Listen.: adapted from lost my childhood to Harry Potter: The actor who plays Draco Malfoy reveals his on chamber of secrets, Nicole Lampert / 9 Nov 2010; Unit 3 Read.: adapted from http://www.independent.co.uk/arts-entertainment/tv/features/they-will-rock-you-the-rise-of-rock-choir-2303153.html, 27 June 2011; U. of E. 3 Part 3: adapted from Sunday Times Style Magazine, 55 (Lydia Slater), Sunday Times; Unit 4 Read.: adapted from http://www.guardian.co.uk/environment/2009/oct/12/himalayas-nepal-climate-change, John Vidal 12 October 2009; Unit 4 Read.: adapted from http://www.guardian.co.uk/books/2001/jan/28/society, Ros Coward 28 January 2001; Unit 4 Read.: adapted from http://www.guardian.co.uk/environment/2009/sep/11/aboriginal-fire-co2-australia, Dean Yibarbuk 11 September 2009; Unit 4 Gram. Focus: adapted from http://icestories.exploratorium.edu/dispatches/preparing-for-the-expedition/ Cassandra Brooks Sat Feb 9 2008; Unit 5 Read.: adapted from http://www.telegraph.co.uk/finance/yourbusiness/startingout/2811916/Starting-out.html, Jamie Oliver 10 July 2007,copyright (c) Telegraph Media Group Limited; U. of E. 5 Part 1: adapted fromhttp://sportsmedicine.about.com/od/sportspsychology/a/superstitions.htm, Elizabeth Quinn Updated June 04, 2010; U. of E. 5 Part 2: adapted from http://wiki.answers.com/Q/How_does_motivation_effect_a_sports_performer, Denidowi; Unit 6 Read.: adapted from http://www.guardian.co.uk/lifeandstyle/2011/jul/02/harry-potter-james-oliver-phelps-weasley-twins, Emine Saner 2 July 2011; Unit 10 Read.: adapted from http://www.guardian.co.uk/lifeandstyle/2010/nov/27/how-to-lose-friends-hannah-pool?INTCMP=SRCH, 27 November 2007; Unit 11 Read.: adapted from http://www.guardian.co.uk/lifeandstyle/2010/feb/21/johnny-budden-parkour-freerunning-paris, 21 February 2010; Unit 12 Read.: adapted from http://www.guardian.co.uk/environment/bike-blog/2011/jul/06/brick-lane-reclaim-stolen-bike, 6 July 2006; Unit 12 U. of E.: adapted from http://www.guy-sports.com/months/bungling_burglars.htm, http://www.guy-sports.com/humor/jokes/latest.htm; Unit 13 Read.: adapted from http://www.nytimes.com/2010/12/07/science/07memory.html?ref=amnesia, 6 December 2010; Unit 13 U. of E.: adapted from http://homeworktips.about.com/od/timemanagement/a/sleeptime.htm (About Guide) Grace Fleming, © 2011 Grace Fleming (http://homeworktips.about.com). Used with permission of About, Inc. which can be found online at www.about.com. All rights reserved. ; Unit 14 U. of E.: adapted from http://www.the-happy-dog-spot.com/dog-communication.html Copyright: The Happy Dog Spot; Unit 14 Listen.: adapted from http://carly-taylor.com/self-development/how-to-be-a-good-communicator, April 2010, Carly Taylor - Internet Entrepreneur & Life Coach 33 Cambridge UK - www.carly-taylor.com and www.socialdivamarketing.com; Practice Test U. of E. Part 2: adapted from http://www.dailymail.co.uk/sciencetech/article-1041944/Can-dog-attack-yawns.html#ixzz1TtxituFo, The MAIL Fiona Macrae 6th August 2008; Practice Test U. of E. Part 3: adapted from Skies of the World In flight magazine Aerolineas Argentina (Leonardo Tarifeno);

In some instances we have been unable to trace the owners of copyright material, and we would appreciate any information that would enable us to do so.

Picture Credits

The publisher would like to thank the following for their kind permission to rproduce their photographs.

(Key: b-bottom; c-centre; l-left; r-right; t-top)
Alamy Images: Chuck Place 126cl, Huntstock, Inc 98r, Brian Jackson 82r, Tom King 56, Tom Merton / OJO Images 126bl, Powered by Light RF 82l, John Robertson 36, Travelfile 80b, Valentyn Volkov 34, Janine Wiedel Photolibrary 126br; **Corbis:** George Shelley / Flirt 50b, Paul A. Souders / Encyclopedia 80t; **Getty Images:** Barcroft Media 76, ColorBlind Images / Iconica 39l, Brett Froomer / The Image Bank 63, Image Source 12, Eamonn McCormack / WireImage 43, Alejandro Pagni / AFP 126tr, Panoramic Images 28, Tim Platt / Iconica 26, Joe Raedle 24l, Mel Svenson / Digital Vision 39r, Chris Whitehead / Cultura 24r; **Photostage Ltd:** Donald Cooper 92t; **Rex Features:** 7, EDPpics / K Tovell 98l, FoxSearch / Everett 92b, Top Photo Corporation 50t

All other images © Pearson Education

Every effort has been made to trace the copyright holders and we apologise in advance for any unintentional omissions. We would be pleased to insert the appropriate acknowledgement in any subsequent edition of this publication.

Illustrated by Oxford Designers & Illustrators